Walking London's
Parks and Gardens

H(

1

WALKING LONDON'S PARKS AND GARDENS

Geoffrey Young
and Roger Tagholm

TWENTY-FIVE ORIGINAL WALKS AROUND
LONDON'S PARKS AND GARDENS

NEW HOLLAND

First published in 1998 by
New Holland (Publishers) Ltd
London • Cape Town • Sydney • Singapore

Garfield House
86–88 Edgware Road
London W2 2EA
United Kingdom

80 McKenzie Street
Cape Town 8001
South Africa

Unit 1, 66 Gibbes Street
Chatswood, NSW 2067
Australia

218 Lake Road
Northcote
Auckland
New Zealand

ISBN 978 1 84773 617 8

Editor: Penny Phenix
Proofreader: Brackley Proofreading Services
Design: Lucy Parissi
Cartography: ML Design and William Smuts

Reproduction by PDQ Digital Media Solutions Ltd, UK
Printed and bound in Singapore by Tien Wah Press (Pte) Ltd

Photographic Acknowledgements
All photographs were taken by Jon Meade Photography

CONTENTS

Preface   6
Introduction   7
Plant Introductions   12
Key to Route Maps   13
Map of London Parks   14

The Parks and Gardens:
Osterley Park   16
Syon Park   22
Fulham Palace Gardens   29
Holland Park   35
Kensington Roof Gardens   40
Kensington Gardens   45
Hyde Park   52
The Regent's Park   61
Kenwood and Hampstead Heath   67
Greenwich Park   73
Victoria Embankment Gardens   80
Victoria Tower Gardens and the Tradescant Garden   87
Green Park   93
St. James's Park   99
Battersea Park   105
Chelsea Physic Garden   112
Richmond Park   119
The Royal Botanic Gardens, Kew   125
Ham House Gardens   135
Marble Hill Park   141
Victoria Park   145
Mile End Park   152
Dulwich Park   159
Cannizaro Park   166
Lincoln's Inn Fields, Lincoln's Inn and Inner Temple Gardens   174

Further Information   182
Index   186

PREFACE

London is loved for its parks and gardens, and we have chosen the best of them for this book. These are the ones with the most historic interest, each with a fascinating story to tell and countless byways that bestow a particular charm and individuality to every one of them. They have also been selected because of the beauty and variety of trees or plant displays, and many have magnificent views – some natural, others contrived – framed by planned landscapes that are unmatched anywhere in the world. Then there is the added appeal of the concerts, shows and other events that these lovely green spaces host.

The routes in this book link the most interesting features of each park or garden, but there are likely to be others, and in the case of large parks, such as Holland Park or The Regent's Park, several very different routes are possible. If, after following the designated walk, you feel like exploring further, this book will have succeeded, and though we do give precise directions, we would hate you to resist the temptation to walk on the grass. The detailed map that accompanies each walk shows the major features along the route, which should ensure that if you do leave the path you won't get lost.

We have given some guidance on the distance of each walk and the time it will take, and these range from the very short Kensington Roof Gardens walk to a trek of around two or three hours in Richmond Park, or the tour of Kew Gardens, where there is also much to see. The routes have been timed at a slow walk, allowing for a breather after an uphill stretch, perhaps, and giving time to look at interesting features, but extra time will need to be allocated for having tea in a café or protracted sitting on a bench chatting.

Admission to the majority of parks and gardens in this book is free, but where a charge is made the ticket prices are given in information panels at the beginning of each chapter. The panels also give such information as the location of the park and its distance from Central London, convenient buses or other transport, the opening times of cafés, seasonal features, and events that take place in the park.

At the back of the book, the Further Information section gives the opening times of associated houses or museums, together with useful telephone numbers, such as information lines and contact numbers for societies related to the parks. Many, for instance, have 'friends of the park' groups, and they welcome new members. This information, together with the walk details and the maps, was up to date when the book was printed, but do remember that parks and gardens are dynamic places with active management and restoration and planting programmes. This may lead to some details changing, so be prepared to improvise at times when following the route map.

GEOFFREY YOUNG

INTRODUCTION

London has some of the most marvellous parks and gardens in the world and they are yours to enjoy. They offer more grass to walk on than you can usually find in the countryside, and many have a great deal more wildlife. But London's parks are not just green places, they are also memorials to the people who created them, worked in them, used them and wrote about them: to kings and queens; landscape gardeners and plant-hunters; diary-writers and duellists; and (in one case) star-gazers. And they are all dotted with discoveries: a very personal secret garden, for instance (in The Regent's Park – *see* page 65); one of the most unusual private houses in London (in Hyde Park – *see* page 59); what is undoubtedly the most pert statue in London (in Green Park – *see* page 98). To discover the secrets and beauties of London's parks and gardens you have only to walk them, and see for yourself what's round the bend in the path. Happiness on the hoof, you could say.

THE PARKS

London's parks are museums of their own history. Some of the oldest are the royal parks, which were originally deer parks, enclosed, in the main, by the hunt-mad Tudors, notably Henry VIII (1509–47). Here the deer were coursed (chased by hounds) or released into what was then open countryside beyond, to be hunted on horseback. Country mansions also had their deer parks. Being heavily grazed, they took on what we have come to know as the 'parkland' look, still to be seen unaltered in Richmond Park.

Hunting in London's parks largely ended in Stuart times and several of the deer parks were then opened to the public. For example, James I (1603–25) first allowed his courtiers access to Hyde Park, and Charles II (1660–85) later opened it up freely. The word 'park' then became used for any large green area open for public enjoyment, including custom-built Victorian examples such as Battersea Park. By then parks usually also contained garden features.

THE GARDENS

The Romans had formal gardens, but after the fall of the Roman Empire it was well into medieval times before anything similar was seen again. Tudor mansions had plots for medicinal herbs and for nosegays to ward off the noxious stench inside the house – there is a delightful example of a 17th-century-style herb garden at Kew Gardens (*see* page 127). By that time flowers such as iris, pansy and cowslip were also being grown for pleasure, and were often charged with innuendo, since the concept of the garden was becoming imbued with symbolism. The wallflower, for example, represented love.

THE KNOT

By the 16th century the knot was an important part of garden formalism, perhaps developing from a square bed with raised plank edges. It was a geometrical pattern within the square. At first, the pattern was created with close-clipped lines of hyssop, lavender, rosemary and other plants, separated by paths of coloured sand or crushed brick. The compartments may have been filled with 'gillyflowers' (clove-scented carnations, first mentioned in the 14th century) and other flowers, but this was not always the case. A development took place with the introduction in Tudor times of the dwarf Dutch box (*Buxus sempervirens* 'Suffruticosa') which could be neatly close-trimmed. It then became more usual to plant flowers or herbs within the knot hedges, and the planting of one variety to each compartment was used to good effect.

Knots have been recreated at many places – at Fulham Palace, Kew Gardens and Ham House – though not many have authentic plantings. The one at Ham was featured in the film *Young Victoria* (2009).

THE PARTERRE

From the knot evolved the more elaborate and larger parterre, with a highly complex arabesque geometry. Flowers or coloured earths could still separate the box hedges and there might be sanded paths, but trimmed grass often played a part, and in one variation, the pattern was cut in the turf. Ornamental fountains, urns, statues, or tall trimmed yew and box trees could be dotted through the design. The parterre was perhaps at its most elaborate by around the end of the 17th century, partly as a result of Dutch influence.

THE PHYSIC GARDEN

Another type of garden had also evolved, probably from monastic gardens, by the late 17th century. This was the Physic Garden, a specialized apothecaries' garden (apothecary being an old name for those who dealt and dabbled with medicines). In addition to producing medicinal plants for use in remedies, it was also a teaching garden, where student apothecaries could learn to recognize medicinal (and poisonous) plants growing in the ranked beds. In time, plants from around the world were grown, also for teaching purposes. Not all these plants were medicinal, and the gardens became known as botanic gardens, but the marvellous Chelsea Physic Garden (*see* page 112) keeps its ancient title.

SPECIALIZED BUILDINGS

By the time the great parterres were laid and planted, the gardens of great mansions might also contain specialized buildings. Orange trees had first been introduced into England during the reign of Elizabeth I (1558–1603) and, in time, orangeries were built to protect them from cold weather. The one at Ham House (*see* page 135), built in 1670, is among the oldest in Britain. There might also have been a banqueting house, where family and guests might take snacks or desserts of wine and sweetmeats.

Also during the 17th century, 'wilderness gardens' were a popular addition to the grounds of England's great houses. These took the form of a plantation of hedges and trees in such a way as to create outside 'rooms', and they were treated as an extension to the house. Ham House has also preserved a fine example.

THE AVENUE

The Tudor mansion, with its walled, inward-facing gardens, was rebuilt or replaced in the early 17th century by the outward-looking Jacobean building, with large windows which begged a view. And when, after the end of the Commonwealth of 1649–58, the monarchy was restored under Charles II in 1660, the new king brought with him from exile in France a fancy for long vistas and avenues of trees. Such avenues could be regarded as a symbol of authority, reaching out into the park and uniting it with the house in a new way. Tree alleys (sometimes in the splayed form of a 'goosefoot') were planted at Greenwich (*see* page 73). There is a late (Victorian) example of the kind at the Royal Botanic Gardens at Kew (*see* page 125). Hedged alleys were also planted in the form of a goosefoot or *patte d'oie*.

THE CANAL AND THE LAKE

The grand avenue could edge a straight canal, and one example of this can be seen in Victoria Park in Hackney (*see* page 146). The canal originally built in St. James's Park (*see* page 100) was subsequently adapted to have a more curvilinear outline during the 18th century. From that time, the 'natural' look was adopted, when lakes became a customary feature of park design everywhere. The lakes of Hyde Park (*see* page 57) and Syon Park (*see* page 24) are two of many examples to be seen in London.

THE NATURAL LOOK

The royal parks tended to set or follow the latest landscape fashions, often as a result of changes introduced by royalty, such as Queen Mary (1662–94), wife of William III; Queen Anne (1665–1714); Queen Caroline (1683–1737), wife of George II; and Queen Victoria's consort, Albert (1819–61). They employed influential landscape designers and gardeners. During the 18th century a number of key figures transformed the appearance of London's parks and gardens by replacing the formal layouts that had prevailed during the 17th century with a much more 'natural' look. This style became synonymous with English landscaping and garden design.

Charles Bridgeman and William Kent. Some first steps towards 'natural' landscaping were taken by Charles Bridgeman (1690–1738), who worked at Chiswick Park and Kensington Gardens. However, the most notable person in this development was William Kent (1685–1748), whose great contribution to the transformation of landscape design was to see nature as a garden. Kent was an artist, and his 'natural' garden style was composed of set pieces reminiscent of a painted scene: not only were there trees and swathes of grass in his landscapes, but temples and other classical eyecatchers were set among them. Quaint additions to the grounds (now called the park) subsequently became the norm, from the grottoes of Marble Hill Park (*see* page 143) to the temples and the Pagoda at Kew (*see* page 130), which were constructed in 1761 to the designs of the influential architect, William Chambers (1723–96).

Lancelot ('Capability') Brown (1716–83). By the 18th century, poets such as James Thomson (1700–48) were opening eyes to the beauties of nature, to scenery 'embosomed thick with trees', for example, a liking we take for granted today. One famous gardener and landscape designer who was infected by this enthusiasm was Lancelot Brown. He gained his nickname 'Capability', from his habit of extolling an estate's capabilities for improvement in this way, and his creations took the form of unified 'landscape gardens'. He worked at Kew Gardens and Syon Park.

Brown's trademark features were natural-looking swells of ground and grass, trees in apparently natural clumps, and lakes with serpentine banks having all the appearance of being a creation of nature, but which gave shifting vistas as you walked past (rather like countryside as seen from a moving vehicle). He often went so far as to fell the formal avenues of trees and tear up the terrace parterres of earlier ages, bringing grass right up to a house. He would also eliminate the need for restrictive walls or railings by using a ha-ha, a ditch that formed a barrier to straying animals, like the one at Ham House Gardens (*see* page 138).

Humphry Repton (1752–1818) was Brown's natural successor, famous for his 'red books' with overlays showing views before and after his improvements. In fact, he invented the phrase 'landscape gardening'. He has left a classic landscape at Kenwood House (*see* page 67). Repton heralded the great changes of Victorian times, reintroducing the planting of flowers beside a house (though not as part of the main vista) as he did at Kenwood. By the time John Nash (1752–1835) was working at The Regent's Park and St. James's Park, flowers were firmly back in fashion as part of the Grand Design.

William Nesfield (1793–1881) was one of many notable Victorian plantsmen and garden designers. By the 19th century there was renewed interest in flower gardens and regret at the destruction of the formal layouts of the past. This resulted in a backlash of a kind, with the creation of formal gardens inspired by Italian Renaissance gardens.

To make an Italian garden, an area might be taken from a lawn close to the house, and parterre-like beds cut, to be filled with greenhouse-raised bedding plants. The corners were sometimes marked by dwarf trees, but tall trees were kept out. If the fall of the land allowed, there could be terraces and Italianate stone balustrades, perhaps with a few statues, but no attempt was made to recreate the magnificence of Italian Renaissance gardens. Instead there was reliance on massing the colours of bedding plants. In The Regent's Park there is a notable recreation of Nesfield's style (*see* page 61). At this time, as a result of this influence, it became customary to add statues and memorials to parks and gardens, some as drinking fountains.

During the late 19th century, the herbaceous border became the latest enthusiasm. There is an example in The Regent's Park (*see* page 66), and a luxuriant representation of the style on Victoria Embankment (*see* page 80). Also, for a new type of gardener – the occupant of a small middle-class villa – the cottage garden was reinvented. This style is, in essence, based on individual plants or clumps of them, rather than the massed bedding beloved of the Victorians.

PLANTS FROM ABROAD

Few plants or shrubs in a garden today are natives by origin, since for centuries plants have been imported from other regions. The discovery of the New World in the mid-16th century was perhaps a turning point. The tomato and sunflower are two examples of plants that first reached Europe at that time, and which are now familiar to all. Key figures of this age of discovery were the Tradescants, father and son, whose work spanned the years 1570–1662. They brought the Virginia creeper to Britain, and very many other plants. The Garden Museum in the Church of St.-Mary-at-Lambeth (*see* page 89) is devoted to them, and many of the plants they collected can be seen in the 17th-century Tradescant Garden which now occupies the churchyard where they are buried.

In the 17th century, the Reverend John Banister sent back from America to Fulham Palace, the country residence of the Bishops of London, the first magnolia to be seen in Britain, and liquidambar *(Liquidambar styraciflua)*, the sweet gum. Descendants of trees and plants he introduced still grow in the garden at Fulham Palace (*see* page 29). Exotic botany became not just a hobby but a profession. In the 18th and 19th centuries, the botanist Sir Joseph Banks (1743–1820) and later William and Sir Joseph Hooker were sponsoring plant-collecting expeditions, in part to fully exploit the new lands of the Empire for crop and medicinal species. Plants they collected are on show at Chelsea Physic Garden (*see* page 112) and at the Royal Botanic Gardens, Kew (*see* page 125). Heated plant houses, called stoves and conservatories, were built by those rich enough to nurture new flowers and shrubs, camellias (from China and Japan) being one passion. These conservatories, which can still be seen at Syon Park (*see* page 27) and Kew, were virtual temples to the new religion of plantsmanship.

BEDDING PLANTS AND EXOTICS

The climax to this development was the building of greenhouses for large-scale raising of exotics, destined for planting out in planned park and garden beds. At Hyde Park for example, plants were being shown in bulk bedding barely two years after first being seen in Britain, and the first great flower shows were held in the Temple Gardens (*see* page 81). This appearance of bedding plants led to today's garden industry and the breeding and raising of new hybrids and varieties that we now take for granted. The 20th century has seen developments not only in the production of plants but also in the embracing of different garden designs and styles, of which the Kensington Roof Gardens (*see* page 40) and the Kyoto Garden in Holland Park (*see* page 38) are outstanding examples.

A NOTE ON GEOFFREY YOUNG

Acclaimed wildlife writer Geoffrey Young passed away in 2001. This new edition, updated by Roger Tagholm, is dedicated to his memory.

PLANT INTRODUCTIONS

The table below gives the date of introduction of some of the trees and plants referred to in the following pages:

DATE (approximate)	TREES	FROM
1500	Holm oak	Mediterranean
1500	(Red) mulberry	Iran
1550	Strawberry tree	Mediterranean/Ireland
1550	Stone (Umbrella) pine	Mediterranean
1580	Plane tree	Southeast Europe
1640	Horse chestnut	Balkans
1640	Swamp cypress	North America
1660	Cedar of Lebanon	Lebanon
1750	Tree of heaven	China
1760	Maidenhair tree	Japan
1760	Lombardy poplar	Italy
1795	Monkey puzzle tree	Chile
	OTHER PLANTS	
1550	African marigold	Mexico via Africa
1580	Hyacinth	Turkey via Italy
1580	Tulip	Turkey via Holland
1600	Yucca	Central America
1600	Nasturtium	South America
1710	Red hot poker	South Africa
1710	Pelargonium (geranium)	South Africa
1790	Hydrangea	China
1880	Cotoneaster	China
1890	Russian vine	Russia
1900	Buddleia	China

KEY TO ROUTE MAPS

Each of the walks in this book is accompanied by a detailed map on which the route of the walk is shown in green. Places of interest along the walks – such as historic houses, museums and churches – are identified by the symbols in the list below. The opening times of houses and museums linked to the park are listed in Further Information at the back of the book, starting on page 182.

The following is a key to symbols and abbreviations used on the maps:

SYMBOLS

route of walk
footpath
railway line
railway station
Underground station
building
church
public toilets
viewpoint
café
flower bed
specimen tree
woodland
parkland
statue
fountain
monument
bandstand
stairs
car park

ABBREVIATIONS

APP	Approach	PL	Place
AVE	Avenue	RD	Road
CLO	Close	S	South
COTTS	Cottages	SQ	Square
CT	Court	ST	Saint
DLR	Docklands	ST	Street
	Light Railway	STN	Station
DRI	Drive	TER	Terrace
E	East	UPR	Upper
GDNS	Gardens	VW	View
GRN	Green	W	West
GRO	Grove	WD	Wood
HO	House	WHF	Wharf
LA	Lane	WLK	Walk
LWR	Lower	WY	Way
MS	Mews		
MT	Mount		
N	North		
PAS	Passage		
PDE	Parade		
PH	Public		
	House (Pub)		
PK	Park		

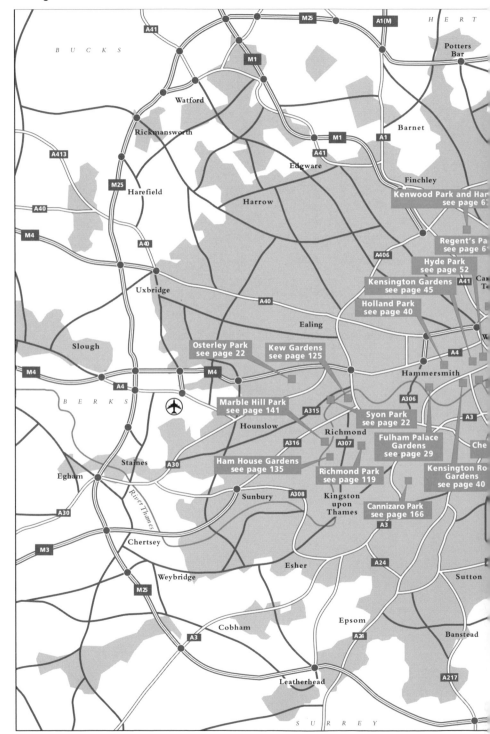

_H E R T_

Potters
Bar

_B U C K S_

Watford

Barnet

Rickmansworth

Edgware

Finchley

Harefield

Kenwood Park and Har
see page 6

Harrow

Regent's Pa
see page 6

Hyde Park
see page 52

Kensington Gardens **Ca**
see page 45 **Te**

Uxbridge

Holland Park
see page 40

Ealing

W

Slough

Osterley Park **Kew Gardens**
see page 22 **see page 125**

Hammersmith

_B E R K S_

Marble Hill Park
see page 141

Syon Park
see page 22

Hounslow

Richmond

Fulham Palace
Gardens
see page 29

Che

Ham House Gardens
see page 135

Richmond Park
see page 119

Kensington Ro
Gardens
see page 40

Staines

Egham

Sunbury

Kingston
upon
Thames

Cannizaro Park
see page 166

Chertsey

Weybridge

Esher

Sutton

Cobham

Epsom

Banstead

Leatherhead

_S U R R E Y_

Cheshunt

Epping

M11

M25

A10

Chingford

E S S E X

A12

A406

A104

eath

A12

Romford

A127

A10

Victoria Park
see page 145

A503

A406

A106

M25

een Park
page 93

A11

A102(M)

Hackney

Barking

A13

James's Park
see page 99

Mile End Park
see page 152

Rainham

Lincoln's Inn Field,
Lincoln's Inn &
Inner Temple Gardens
see page 174

A206

Aveley

A13

Victoria Embankment
Gardens
see page 80

Woolwich

River Thames

Victoria Tower Gardens
see page 87

ersea Park
e page 105

Greenwich Park
see page 73

Lewisham

A2

Dartford

A2

Garden
112

A205

Swanley

Dulwich Park
see page 159

A20

M20

Bromley

A225

oydon

M20

A21

A22

K E N T

Biggin
Hill

A21

Sevenoaks

Caterham

M25

Westerham

OSTERLEY PARK

LOCATION	About 9 miles (14.5 kilometres) west of Charing Cross.
TRANSPORT	Osterley Underground Station (Piccadilly Line) is 15 minutes' (signposted) walk away. There is a car park (fee £3.50) at the end of South Avenue.
ADMISSION	Open daily 08:00 hours–18:00 hours (to 19:30 hours late Mar–late Oct). Admission to the house and garden is £7.60, the garden alone is £3.35 and the park is free.
SEASONAL FEATURES	Spring blossom and autumn tree colour. Regency garden in summer.
EVENTS	Dawn walks with the Royal Society for the Protection of Birds, spring Plant Fair, National Gardens Scheme Day, Community Fun Week in July with theatre, dancing and poetry. Concerts are held regularly near Middle Lake.
REFRESHMENTS	Stables Tea Room and Tea Garden open 11:00–17:00 hours when the house is open (see page 182).

For some 300 years Osterley Park, an estate of 650 acres (263 hectares) was the largest park near London. At its core was a 'faire and stately building of bricke', completed by Sir Thomas Gresham, Chancellor of the Exchequer to Queen Elizabeth I, by about 1577. In 1761 Francis Child (or Childe), one of a family of wealthy bankers, commissioned the neoclassical architect Robert Adam to redesign it. Child died in 1763, but his brother Robert maintained the work. Adam retained the four Tudor turrets, but closed the front with the magnificent portico, and much of the interior was also transformed. The result was described by the writer Horace Walpole (1717–97) as 'a palace of palaces'. The house has remained virtually unchanged outside and in since Adam's day, the brightness of its interior decoration a surprise to modern eyes. The park had 'manie fair ponds', with the customary Tudor walled gardens beside the house. The Child family called in the architect Sir William Chambers (1800–83) to replace this formality with a looser, more natural style, and lakes were created from the small ponds.

In 1949 the 9th Earl of Jersey (a daughter of the Childs married into this family in 1802) gave the house and the park to the National Trust. The house was initially let to the Department of the Environment to cover management costs, but it reverted to trust control in 1988, backed with management funds. The Trust has plans to restore more of the park's 18th-century character. In the 1960s the estate was bisected by the M4 motorway. The southern half – covered on this walk – is 140 acres (57 hectares). This great reduction in area had no visual impact on the core of what is a unique survival, a great country estate within the embrace of London.

THE OSTERLEY PARK WALK

Start and finish South Avenue. **Time** Allow 1¼ hours.

South Avenue, the main drive leading to Osterley Park House, passes through fields of wheat and pasture, a rural touch which sets the scene for the character of its surrounding park. The drive was created in 1870, when the new West London Railway built a station almost at the park gates. It is lined with trees such as limes and horse chestnuts, with drifts of daffodils beneath them in spring. There are some liquidambars (*Liquidambar styraciflua*), or sweet gums, along the path from the car park at the end of the drive. This tree was first brought to Britain in 1681 for Bishop Henry Compton (*see* page 29). It looks similar to maple, its autumn leaves equally colourful, but has bobble fruit instead of the maple's winged fruit.

Garden Lake

The path rounds the end of Garden Lake and turns left along its north bank. Middle Lake, a larger stretch of water, lies to the right behind trees. These lakes are part of the improvements carried out by Chambers around 1750, when the Park was 'naturalized' in the manner that was popular at the time. Before then, there was a formal, straight canal, partnered by avenues of trees.

There are likely to be black-necked Canada geese, mallard duck and coot on the lake, all reasonably tame. In summer, white waterlilies float on its surface. Some maps still show a curious Chinese pavilion out on the water. It was a gift from a Hong Kong company following a Chinese festival held in the grounds, but the wooden structure rotted away in the early years of this century. Interestingly, there is a record of a Chinese tea house at Osterley which has now disappeared.

The Cedar Lawn

Follow the path along the lakeside, keeping tight to the water's edge, and when you near the house, take a detour round the Cedar Lawn to the right. Its magnificent cedars of Lebanon (*Cedrus libani*) were planted in the 1760s, which makes them over 240 years old, and experts at the National Trust think they were probably planted to commemorate the birth of Sarah Sophia Fane, a granddaughter of Robert Child.

Cedars of Lebanon have become firmly linked with the country house image; they were not planted around town mansions because they cannot tolerate much smoke pollution. Although the diarist John Evelyn (1620–1706) makes no mention of them in his book *Sylva*, which was published in 1664, they were introduced at about that time, perhaps via France – there is a delightful story of a Frenchman bringing the first seedlings to Paris using his hat as a flower pot. They come from Syria as well as from the Lebanon, and became popular not only for their tiered shape but also for their Biblical links – they are mentioned in the Book of Psalms, for example – which made them a popular choice for commemorative planting. These Osterley Park cedars miraculously escaped damage in the two great night-time storms of October 1987 and January 1990, which cut swathes across the trees of southern Britain. Prudently, replacements have subsequently been planted. Other closely related trees on this lawn are the Atlantic cedar (*Cedrus atlantica*) from the Atlas Mountains in North Africa, with upward-angled branches and bluish needles, and the deodar (*Cedrus deodora*) from the Himalayas, with a pointed crown. At the southwestern corner is a venerable cork oak (*Quercus suber*) with massive horizontal branches, its trunk protected by railings. This Mediterranean tree, planted as a curiosity a couple of centuries ago, is a real find.

From this gnarled oak retrace your steps and pass the grand portico of the front of the house. Osterley House and its grounds have been used in many films, among them *Amazing Grace* (2006) where interiors were used for William Wilberforce's Wimbledon home, *Miss Potter* (2006), where the grounds became Hyde Park, and *Mrs Brown* (1997) where the house represented Buckingham Palace.

Ancient trees

Turn left for the entrance to the gardens and once through the gate, turn right to find a magnificent Oriental plane tree (*Platanus orientalis*) planted in around 1755 and now, understandably, supporting itself with its own branches. The seed heads of planes look like natural baubles on a giant Christmas tree, and it has been reported that in Beckenham, south London, school children have used the hairy seeds as an itching powder.

Before the pretty white garden house, take the path to the right to the Walled Garden, a common feature of the Tudor period. This is now the cut flower garden and provides the displays used inside the house. Retrace your steps around to the Adam Garden House, designed by Robert Adam (1728–92). This is an attractive, semicircular building with round-arched windows and paired pilasters (projecting rectangular pillars). In front of it a Regency flower garden has been recreated.

Follow the path that leads in front of the house and as it bears round to the left, you will pass the Pinetum, a collection of exotic evergreens. The area to the left of the path is known as the Pleasure Grounds and boasts an arboretum, where trees of special scientific interest grow. There is a stunning Cedar of Lebanon here, marked with a plaque. Lebanon cedars are a source of hard, fragrant timber and legend has it that it was wood from these trees that was used in the construction of Solomon's Temple. Certainly, there is something of the majesty of that famous building in the way this tree rises and spreads, its branches forming green islands above you.

The Temple of Pan

The path now heads toward the Temple of Pan, a kind of summer house where the family might picnic. It was designed by William Chambers and is in Doric style – the oldest form of classical Greek architecture, with simple capitals at the tops of the pillars. Pan was the god of flocks and gardens, and the ruler of Arcadia (a province of Greece since ancient times). The temple is usually open in summer, when visitors can appreciate the fine decoration of the interior walls, with Wedgwood-style swags in green and white. Behind the temple, evergreens have been planted to recreate its original setting.

OSTERLEY PARK

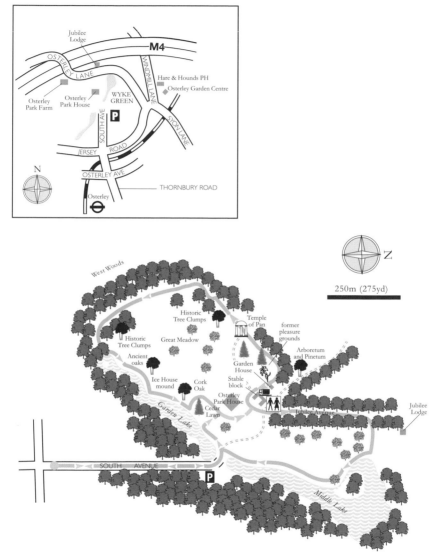

The Long Walk

Now, to the right of the temple, follow the shady Long Walk, which was created as a place for the Child family to stroll.

There is a detour to the left to view restoration work, but keep on the path until a wider clearing appears on your left which better demonstrates this ongoing project. In 2007, the National Trust began work to remove cherry laurel which was stifling woodland growth. Using a machine called a 'forest mulcher' and a process known as 'hallowing', in which vegetation around trees is carefully cut back, new growth is being allowed and the original, splendid views of the house can once again be enjoyed.

Views extend across the Great Meadow which is grazed by cattle – usually the massive but benign French Limousins, with whitish coats – from September to December. There are three large clusters of trees out on the Great Meadow, but they are difficult to see. Known as Historic Tree Clumps, they were planted as part of Chambers' landscaping of the 18th century, with a mixture of trees, such as horse and sweet chestnut, oak and hornbeam, with hazel and hawthorn below.

The walk continues into the West Woods. There are some interesting trees here, which were planted more than 100 years ago by the 7th Earl of Jersey. They include Hungarian oaks (*Quercus frainetto*), distinguishable by their large leaves with many wavy lobes, and red oaks (*Quercus rubra*), from North America, which are spectacular when a cold snap in autumn turns the leaves to fiery colours.

Displays of bluebells are splendid in this part of the walk during the spring, and there would be a true feeling of being deep in the countryside, were it not for the aircraft overhead. Nevertheless, parts of the Long Walk do offer the pleasant sensation of being a long way from anywhere.

The Boat House

Continue along the Long Walk and after it bears to the left, you come to the sunken Boat House – effectively a grassed-over tunnel – from which the Child family would take small boats back to the house after their constitutional. You can see the narrow steps down to the water. Follow the meandering path along the water's edge, noting, to your left, the two unmistakable stag-headed oaks growing on a rise above wet ground. Just beyond them, a mound marks the site of an 18th-century ice house, domed in brick, within which lake ice was packed in straw to last through the summer, enabling food to be chilled and preserved and even allowing for the creation of ice cream and other chilled desserts. This giant, outdoor fridge was filled in for safety reasons in 1939.

Now head left and pass the west front of the house, with its elegant, sweeping staircases and raised entrance – a perfect place for plane spotting, for anyone so inclined. There are camellias planted against the wall of the house.

You will leave the gardens by the same gate as you entered, passing the stable block on the left. This is a Tudor building, part of Sir Thomas Gresham's mansion of the 1570s, although it has since been altered. The clock by Richard Street dates back to 1714 and the Tuscan porch below it was built in the 1750s.

Middle Lake

Walk on toward the east front of the house and then head along the avenue of trees you will see to your left (running northward). Do not take the path near the well. The path that you are now following is Jubilee Avenue, planted to commemorate Queen Victoria's Diamond Jubilee in 1897. It leaves the grounds at Jubilee Lodge, on a bridle path leading to Wyke Green, but turn right before you reach the park's eastern boundary and walk across the open grass to Middle Lake.

The lake area is not quiet, since the M4, which runs around part of the park's boundary, is fairly close by, but it is relatively undisturbed, so a great deal of interesting wildlife can be seen at the western end. Great crested grebe and herons compete with the fishermen, who claim that the waters of the lake contain pike. The ridge and furrow of medieval ploughland that was enclosed by the park are visible in the turf around the lake.

Turn right along the bank and stroll back toward some collapsed willows. Look carefully at the water's edge just beyond and you will see the footings of the wooden bridge which stood here from Victorian days until the end of the 20th century. There is a splendid view up to the house as you return along the lakeshore and turn left to reach the car park, where the walk ends.

SYON PARK

LOCATION	About 8 miles (13 kilometres) west of Charing Cross.
TRANSPORT	Syon Lane and Kew Bridge stations (overground trains from Waterloo and Clapham Junction); 267 bus from Kew Bridge to Brent Lea.
ADMISSION	Gardens open daily 10:30–16:00 hours (to 17:00 hours or dusk Mar–Oct). Admission £4.50 adults, £2.50 child.
SEASONAL FEATURES	Spring blossom; displays of azaleas and rhododendrons in spring. Trees in autumn colours. Rose garden in summer.
EVENTS	Woodland walks, study days and talks, Bonfire night displays, Christmas carols by candlelight.
REFRESHMENTS	Refectory open daily, same hours as gardens.

The grounds of Syon House, London's only ducal residence, provide one of the most attractive London walks. Its 55 acres (22.2 hectares) of gardens and parkland are noted for their fine native and exotic trees. They number more than 3,000, of which about 40 per cent are more than 100 years old, and close to 200 are 200 years old. The grounds were opened to the public in 1837, and a century ago the prestigious *Gardener's Chronicle* could write of Syon: 'Its History up to the present day is almost the most brilliant on record as regards practical horticulture, to say nothing of the interest attaching to the large and choice collection of rare trees ...'.

During the 1400s, a convent stood on the site of Syon House, but after 1539, when Henry VIII dissolved the religious houses, the convent buildings fell into disuse. Their last use was as a prison for the hapless Catherine Howard, the king's fifth wife, before her execution in 1542. The Duke of Somerset, Lord Protector, subsequently built the core of the house that stands today on the cloisters of the convent, but he was beheaded in 1552, charged with wishing to fortify it, a crime of treason at the time. In 1594 Elizabeth I leased the estate to the powerful Percy family, earls and later dukes of the northern province of Northumberland, who were eventually given freehold ownership.

The interior of the house, then, is basically Tudor and there would have been formal terraces and gardens near the house in Tudor times, sheltered by brick walls. One of these seems to have been an early botanical garden, for a Dr. William Turner, author of a famous herbal and often described as 'the father of English botany', lived on the opposite bank of the Thames in the 1540s, in the area which is now Kew Gardens, and rowed across the river to work at Syon. In the 1630s, the 10th Earl commissioned the Renaissance architect Inigo Jones to improve the house, but it subsequently became a prison again, this time for

SYON PARK

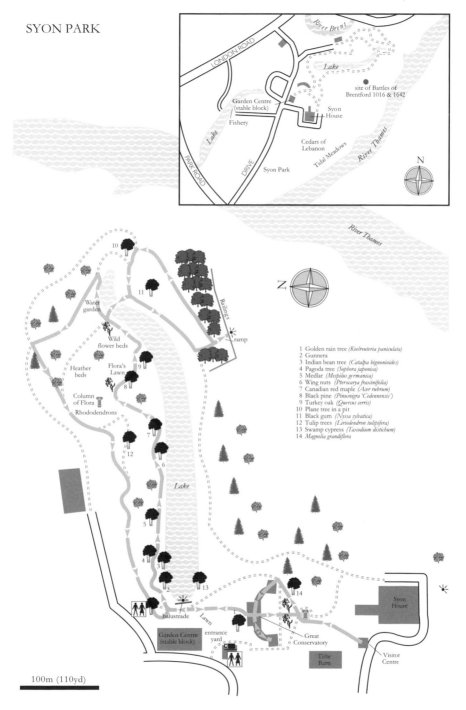

River Brent

London Road

Lake

site of Battles of
Brentford 1016 & 1642

Garden Centre
(stable block)

Fishery

Syon
House

River Thames

Cedars of
Lebanon

Tidal Meadows

Park Road

Drive

Syon Park

N

River Thames

10

Water
garden

11

Railings

ramp

Wild
flower beds

Heather
beds

Flora's
Lawn

9

8

Column
of Flora

Rhododendrons

N

7

12

6

Lake

5

4

3

2

13

balustrade

Lawn

1

Garden Centre
(stable block)

entrance
yard

14

Great
Conservatory

Syon
House

Tithe
Barn

Visitor
Centre

1 Golden rain tree *(Koelreuteria paniculata)*
2 Gunnera
3 Indian bean tree *(Catalpa bignonioides)*
4 Pagoda tree *(Sophora japonica)*
5 Medlar *(Mespilus germanica)*
6 Wing nuts *(Pterocarya fraxinifolia)*
7 Canadian red maple *(Acer rubrum)*
8 Black pine *(Pinus nigra 'Cedennensis')*
9 Turkey oak *(Quercus cerris)*
10 Plane tree in a pit
11 Black gum *(Nyssa sylvatica)*
12 Tulip trees *(Liriodendron tulipifera)*
13 Swamp cypress *(Taxodium distichum)*
14 *Magnolia grandiflora*

100m (110yd)

the children of Charles I after the beginning of the Civil War in 1642. During the 1760s the 1st Duke – then the richest man in the kingdom – had further improvements made by Robert Adam. His magnificent decoration remains, although in the 1820s the exterior of the house was fronted in Bath stone, which was then considered an improvement.

Around the time when Adam was redesigning the interior, the Tudor gardens were swept away by the 1st Duke. A painting by the Venetian painter Canaletto (1697–1768) of around that time shows that they had already gone. The landscape designer Lancelot 'Capability' Brown (*see* page 10), who was born in Northumberland in 1716 and who worked for the family in the north, was also employed. He introduced a new style, replacing formal gardens with grass and planting lawns right up to the house. He had serpentine lakes dug out and planted trees in clumps that were carefully positioned to look natural. A good many of the estate's fine trees have been planted since 'Capability' Brown's time. They have been sensitively selected and sited to add to the appeal of his basic plan, and many are unusual or especially interesting.

Some of the more interesting trees along the walk are marked on the map and described below, but most of the exotic trees in these grounds have name-tags. Some are quite hard to see, however, and they give the scientific name only, so it is a good idea to take with you on the walk one of the species recognition guides listed on page 185.

Much of the pleasure of this walk comes from seeing the inventive work of the gardeners, and this is particularly so along the lake's edge. Alterations to the gardens were carried out during 2009, including extending the lake and the installation of an elegant new bridge. On a rather more prosaic note, Syon House is also home to the U.K.'s very first garden centre, which opened in 1965.

THE SYON PARK WALK

Start and finish The Entrance Yard. **Time** Allow 2 hours.

The entrance to the gardens lies near the house and is found by passing through the gift shop and turning left. Follow the signs to the Great Conservatory and pass it to the right, beneath a fine oak. Cross to the far side at the back of the conservatory to note an attractive Golden Rain tree (*Koelreuteria paniculata*) from Asia, with handsome clusters of yellow flowers in July and August, and papery, bladder-like fruits. It is near the conservatory's central door and close to two elegant lampposts.

The Lake

Follow the path down and over the arched wooden bridge, which was installed in 2009 when the lake was extended. This water feeds the Duke of Northumberland's river, which runs away to the north and takes quite a journey. It passes beneath West Middlesex Hospital and under Heathrow Airport – the Duke's permission had to be obtained when Terminal Five was built, since the river had to be re-routed – until it eventually joins the River Crane. From the bridge there is a lovely view eastward along the lake. 'Capability' Brown was certainly employed at Syon, since there are records of payments made to him in the 1750s, but there are no plans or other paper evidence for what he did. However, this lake can be safely regarded as a 'Capability' Brown feature; the serpentine, natural-looking lake with carefully sculpted banks is his signature. The park had been extended to the north, and the old and new areas were separated by this manufactured stretch of water. 'It is well stored with all sorts of river fish and can be emptied and filled by means of a sluice ...', an observer noted at the time.

Follow the path right around the curve of the lake and continue along the north bank, passing a stand of gunnera (it looks like giant rhubarb, though the foliage dies down in winter) with its feet in the water. This is a waterside plant from Brazil, but it is relatively hardy in the cool temperate climate of Britain. Note the swamp cypress (*Taxodium distichum*), with roots that are trying to burst through the path. This species hails from the southeastern U.S.A. and was first recorded in Britain in 1640 after John Tradescant junior (*see* pages 11 and 87) introduced them. In wet or waterlogged ground these trees grow curious root knobs, sometimes called 'knees', above ground to get air to the roots and some are visible near the water. When they were planted the water table was higher and the lake edges probably deeply marshy. An even finer example appears later in the walk. Ahead of it, sprawling beside the lake, is an Indian bean-tree (*Catalpa bignonioides*), a showy tree with broad, pale green leaves and masses of white flowers in upright clusters in summer, followed by hanging beans, which remain through the winter. In summer its branches are a favourite sunbathing spot for the lake's many terrapins.

Syon's Trees

The meandering lakeside path ahead of you contains many gems along the shore. All the way along, Simon Hadleigh-Sparks and Syon's four other gardeners have cleverly created little 'rooms' and vignettes – a miniature five-bar gate here, a tiny secret path through bamboo there, a hanging sculpture here, a seat furnished from a collapsed trunk there. These delightful little displays are constantly being changed and show great imagination. One other example: a tree surgeon who used to work in the gardens has created a gondolier from a tree trunk at the water's edge, complete with curved decorations that look like sorcerers' shoes. Children love this walk. To the left is a grassy woodland area planted with magnificent trees. Growing just beside the path, beyond the Indian bean-tree, is a fine pagoda tree (*Sophora japonica*), a mountain tree from Asia with panicles of white flowers; and a little way past it is a medlar (*Mespilus germanica*), a small tree native to southern Europe, with rather twisting branches, pretty spring blossoms, and autumn fruits like large brown rose hips. It was a common feature of gardens from Tudor days.

As you continue along the walk, the path curves down to the shore of the lake, where you will notice that areas of the waterside are planted with an unusual border of herbaceous flowers and foliage plants. There are coots, mallards and Canada geese on the lake, and terrapins can often be seen basking at the waterside on warm days. Look also for a clump of wingnuts. These trees are, in fact, the suckers of a Caucasian Wingnut (*Pterocarya fraxinifolia*), which have grown tall; they have huge leaves composed of paired leaflets, and straight hanging chains of winged fruit.

The Column of Flora

Away to your left you will soon see a classical pillar and statue, the tall Column of Flora. The statue is the third version to stand atop the column. The first fell off and the second was struck by lightning. The column is Doric, the oldest and simplest classical Greek style, and is probably an 18th-century original, but the figure of Flora, the Roman goddess of flowers, on top of it is a fibreglass replica that was made in 1968.

The South Bank

At the end of the lake, cross the footbridge and turn right. In summer, look down into the water to see native yellow waterlilies floating on the surface. Follow the path by the water and note the dark masses of some strawberry trees (*Arbutus unedo*) at the water's edge. These are followed by the unmistakable crowns of a stag's horn sumach (*Rhus hirta*) which has flame-like foliage in the autumn, and a little further on some magnificent swamp cypress roots which look like wooden stalagmites. Head through the gate and up toward the wooden platform, from where you can look out across the Tide Meadow or flood plain. This is the only S.S.S.I. (Site of Special Scientific Interest) beside the Thames and the only remaining unbanked part of the river.

The open ground of the Tide Meadow may be a relic of the work of 'Capability' Brown. A guidebook to London and its environs that was published in 1761 reported that 'a fine lawn extending from Isleworth to Brentford' had been created and that 'by these means also a beautiful prospect is opened into the King's gardens at Richmond [now Kew Gardens] as well as up and down the Thames ... even the Thames itself seems to belong to the gardens, and the different sorts of vessels which successively sail as it were through them, appear to be the property of their noble proprietor ...'. More ancient history lies buried beneath Brown's work. Somewhere on these tidal meadows are the sites of the battles of Brentford of 1016 and 1642, and some historians claim that this is the spot where Julius Caesar fought his way across the River Thames in 54BC. Wooden stakes found in the river mud could match his description of the defences of the Celtic tribes.

Retrace your steps through the gate to a giant plane tree which you will see ahead, surrounded by railings. This old tree stands in a stone-lined pit. One possible reason is that it was growing there before the soil was piled up from the lake excavations. Walk back along the path and across the footbridge to the north bank of the lake.

The Water Garden

Take the path that leads to the right from the footbridge, and follow its twists and turns through a picturesque water garden, planted with an attractive mixture of deciduous and evergreen foliage. A small stream winding through its midst splashes over shallow water drops, and is crossed by a humpbacked stone bridge and stepping stones. On hot summer days this water garden is blissfully cool and very peaceful. After the stone bridge, turn left and then go left again on a broad walk. From here, turn onto the path leading to the right. Follow this path through the parkland on the south side of Flora's Lawn and around the back of the Column of Flora.

The Woodland Walk

Just past the Column of Flora you pass a majestic *Zelkova carpinifilia* in an Eastern-style garden. Follow the path to enter an area of woodland planted with rhododendrons. In spring it is aflame with brilliant colour. The path takes you through the northern part of the grassy area planted with specimen trees through which you walked earlier. Down by the lake there are beds of orange, pink and yellow azaleas.

Leave the path from time to time and wander through the trees in order to see them more closely. Look in particular for a lofty copper beech, a tall-trunked hybrid Indian bean-tree, and the dark-leaved Mediterranean oaks. Some of the trees in this park became popular because of their colourful autumn foliage: the North American liquidambar (*Liquidambar styraciflua*), or sweet gum, and the maples are notable examples. Others found favour because of their unusual or striking insect-pollinated flowers, since native British trees, such as the oak, the ash, and the beech, have only small, inconspicuous flowers because they are wind-pollinated.

There are many other delightful 'rooms', hidden areas and wooden sculptures in this part of the garden which well reward the time taken to explore them. In the middle of this woodland area, close to a beehive, is an enormously tall tree with a primeval-looking trunk. This is a tulip tree (*Liriodendron tulipifera*). Its foliage is far out of reach, but a younger one is growing nearby, and you can inspect the unusual shape of its leaf. Unlike that of any other tree, it has a rather abruptly notched tip, looking as if it has been scissored across. The tulip tree was one of the first exotic trees to be brought from North American in the 1600s. It has yellowish flowers above folded-back sepals, which are somewhat cup-shaped, but do not look much like tulips. Past the tulip tree is an ancient sweet chestnut, very likely a tree planted by 'Capability' Brown. His plantings were mainly of native or long-established trees, and the sweet chestnut was brought to Britain in Roman times.

Rejoin the lakeside path, re-cross the bridge and head for the Great Conservatory.

The Great Conservatory

In the past, Syon had not only its magnificent Conservatory, but also a vast area of glasshouses dedicated to horticulture over toward the River Brent. Exotic flowers were grown in them, pineapples, bananas and figs were ripened, and it was here that Britain's first mangosteens (a fruit from the East Indies) were raised. The glasshouses have gone, but the Great Conservatory remains. Erected in 1820–30 by Charles Fowler, the architect of Covent Garden Market in central London, it is a mansion of its kind, in Bath stone, cast iron and immense areas of glass.

Conservatories have an important place in British garden history. They first appeared in the 17th century, when, furnished with a stove to keep frosts at bay, they were called 'winter houses'. Soon after, when orange trees became a prized status symbol, they evolved into orangeries, and a new term, 'greenhouse', was coined for these buildings, since they protected tender 'greens', as orange trees and other tender shrubs, such as pomegranates, myrtle and bay, were called. Later, a new word – 'conservatory' – became used to describe places to display prized plants, and 'greenhouse' became the name for the glasshouses where they were propagated.

The first conservatories were stone or brick buildings, with a solid roof, for the importance of light as well as heat in plant biology was not yet fully understood. However, by the early 19th century new technology brought a revolution in plant propagation. Curved iron glazing bars, which enabled walls and roofs to be glazed with small panes of glass, were invented by J. C. Loudon in 1816, and although all windows carried a prohibitive tax until 1845, it became cheaper to manufacture glass. The scene was set for the creation at Syon of this vision of curved tracery with a vista of the sky.

Walk through the north door and stand beneath the central dome. The scale of the Great Conservatory is astounding. It measures more than 100 yards (90 metres) from one end of its curved wings to the other, and the dome above is 60 feet (18 metres) high. Walk along the west wing, to the right, to see a commemorative vine threading through its ceiling. It was grown from a cutting donated by the Australian government, to commemorate 36 cuttings sent from Syon to Australia in 1832 to start the white wine industry there. At the west end is a lily pond. Now walk along to the east wing, which is stocked with bedding plants and climbers, some of which are beautifully perfumed. At the end is a delightful cactus room.

Exit the Conservatory by the south door and you step out onto a raised terrace. Embraced by the Conservatory's two wings is a formal garden, its lawns set with yews that have been clipped into cone shapes. You will also see lavender beds and wisteria. Descend the steps and walk along the path through the centre of the garden, where there is a pool with a fountain topped by a statue of Mercury.

Now retrace your steps back to the visitor centre where the walk ends.

FULHAM PALACE GARDENS

LOCATION	About 4½ miles (7 kilometres) west of Charing Cross.
TRANSPORT	Putney Bridge Underground Station (District Line) is ten minutes' walk away. Putney Station (overground trains from Waterloo) is 20 minutes' walk away. Buses 220, 430 stop on Fulham Palace Road, and 14, 22, 85, 93, 414, 265 near Putney Bridge. There is a small car park.
ADMISSION	Fulham Palace Gardens and Bishop's Park open daily dawn–dusk. Admission to both is free.
SEASONAL FEATURES	Spring blossom, magnolias April–May; herb garden in summer; fruit in Oct, and autumn colour.
EVENTS	Tours of the grounds and the palace.
REFRESHMENTS	Drawing Room Café open daily 10:00–16:00 hours.

From the 8th century until 1973, Fulham Palace was the residence of the Bishops of London, and its beautiful gardens were largely the creation of the many keen gardeners among them. They have the atmosphere of very personal gardens – indeed, one Bishop Blomfield loved Fulham Palace and its gardens so much that a special Act of Parliament was passed to allow him to live there in retirement. Before that, bishops did not retire, but died in office. Many are buried in All Saints Church by Putney Bridge, which from medieval times was the local parish church.

The site of the palace, beside the River Thames, is a more ancient settlement, however. Archaeologists have discovered traces of Neolithic people and Roman defensive earthworks. The Manor of Fulham was granted to Bishop Waldhere in 704, and from the 11th century the bishops had a country residence on the site. The palace is at heart a Tudor mansion with later additions and alterations, but beneath the Great Lawn traces have been found of its predecessors. In medieval times, the site was surrounded by a massive defensive moat, the longest in England, which remained until the 1920s. Beyond it stretched Thameside water meadows, and the manorial farms and fields. Today, the buildings and gardens that were enclosed by the moat are classified as an Ancient Protected Monument.

A key figure in the development of the gardens was Henry Compton, Bishop of London (1675–1713), and, incidentally, the only bishop to sign the document inviting the Dutch Prince William of Orange and Queen Mary to become King and Queen of England in 1688. The diocese of this bishop included the North American colonies and he sent a botanist from Oxford, the Reverend John Banister (*see* page 11), to Virginia as a missionary, with instructions to send interesting plants to Fulham. During his bishopric the palace gardens were planted with new trees and shrubs from America, the West Indies, India and Africa. Early stove houses (greenhouses) were built in the gardens and filled with 'exoticks', and people came from all over England to see them.

John Banister went to Virginia in 1680 and collected plants there until his death. In 1688 he sent back to Britain sweet bay (*Magnolia virginiana*), the first magnolia to be grown in England. He also sent the sweet gum (*Liquidambar styraciflua*), scarlet oak and the box elder, or ash-leaved maple (*Acer negundo*) – all trees that are admired for their foliage, and all introduced at Fulham Palace, starting the tradition of fine specimen trees. The original stock has died and been replaced, but some trees in the gardens may date from Bishop Compton's time. The success of his introductions is partly explained by the fact that for some years from 1681 his gardener was George London, who, with his partner Henry Wise, set up the influential Brompton Nurseries (where the South Kensington museums stand today), an important source of exotic plants for British gardeners.

Situated so close to the River Thames, the palace was often flooded, and when in the 19th century the bishops presented two water meadows along the riverside to the people of Fulham as a public park, in return an embankment was built to prevent further flooding. This was soon planted with a fine avenue of London plane trees.

After World War II the palace was divided, the bishops retaining one part from which the diocese was run, and the remainder being used as offices. By the 1970s the gardens had fallen into disuse and in 1973 they were leased to the Borough of Hammersmith and Fulham, which opened them to the public the following year.

Many of the splendid trees in the 13-acre (5.2-hectare) gardens are name-tagged. Those described on the walk are located on the map on pages 32–3, and a detailed map of the trees in Fulham Palace Gardens is available from the Museum shop, but it is a good idea to take on the walk one of the tree identification guides listed on page 185.

THE FULHAM PALACE GARDENS WALK

Start and finish The main gate on Bishop's Avenue. **Time** Allow 1½ hours.

The walk begins at the old gateway to the palace on Bishop's Avenue, found by continuing from the main road and down past the tennis court. The stone gateposts date from the early 19th century. As you pass through them you are, in fact, walking onto a bridge across the ancient moat which for centuries surrounded the palace and its grounds. It was originally dug around a pre-Norman settlement, which occupied the site between the River Thames and the present palace. If you look through the railings on either side you can see the line of the moat, which existed until the 1920s, when it was filled in at the orders of Bishop Winnington-Ingram. The moat also ran along Moat Gardens beside Fulham Palace Road, and along the boundary between Fulham Palace Gardens and Bishop's Park.

The quaint Porter's Lodge which marks the end of the bridge just ahead to the left was designed in 1815 in the fashionable Gothic style. Opposite is the Coachman's Lodge, faced with black clapperboard, a rural touch, and designed by the Victorian architect William Butterfield (1814–1900). Continue straight ahead, passing on the right a lime tree with floodlights, perhaps planted to commemorate an avenue of limes that were planted along this road – the main drive up to the palace – by Bishop Compton. Walk right up the drive to the red-brick façade of the palace, and over the cobbles beneath a Tudor archway. Notice the great medieval wooden gates. The archway leads into the intimate West Court, a rare example of a Tudor courtyard, although the central fountain, on the site of the old well, was built in Victorian times. Vines clad the walls in places, benefitting from the sun trap.

Leave the courtyard through the Tudor archway, turn right along the palace's outer wall, then right again onto the path that leads to an open lawn planted with trees. To the left is an unusual environmental sculpture, nicknamed 'the Bishops' Tree', which commemorates local resident Peter Moorhouse who loved the park and who died in 2005. It makes clever use of the trunk of an ancient Cedar of Lebanon, into which have been carved the figures of four of the bishops who have lived at Fulham Palace.

The Great Lawn

Continue past the palace on your right. Ahead of you and to the right, spreading around the palace, is the gracious Great Lawn, dating from the 18th century. Take the path that skirts it on the left. Many of the trees on the lawn were damaged during the hurricane of October 1987, among them the Judas tree (*Cercis siliquastrum*) to your right, which is now regenerating. To your right at the point where the path starts to bend is a statuesque black walnut (*Juglans nigra*), which is probably around 150 years old, a tree native to North America.

Just ahead, turn onto a small path leading off to the right and turn to look at the garden façade of the palace. It was added to the Tudor core in 1814 by Bishop Howley (1813–28), who disliked the 'Gothick' taste of his 18th-century predecessors. Ahead of you is an Atlas cedar (*Cedrus atlantica*), from North Africa. With somewhat upgrowing branches, it is another tree probably planted about 150 years ago. Ahead, in a coppice just to the right, is an ancient sweet chestnut (*Castanea sativa*) with a beard of twigs on a goitred, swollen-looking trunk. It is tree of distinct personality, very likely planted by Bishop Compton.

Return to the main path and turn right. Across the yew hedge on your left, you catch glimpses of an allotment area. Despite its proximity to the Bishop's Palace, in Tudor days, this area was the site of pleasure grounds and Elizabeth I was a regular visitor. The land was made over for use as allotments during World War I, so these are quite early examples of their kind. At the end of the path you come to a dinosaur of a tree trunk with no branches. This is a London plane, seemingly dead a few years ago, the victim of the 1976 drought, but now growing a sturdy young limb.

The Kitchen Garden

In front of the plane the path veers right and you will soon see to the left an isolated length of brick wall. This wall reminds the curator of the museum, Miranda Poliakoff, of a pine pit – a place where pineapples were grown in pre-Victorian times. It consisted of a cold frame with a brick trench outside, heaped with manure. The heat from fermentation warmed the bricks, which radiated warmth into the cold frame, helping to ripen the fruit.

Beyond the pine pit, pass through the gateway in the wall ahead into the Kitchen Garden. This large enclosure was probably converted from an orchard in the 18th century (the area

FULHAM PALACE GARDENS

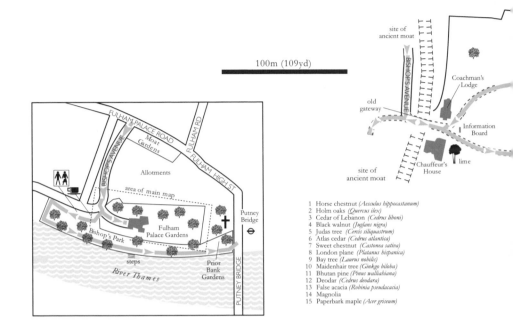

100m (109yd)

1 Horse chestnut (*Aesculus hippocastanum*)
2 Holm oaks (*Quercus ilex*)
3 Cedar of Lebanon (*Cedrus liboni*)
4 Black walnut (*Juglans nigra*)
5 Judas tree (*Cercis siliquastrum*)
6 Atlas cedar (*Cedrus atlantica*)
7 Sweet chestnut (*Castonea sativa*)
8 London plane (*Platanus hispanica*)
9 Bay tree (*Laurus nobilis*)
10 Maidenhair tree (*Ginkgo biloba*)
11 Bhutan pine (*Pinus walliahiana*)
12 Deodar (*Cedrus deodara*)
13 False acacia (*Robinia pseudacacia*)
14 Magnolia
15 Paperbark maple (*Acer griseum*)

is shown blank on a map of 1745). Turn right across the grass to pick up a small path which passes a range of decaying greenhouses, their glass long gone. This was at one time the Palace Vinery, and though the grape vines are still surviving gamely, the Vinery itself is marvellously tumbledown and romantic in decay. It is anticipated that restoration work will begin here in 2010.

To the left of the path is an oval-shaped knot garden which was laid out in the 1830s. Its beds, edged with dwarf box, are densely planted with herbs used for culinary, household and medicinal purposes, such as purple sage, sorrel, salad burnet, lavender and feverfew, many of which scent the air. At each end is a golden bay and a tall green bay tree. At the far end of the knot garden, beside a fine Tudor gateway, a metal map in Braille identifies the herbs planted within. Pause here to look across the Kitchen Garden at the line of fruit trees, among them cherries, plums, quinces, pears and medlars. The latter is somewhat unusual, in that its fruits cannot be eaten until the first frost has softened them. Beds here once supplied the palace kitchens with fruit and vegetables.

The walk now turns sharp left, across the grass, and takes you back along the knot garden's crowning glory, the magnificent wisteria pergola which encloses it, bearing cascading lilac-coloured flowers in spring. Its age is not known exactly, but it was planted before 1899, since it features in a photograph taken in that year.

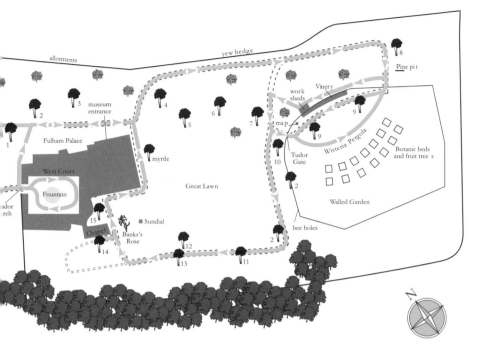

Retrace your steps toward the pine pit and follow the path. Before you turn left in front of the palace, notice, to your left, behind a screen of trees and shrubs, the once-busy work 'bothies', and the buildings used by the staff who tended the stoves that heated the greenhouses, which had to be fed day and night. For safety reasons, this part of the garden is closed to the public.

The Tudor Gate

Turn left as you see the palace and continue straight ahead until you are level with the Tudor Gate at the end of the knot garden in the Kitchen Garden wall. Facing the palace across the lawn, this gateway was once the exit from the formal garden to the orchard. During restoration work it was found that the lower brickwork courses were laid in about 1480, and most of the remainder around 1500, with some Victorian additions at the top. The arms at the top are of Bishop Fitzjames, a bishop under Henry VIII.

There are some interesting trees in this area. To the right near the Tudor Gate is a young Maidenhair tree (*Ginkgo biloba*), with leaves like no other coniferous or deciduous tree. These leaves turn a buttery yellow in the autumn and the small fruit (this tree is a female) have a rather unpleasant scent. Further along the wall is a magnificent Holm or evergreen oak from the Mediterranean, and just past it you will notice some bee boles in the old brick wall. These semicircular niches held round straw or cane skips, which were the beehives of the age (the slatted wooden hives that we know today are a Victorian invention). However, the niches have now been filled in.

Toward the river, where the path bends right, is a magnificent evergreen oak with a sculptural contortion of riven trunks which are probably the branching of one tree, its original trunk now dead and rotted away. It is thought to have been planted in Tudor times and it has official Great Tree of London status. Today, it leans over, bent like an aging dowager. To the left a woodland walk has recently been opened, but the route we will follow takes the path to the right, beneath the oak, to find on the left a pretty Bhutan pine (*Pinus wallichiana*) from the Himalayas. Traces of the ancient moat can be seen in the shrubbery to the left, while to the right of the path is a deodar, a Himalayan cedar (*Cedrus deodora*).

Carry on up the path until you reach the chapel built onto the east façade of the palace in the 1860s. As the path turns to the right, there is a false acacia (*Robinia pseudacacia*) on the left. The chapel, by William Butterfield (1814–1900), is an example of Tudor Revival architecture. Along its wall is a spreading Chinese evergreen magnolia (*Magnolia delavayi*), a native of Southern China, while around the corner, on the front lawn, is a Banks rose (*Rosa banksiae* 'Lutea'), with small yellow flowers. Opposite this, to your right, is the base of an 18th-century sundial (the dial itself is in the museum). Round the corner ahead is a paper-bark maple (*Acer griseum*), which originated in China, but is now thought to be extinct in the wild. Its name is derived from its thin, peeling, orange-red bark. The last stop is before the house front, where strong growths of scented myrtle are said to have been grown from cuttings used for Queen Victoria's wedding bouquet.

Return through the car park, once a farmyard and the site of the tithe barn. The building to your left is the old stable block. Follow the drive back and left to the main gate, where the walk ends – perhaps with thanks to the three gardeners who maintain this magic garden. Outside the gate to the left is the entrance to Bishop's Park, which offers the pleasant prospect of a stroll around its beds and shrubberies, and a delightful walk along the embankment, past All Saints Church to Putney Bridge.

HOLLAND PARK

LOCATION	About 3 miles (4.8 kilometres) west of Charing Cross.
TRANSPORT	Holland Park Underground Station (Central line) is ten minutes' walk from the park. Three Underground stations: High Street Kensington (District and Circle lines), Notting Hill Gate (Central line) and Shepherd's Bush (Central and Hammersmith and City lines) are a short bus ride away. Buses along Kensington High Street are 9, 10, 27, 28, 49, 328; along Holland Park Avenue are 12 and 88. There is a car park on the west side of the park.
ADMISSION	Park open daily 07:30–dusk. Admission is free.
SEASONAL FEATURES	The Camellia Border and Azalea Walk in spring; The Napoleon Garden, Iris Garden and Rose Garden in spring and summer; the Dahlia Garden in summer. Spring blossom and autumn colour in the woodland enclosures.
EVENTS	Open-air theatre, opera and concerts in summer; art exhibitions and other events in the Orangery April–October, and in the Ice House; displays and exhibitions in the Ecology Centre.
REFRESHMENTS	Holland Park Café open daily 10:00–19:00 hours or later.

This 54-acre (21.8-hectare) park, with white peacocks in the Japanese garden, rabbits in the Fox Enclosure, open-air theatre, art exhibitions, and woodland walks can seem like a world of its own. It surrounds what remains of Holland House, a splendid Jacobean mansion built on one of the natural terraces of the River Thames, with views south over what was then open countryside. The house was built to an H-plan, with formal gardens alongside and a wilder area of woodland divided by paths to the rear.

Holland House was built around 1608 for Sir Walter Cope, Chancellor of the Exchequer to James 1, and was originally called Cope Castle. After his death it passed to his daughter, whose husband was created Lord Holland in 1624. Under Henry Fox (1773–1840), the 3rd Lord Holland, and his imperious but witty wife, it became something of a court in its own right – London's established centre of literary and political society. To Lady Holland's salon came the literary luminaries of the day, including Lord Byron, Macaulay, Sir Walter Scott and, when he was fashionable, Charles Dickens, to mingle with the politicians of the day, such as Melbourne, Palmerston and other Whigs (the political party that evolved into the Liberals). In the 1840s, part of the Jacobean stable wing was converted into the Garden Ballroom, and this and the Orangery were linked to the main house by the terraces and arcades which can still be seen today.

This fine house was bombed and gutted by fire during World War II, leaving only the east wing worth restoring. The remains of the house and the estate were purchased in

1952 by the then London County Council and the east wing was renovated in 1959. It now forms part of what must be London's best-sited youth hostel. In 1986 ownership of the estate passed to the Royal Borough of Kensington and Chelsea, which has been active in restoring the gardens and creating new interest.

THE HOLLAND PARK WALK

Start and finish The Kensington High Street gate. **Time** Allow 1½ hours.

Fine wrought-iron gates dating from the 1840s mark what was the main entrance to Holland House. The flanking stone piers were inspired by a design of Inigo Jones. From this gate, stroll along the handsome avenue of plane trees and chestnuts leading past the Commonwealth Institute and a public sports field which is very busy in summer. The path swings left to pass the front of the Jacobean house. Parts of it form a backdrop to the Open-Air Theatre, which opened in 1964.

The Ice House

Passing the theatre and the café terrace beside it, walk through the portal on the right. To the left is the Ice House, a round brick building of 1770 with a handsome domed and tiled roof. This ice house is unusual in being above ground – these buildings were usually partly buried to improve their insulation. It was restored in 1979. To the right is a small lawn with a sculpture of a boy with bear cubs by the English animal sculptor, John Swan, which was erected in 1902. Follow the path past the sculpture to reach the Dutch Garden.

The Dutch or Formal Garden

This garden, stretching westward from the house, was first created in 1812 by one Buonaiuti, librarian to the Holland family. Originally, and until a souring of Britain's relations with Portugal, it was called the Portuguese Garden. The name 'Dutch Garden' does reflect its layout, however: neat, geometric parterre hedging of miniature box separated by paths, although these are probably broader now than they would have been in the original design. Within the hedging two main displays are bedded out over the course of the year. There is a spring show of overwintering wallflowers and tulips and a summer one with geraniums and other bedding plants, perhaps yellow calceolarias and scarlet or blue salvias. The plants that are usually referred to as geraniums are really pelargoniums. They came originally from South Africa and were the key to much Victorian and subsequent planting. The first dwarf 'Tom Thumb' variety, ideal for bedding such as this, was available by 1840.

The walk takes you up to the east end of the garden and then along the paths through the centre to the west end, where there is an armillary-sphere (hollow hoop) sundial, one of the donations of the fund-raising Friends of Holland Park. Other donations from this body include £5,000-worth of snowdrops, an engraving machine for labelling trees, bird boxes and eight hedgehogs. Turn to walk eastward along the warm brick wall, once part of the Jacobean stables, offering shelter on the garden's north side. Turn left up the steps at the end of the path and leave the Dutch Garden through the wisteria-covered brick arch.

The North Lawn and Azalea Walk

To the right you can now see remnants of the walls and windows of the house, running toward the youth hostel in the restored east wing. Cross the North Lawn, a favourite area for relaxing in the sun in summer. Directly ahead, in the top left-hand corner, is a young Cedar of Lebanon (*Cedrus libani*), planted in 1996 by the U.K. Alumni Association of the American University of Beirut. Bear right toward what was once a rose walk leading off the lawn, but was replanted with azaleas around the turn of the 19th century – it is usually at its most dazzling in May when the azalea varieties, many of them scented, are in full flower. Turn left along the Azalea Walk. To the right is the Arboretum, planted in the 17th and 18th centuries and well known for its many exotic trees cultivated for their scientific interest. It is carpeted with bluebells in spring.

At the end of the Azalea Walk you will reach a pond which has a commemorative statue of the 3rd Lord Holland, the statesman Henry Fox, who was responsible for some of the tree-planting in the park. Sculpted by G. F. Watts in 1840, Lord Holland sits at ease (note the comforting spats), his head and hands much favoured by perching London pigeons. There is a fine copper beech nearby, and as an example of the more exotic trees, behind the statue is a pin oak (*Quercus palustris*) from North America, one of the oaks that has handsome red leaves in autumn.

The Woodland Enclosures

Continue along the path directly ahead. In this area, behind the North Lawn, are some of the park's ten woodland enclosures in what was originally designated a 'Wildernesse'. Over to the right is the Beech Enclosure, planted not only with beech trees but also with holly, which would be present in natural beech woodland.

At the top of the Beech Enclosure turn left into a long walk lined with fine horse chestnuts (*Aesculus hippocastanum*), which were planted in the 19th century. Introduced from the Balkans in the 16th century, these trees are common enough to be taken for granted, but the flowers, which appear from May to June, are as intricate as orchids. They are usually white, but there is a variety with red flowers and one with double flowers which does not produce conkers.

To the right is a wildlife reserve. Holland Park has a marvellous wildlife tally for its location deep in a city. Sixty different wild bird species have been seen here, 30 of them nesting in this reserve or elsewhere in the park. They include the tawny owl, the sparrowhawk and the great spotted woodpecker. There are many voles and mice, although they are rarely seen. Halfway along the path is a pond, which was established as recently as 1991 but is now a major feature. It attracts newts, frogs and toads, and is usually busy with dragonflies in summer.

The ground falls away down the line of the path, which is set with commemorative benches. At the end, to the right, is the 'D' Garden, so named because of its shape, which comprises an open lawn enclosed with bushes.

Take an abrupt left turn, not the tarmac path, into the Lime Tree Walk, originally planted by one Lady Holland in 1876. Many of its trees were lost in the great storm of October 1987, but they have been replaced with new trees. To the right is the Fox Enclosure, named after

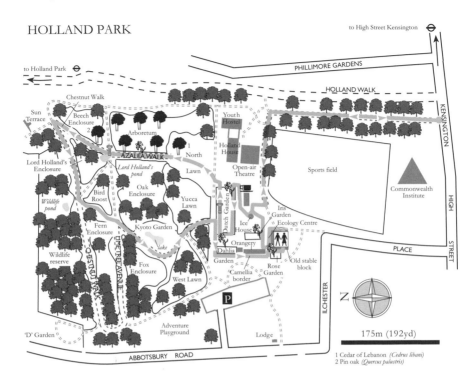

HOLLAND PARK

to High Street Kensington

to Holland Park

PHILLIMORE GARDENS

HOLLAND WALK

KENSINGTON

Chestnut Walk

Sun Terrace

Beech Enclosure 2

Arboretum

Youth Hostel

Lord Holland's Enclosure

Lord Holland's pond

1

North Lawn

Holland House

Open-air Theatre

Sports field

Commonwealth Institute

HIGH

Oak Enclosure

Bird Roost

Wildlife pond

Yucca Lawn

AZALEA WALK

Fern Enclosure

Kyoto Garden

Dutch Garden

Iris Garden

Ice House

Ecology Centre

Orangery

Wildlife reserve

Fox Enclosure

lake

Dahlia Garden

Camellia border

Rose Garden

Old stable block

PLACE

STREET

CHESTNUT WALK

CHESTNUT AVENUE

West Lawn

ILCHESTER

N

'D' Garden

Adventure Playground

Lodge

175m (192yd)

ABBOTSBURY ROAD

P

1 Cedar of Lebanon (*Cedrus libani*)
2 Pin oak (*Quercus palustris*)

Henry Fox rather than the bushy-tailed hunter – which is fortunate for the good many tame, fat, sassy rabbits that inhabit these woods and enclosures.

The Kyoto Garden

A left turn at the end of the Fox Enclosure brings you to the Kyoto Garden, a sanctuary created and donated in 1991 by the Chamber of Commerce of Kyoto, 'the Athens of Japan', that country's imperial and cultural capital for 1,000 years. Climb the steps and follow a path paved with smooth stone that winds through the garden. After the natural tangle of the woodland walks, this garden is a sudden contrast, a dream of order, with smooth, vivid green lawns set with lime and other trees, a small lake with a tumbling clear cascade, bamboo-spouted water fountains that are somewhat unusual to Western eyes, and solidly built stone lanterns.

Although the Japanese and the Chinese had some of the most ornamental of plants in their nurseries – peonies, hydrangeas, azaleas – which astounded the first European plant collectors, the key to such a garden is simplicity and correctness. Everything has its proper place in the scheme: the cascade and the symbolic bridge; the humps of natural stone (symbolizing mountains); the grouped foliage of the trees and shrubs. It is an artistic composition, a kind of three-dimensional picture, where, by the careful use of proportion an impression of great space is created. The emphasis is on foliage rather than bright flowers. In late summer, for example, the only touch of flower colour might be from some discreet hydrangeas or pink water lilies. In autumn, leaf colour might be a feature. A garden like this, epitomizing the Japanese value of order is, in its way, as formal as the Dutch Garden.

Leave the garden via the steps again and follow the path as it bends left. It passes an enclosure much favoured by peacocks which have the unexpected habit of roosting in trees.

The Napoleon Garden and the Orangery

Turn right behind the Walking Man statue and left off the path into the Napoleon Garden at the west end of the Dutch Garden. This space for contemporary sculpture was created in 1997 and is believed to be named after a bust, since lost, of the Emperor Napoleon by the Italian sculptor Antonio Canova (1757–1822).

From the Napoleon Garden, turn left along the path leading past the chic Belvedere Restaurant and the lovely old Orangery. Alongside the path is a marvellous tall camellia border. Look through the end windows of the Orangery to see a pair of bronze figures of boy wrestlers, about 4 feet (1.2 metres) tall. Known as the 'Herculaneum wrestlers', they are Roman, from the 4th century AD, and were donated by a London County Council chairman. Turn left at the end of the Orangery; to the right is a rose garden, sheltered by the high walls of the old stables, but the walk takes you left again through an open arcade, and right along a covered walkway.

The Iris Garden

On the left side of the walkway, arches open cloister-like onto a charming Iris Garden with a central fountain. Irises are a flower family that excite passions. An iris (possibly the wild yellow flag) was adopted as a royal emblem in the arms of both France and England, and the flowers have been bred into some unexpected colours – the pinks and browns of the artist Sir Cedric Morris (1889–1982), for example.

Continue to the end of the covered walkway. At the end you will see the café terrace ahead. In the old stable block to the right, there is an information centre and the Ecology Centre, which has natural history displays, including tanks of freshwater fish, invertebrates and reptiles, among them a royal python. Follow the path ahead along the top of the sports field then turn right along Holland Walk to the main gate, where the walk ends.

KENSINGTON ROOF GARDENS

LOCATION	About 4 miles (6 kilometres) west of Charing Cross, on Kensington High Street, W8. The entrance is at the bottom of Derry Street, W8, on the right (west) side. Sign yourself in at the reception desk in the foyer, and take the dedicated lift to the roof.
TRANSPORT	High Street Kensington Underground Station (District and Circle lines). Bus 9, 10, 27, 28, 31, 49, 52. There is an underground car park beneath Kensington Town Hall on Horton Street, W8.
ADMISSION	Open 09:00–18:00 hours whenever the club is not in use (tel: 020 7937 7994 to check). Admission is free.
SEASONAL FEATURES	The blossom in the English Woodland Garden and the wisteria in the Tudor Garden in spring; the Spanish Garden in summer.
REFRESHMENTS	Not available in the Roof Gardens. Muffin Man Tea Shop, 12 Wright's Lane, W8 6TA, open Mon–Sat 08:30–18:00 hours.
EVENTS	Roof Gardens and the adjoining club are privately owned, but are sometimes hired for private events.

These roof gardens are above what was once the Derry & Toms department store. Briefly, during the 1970s, it became home to the fashionable Biba department store, with an art-deco style restaurant overlooking the Roof Gardens. The Virgin Group now operates the gardens and the nightclub and functions complex at the top of the building.

At 1.5 acres (0.5 hectares), this is the largest roof garden in Europe. It was planted in 1936–8 and was the brainchild of Trevor Bowen, then head of the Barker's Stores empire (which had taken over Derry & Toms). The garden was designed by Ralph Hancock, who was the leading gardener of the day. The design is similar to his earlier 'Garden of the Nations', which was laid out on the 11th floor of the R.C.A. building at the Rockefeller Centre in New York.

This is a short walk, and afterward you may have time to visit Kensington Square, at the bottom of Derry Street. It was one of the first new developments when the former village of Kensington became invaded by London's fashionable set seeking pure air. Then, when William III and Queen Mary moved to Kensington Palace in the 1690s, the square was taken over by courtiers – Nos. 11 and 12, built in 1683, are probably the best-preserved houses. Among the residents have been the political philosopher John Stuart Mill (1806–73), who lived at No. 18 (there is a statue to him in Temple Place Gardens, *see* page 81) and the actress, Mrs. Patrick Campbell (1865–1940). The square is planted with some fine old London plane trees.

Osterley Park: *The west face of Osterley House, with its elegant, sweeping staircase and camellia planted against the wall*

Syon Park: *The perfect symmetry of the Great Conservatory*

Fulham Palace Gardens: *The gated entrance that leads to the quiet Tudor courtyard and sun-trap*

Holland Park: *Detail of the 'armillary sphere' sundial; the rings represent the celestial sphere*

Kensington Roof Gardens: *Dappled light plays on the elegant Tudor walkway leading to the Spanish Garden*

Hyde Park: *Plane trees create an arboreal cathedral on one of the carriageways*

Kensington Gardens: *The famous statue of Peter Pan was erected in 1912 and parts of it are now golden, having been touched by so many children over the years*

KENSINGTON ROOF GARDENS

1 Windmill palms *(Trachycarpus fortunei)*
2 London planes *(Platanus × hispanica)*

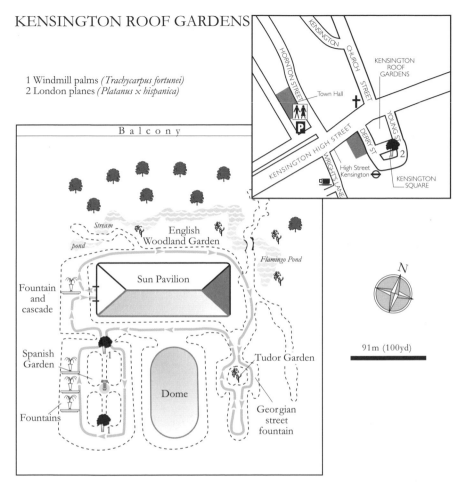

91m (100yd)

THE KENSINGTON ROOF GARDENS WALK

Start and finish The Sun Pavilion.

Time This very short walk can be completed in under ten minutes, but allow half an hour or more to really enjoy these gardens.

The lift opens into the Sun Pavilion, originally a roof restaurant and now the Roof Gardens Club. It was designed by Barker's in-house architect, Bernard George. Turn left to walk out through the swing doors where you will immediately hear the unexpected sound of water from the rockwork fountain and cascade now facing you. The water from the cascade flows away as a stream, and you should follow it to the right (if you turn left you arrive at the Spanish Garden, which will be the climax of the walk).

The Woodland Garden

Follow the stream to the fishpond, which has an almond tree on the far side and a peach and apple tree to the right. During 2008 Head Gardener David Lewis, who has a team of three part-time staff, replanted the gardens extensively, putting in more blossom trees to enhance the year-round interest. The idea of much of the planting has been to mark moments in the gardens' history, and blossom trees were popular when these extraordinary gardens were created in the 1930s.

The stone bridge is an original from 1936 and if you cross it, you can pass through a gate to a viewing platform, with views across central and south London. There is, however, a more interesting viewing post later on. Continue along the path to the lawn, where there is a remarkable sight. Here you could be forgiven for thinking that you were following a woodland stream deep in the countryside. The effect is magical. There are splendid, mature trees here – English oaks, a North American red oak in the centre, limes – as well as borders busy with British woodland hedgerow natives: bluebells in spring, yellow flag iris, bright red lobelia, geraniums and wild garlic. There are also beds with ferns and foxgloves. Odd pieces of pottery and stone adorn the riverbank, while in the water or on the stream's edge a variety of ducks potter about, among them wood duck, mandarin, white-cheeked pintail, ringed teal and pochard. They have had their wings clipped so that they don't fly away. In among them are mallards that have flown in and decided to stay – and who could blame them? This must be the most exclusive pond in the whole of London.

The largest trees are 70 years old and date back to when the gardens were first laid out. It is remarkable that all this life manages to grow in soil just 16 inches (40cm) deep. A drain runs underneath the stream to a gully behind the boundary wall. It is easy to forget that you are high up in the centre of London, until you catch a glimpse of rooftops and horizon through the wall's circular windows.

At the end of the Woodland Garden there is a pretty, Japanese-style wooden bridge with a 70-year-old Japanese acer growing next to it. Cross the bridge and pass under two mature lime trees to find a somewhat hidden viewing platform. Next to the gate there is a plaque to Trevor Bowen, the chairman of Barker's department store, who inspired this 'garden in the sky'. As you leave the viewing platform there is a black mulberry on your left, in the bay by the wall. Now it is time to meet the gardens' most famous residents.

The Flamingo Pond

It is quite startling to see flamingos outside of a zoo, but their presence here is entirely in keeping with the dream-like atmosphere of so much of these unusual gardens. There are four flamingos. Bill and Ben are Chilean pink flamingos and are more than 30 years old; the other two are Greater Flamingos and are more recent arrivals – Splosh and Pecks took up residence in November 2008 as part of the gardens' 70th birthday celebrations. The names were chosen through a competition among the staff, although what former pop singer and model Victoria Beckham ('Posh') and her husband, footballer David Beckham ('Becks'), think nobody knows. The flamingos are fed twice a day with food containing carotenoid which helps keep their feathers pink.

Opposite the pond is the V.I.P. 'moo' room – a fun, decidedly unsophisticated name that alludes to the cow-patterned furnishings within. Now pass through the Laburnum Walk where you immediately come to an original street fountain, probably Georgian in origin and which it is believed Ralph Hancock used for his garden at the Chelsea Flower Show during the 1930s.

The Tudor Garden

This sheltered enclosure has an entirely different atmosphere. It is a walled courtyard with herringbone brick floors and a magnificent, snaking wisteria that dates back to the 1930s. The planting in the bed on the left, just past the water fountain, is based on Biba colours, with plenty of black and white, including white foxgloves (*Aconitum ivorine*), black hollyhocks, black and white tulips and black and white dianthus.

This part of the gardens is where special events take place. Owner Richard Branson celebrated the publication of his book *Business Stripped Bare* here in 2008, and it is frequently hired for private parties.

If you look carefully at the archways you may be able to see the Derry & Toms monogram, the stick of the D also forming the stick of the T. The lime trees in the courtyard are planted in the same place as those on the original 1936 plans.

The Spanish Garden

After circling the courtyard, turn left to follow the arched Tudor Walkway, which has myrtle hedging and plants typical of Tudor England. It brings you out into another world entirely – the atmospheric Spanish Garden, with its reproduction campanile and convent. It may be called the Spanish Garden, but the scope of its planting is much broader. This is, in fact, a glorious Mediterranean garden with more than a touch of Hollywood about it. You could be forgiven for thinking that you had walked onto a film set. It was laid out when few people had visited Spain – Spanish gardens tend to have cooler colours than those found here – but Hancock wanted vibrancy and heat in his colour scheme and this garden doesn't disappoint. In 2008 two shades of pink were used to repaint the walls and buildings. The darker shade is the original colour of the 1930s and the pale pink is the colour Biba chose in the 1970s.

Mediterranean plantings abound – palms, figs, pomegranate, olives and grapes. In the beds are hibiscus, bougainvillea, rosemary, cannas and agaves, while elsewhere there are aliums, lilies and tulips. There is also a mimosa tree that is fabulous in February. Note the pretty tiling everywhere, made up of remnants from a Derry & Toms sale.

Running parallel to the far wall, and lined with pencil-like Italian cypresses, is a long, thin pond. When the fountains are quiet, this becomes a dark reflecting pool – if you stand at the end facing the campanile you can enjoy the faintly hypnotic effect.

There is a Moorish feel to these gardens too, and a hint of the New Mexico of so many Westerns of old. During Hollywood's golden era, it was popular with many film stars of the day, with Raymond Massey, Will Hay, Ava Gardner and John Gielgud among those who visited. It is still something of a celebrity haunt today, with princes William and Harry regular visitors to the roof garden nightclub. The top floor, above the gardens, is home to the exclusive Babylon restaurant.

To the right of the campanile is a small courtyard with vine-covered Moorish arches, cast from the same moulds used those for the gardens at the Rockefeller Centre in New York. Just beyond you can see the spire of St. Mary Abbots, the parish church of Kensington, built in 1872 and in which children's author Beatrix Potter used to worship.

After this taste of rooftop exotica, leave the Spanish Garden to the left to arrive back at the cascade and the door leading to the lift, where the walk ends.

KENSINGTON GARDENS

LOCATION	About 2½ miles (4 kilometres) west of Charing Cross.
TRANSPORT	North side: Lancaster Gate or Queensway Underground stations (Central Line); 12, 94 bus. South side: High Street Kensington Underground Station (District and Circle lines); 9, 10, 52, 70, 452 bus. On foot, 10–15 minutes' walk from the underground car park on Park Lane.
ADMISSION	Open dawn–dusk daily. Admission is free.
SEASONAL FEATURES	The Sunken Garden and the Flower Walk in spring and summer; spring blossom; autumn tree colour.
EVENTS	Evening concerts at the Bandstand on Thu; kite-flying, model boat-sailing on the Round Pond; summer puppet shows on weekdays. Events booklet (*see* page 182).
REFRESHMENTS	The Orangery Café is open 10:00–17:00 from 1 November to 28 February.

Kensington Gardens were originally simply an extension of neighbouring Hyde Park, but in 1689 William III, seeking to ease his asthma with the clean country air of Kensington, commissioned Sir Christopher Wren and Nicholas Hawksmoor to convert the old Nottingham House into a palace-cum-country-retreat for himself and his household. The palace was linked to St. James's Park and his London palaces by the Route du Roi, its name eventually corrupting into Rotten Row, as it is still know today (*see* map on page 54). The palace, an example of domestic rather than florid state architecture (described by John Evelyn in his diary in 1696 as 'very noble, tho not greate'), had 26 acres (10.5 hectares) of Dutch gardens laid out around it, including fine parterres. During the 18th century Queen Anne added the red-brick Orangery; later Queen Caroline, wife of George II, extended the grounds; and Charles Bridgeman (appointed Royal Gardener in 1738) subsequently created long avenues of trees stretching to the distance as they do today, and possibly also the Round Pond. Caroline also had the Serpentine dug out, later extending it as the Long Water.

Under George II, Kensington Gardens was opened to visitors, although Queen Caroline had servants placed at the different entrances 'to prevent persons meanly clad from going into the garden'. When George II died in 1760 the palace fell out of prime use, although various royals lived and were born there, Queen Victoria among them. The gardens were opened up, eventually, even to the hoi polloi, which caused a certain Princess Lieven to write in 1820 that they had been 'annexed as a middle-class rendezvous and good society no longer goes there, except to drown itself' – an allusion to Harriet Shelley's suicide (*see* page 57). Along with the other Royal Parks, Kensington Gardens passed into public hands in the last century and today almost all of it is maintained by the Royal Parks Agency.

THE KENSINGTON GARDENS WALK

Start King's Arms Gate. **Finish** Palace Gate. **Time** Allow 1½ hours.

A dramatic introduction to the gardens is at King's Arms Gate. Cross to the right and walk up Dial Walk toward the magnificent Crowther Gates in front of Kensington Palace. Through them you can see a statue of Prince William of Orange (who later became William III). The drama is created by the tulip trees (*Liriodendron tulipifera*) that line the walk. The tulip tree was one of the first exotic trees to be brought to Britain from America in the 17th century. A close relative was later found growing in China. It has leaves shaped unlike those of any other tree, and yellowish flowers which are cup-shaped, but do not look much like tulips.

Turn right at the Crowther Gates, then left into the Broad Walk. This grand alley, part of Bridgeman's original design, is 50 feet (15 metres) wide. It was originally lined with elms, but by the 1970s these had died of Dutch elm disease and those that remained were felled and replaced with limes and Norway maples.

To the right of the Broad Walk, almost opposite the statue of Prince William of Orange, 'The Hump' can be traced – the edge of a great semicircular terrace with the Round Pond at its centre. This feature, with avenues of trees radiating from it, was the crux of Charles Bridgeman's design. In 1988 a double avenue of 160 lime trees was planted around the plateau, reviving another original period feature, the Great Bow. Occasional and impromptu concerts are staged on the bandstand to the right.

Walk up the Broad Walk until you come to a statue of Queen Victoria to the left. It was unveiled in 1887 to commemorate 50 years of the queen's reign. It shows her as an 18-year-old woman – her age when she took the throne in 1837. It was at Kensington Palace that she was told of the death of William IV, and she held her first Privy Council in the Red Saloon. The statue must have been modelled from a painting, since it was carved by her sixth child, Princess Louise, a respected sculptress. Notice the fine detail in the drapery curls and the thistles and other decoration at the back.

The Sunken Garden

Turn along the next path leading to the left off the Broad Walk, then left again. You are now entering the Cradle Walk, an alley formed by pleached lime trees which surrounds the Sunken Garden. This is a superb example of a Dutch-style garden of the early 18th century, but it was actually laid out in 1906–9. You can see into it through squints cut in the limes. It has three tiers of flower beds leading down to a rectangular pond 50 yards (45.7 metres) long with waterlilies and a line of three handsomely decorated lead cisterns of the period with fountains. The upper bed is devoted to perennial herbaceous flowers, the lower two to seasonal bedding. These display tulips and other bulbs; forget-me-nots; polyanthuses planted in October for flowering in spring; and bedding plants raised in the Hyde Park greenhouses (*see* page 59), which are planted out in May to flower until September. Perennial sword-leaved phormiums with their long, reddish flower spikes in summer add crisp definition to the corners.

KENSINGTON GARDENS

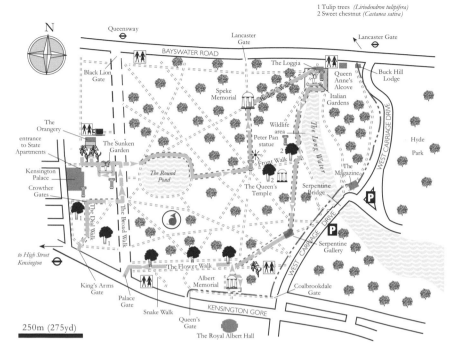

1 Tulip trees *(Liriodendron tulipifera)*
2 Sweet chestnut *(Castanea sativa)*

250m (275yd)

The Orangery

Walk all the way round the Sunken Garden and you emerge to see the 'pepper pots' directly ahead – lines of tall drum topiary with alternating holly and bay trees – marking the path to the Orangery. Follow this path, which is attributed to Sir Christopher Wren although the topiary is, at a guess, only 60 years old. It is not clear whether the Orangery was designed for Queen Anne by Sir Christopher Wren, by Sir John Vanbrugh (1664–1726), or even by Nicholas Hawksmoor (1661–1736), Wren's assistant. It was built in 1704 and has superb brickwork, especially in features such as the rubbed brick columns at the central entrance. Tall windows rise from just above the paved terrace to let in as much light as possible. Inside is a café-restaurant where you can take tea, as Queen Anne did. The decor is coolly white, with good copies of classical busts of the kind favoured in the 18th century, stone urns and dark green orange bushes. Over the archways at each end are swags by Dutch woodcarver Grinling Gibbons (1648–1721), who also carved the tumbles of flowers.

Turn left along the terrace in front, usually set with orange trees in tubs as it would have been when first built. It may be that orangeries were promoted not wholly because of the exotic bushes but also in deference to William III's title, William of Orange (the French city), and anti-Catholic politics; his queen, Mary, was the Protestant daughter of James II, and William, who was Europe's Protestant figurehead, was invited in as joint ruler.

At the end of the terrace turn left again and walk back toward the palace. Ahead is a beautiful Wren doorway and the entrance to the palace apartments. Many rooms suffered bomb damage in World War II, losing details by Grinling Gibbons and other notables, but fine ceilings and wall-paintings by William Kent (*see* page 9) survive. Victoria's bedroom, where she awoke to find herself queen, is one of the rooms on display.

The Round Pond

Turn left again, walk back to the Broad Walk and then continue straight across the grass to the north bank of the Round Pond. Commanding a grand terrace, with wide views and a vast open sky above, the pond is an invigorating place, and the area around it popular for kite-flying. It is not round, but its formal shape is difficult to discern from the ground. It was probably the work of Charles Bridgeman, but perhaps of Henry Wise, the partner of George London, who set the gardening pace in the early 18th century (Bridgeman worked under them for a time). And even though there is no plant cover out on the water, there are always a few water birds swimming on the pond, including swans, coots and gulls. More action comes from the model yachts which dedicated enthusiasts sail on the pond; model speed boats are not allowed.

Walk round the pond to the east side and take the path leading due east through the trees. It takes you to the bronze statue, *Physical Energy*, the creation of the 19th-century Royal Academician, George Frederick Watts, who shows energy as a naked male rider on a rearing horse. The original stands on Table Mountain outside Cape Town in South Africa as a memorial to Cecil Rhodes; this copy was placed at this spot in 1907.

The statue stands on what gardens staff call the Front Walk, one of Bridgeman's key avenues, at the centre of a radiating star of paths. There are splendid vistas across the park from this hub, which Bridgeman crossed with a straight avenue from Lancaster Gate. It was later angled to lead to the Albert Memorial. Some way south of this statue trees still mark the old line. The walk turns left, however, up the straight avenue to the memorial to the 19th-century explorer, John Hanning Speke. It is a pointed column of polished granite inscribed with the terse words: 'In memory of SPEKE. Victoria, Nyanza, The Nile 1864'. Terse, but a cloud hung over his memory: his death may have been not a hunting accident, but suicide; his better-known colleague, David Livingstone, disputed his claim to have discovered the source of the Nile.

The Long Water and the Italian Gardens

From Speke's Monument, turn northeast (right) onto Budge's Walk. A line of sweet chestnuts, planted in 1992, guides you along it to the Italian Gardens at the head of Long Water. This lake had been a series of fishing pools in a natural valley until Queen Caroline had it dug out as an extension of the Serpentine. It is quite shallow, only 4 feet 6 inches (1.4 metres) deep on average. The Italian Gardens were designed by James Pennethorne in 1861, with pools and osprey-plumed fountains, urns and balustrades. The path takes you to the Italian Pavilion at the north end, which was perhaps designed by Prince Albert himself, echoing the Petit Trianon at Versailles.

The plumbing is best Victorian. Water from an artesian well on Duck Island in St. James's Park is piped through a 10-inch (254-millimetre) pipe (fitted with valves to fill Buckingham Palace lake) to feed into Long Water and then into the Serpentine. The massive chimney of the Italian Pavilion is a clue to its former role: it contained a steam engine (now replaced by an electric pump) to operate the fountains, but this also fed the Round Pond and created an 18-foot (5.5-metre) head of water on the fountains, so the royals of the day (on restricted Sunday afternoons) could see them play without the gouts of smoke from the engine. The paved manhole in front of the Italian Pavilion hides a secret, 230-foot (70-metre) deep well shaft of mysterious origin. It is called St. Agnes Well and up to now it has remained unused.

Cross to the east side of the pavilion to see a large, wood-panelled alcove set in brick. It was designed by Wren for Queen Anne and moved brick by brick to this site from near King's Arms Gate. Walk a little further along the path in front of it to Buck Hill Lodge, one of the most attractive of Kensington Gardens' lodges, with a secluded, well-hidden pets' cemetery some 200 yards (183 metres) beyond, up the slope and just before Victoria Palace Lodge. It lies behind dense shrubbery to your left.

Return to the Italian Gardens and turn left along the east side. The Portland stone vases on the balustrades are of five main designs known as swan breast, woman's head, ram's head, dolphin and oval; in 1990 an English Heritage stone carver recarved one of each, offsetting the ravages of weathering. Halfway down, facing the fountains, is an 1858 bronze statue of Edward Jenner (1749–1823). In 1798 Jenner perfected vaccination and fought for its use; his discovery is still saving countless lives.

Peter Pan

Turn right at the southern end of the gardens, pausing to admire the view down Long Water, then left down the path leading south along its bank. Alongside the fence to your left is a wildlife area where the grass is left to grow long for the butterflies, and at the end is an information board with details of some of the diverse waterfowl to be seen on the Long Water.

To the right is the famous statue of Peter Pan by Sir George Frampton. It was commissioned by Sir James Matthew Barrie (1860–1937), the Scottish writer of the children's fantasy play, *Peter Pan*. In 1912 the statue was unveiled unofficially, but once in place it was so popular it could not be moved. It depicts Peter Pan with pipes, and the tortuous design oozes rabbits, mice, squirrels and bronze fairies clad in what look like Edwardian party frocks. One child remarked that Wendy, who is part of the group, looks puzzled. The ensemble is intended for children, many of whom have touched the rabbits' ears – which is why they are now so shiny.

J. M. Barrie lived in a house overlooking Kensington Gardens and it was while walking in these gardens that he met the sons of an impecunious barrister and unofficially adopted them, sending four to school at Eton and one into a British navy cadetship. Royalties from his play, an enduring fairy tale about a boy who never grew up, still go to Great Ormond Street Hospital for Sick Children.

Behind the statue's enclosure is the Leaf Yard, an ecological innovation of the early 1990s. Autumn leaves collected from Hyde Park and Kensington Gardens are shredded, stored, and shredded again to make a rich mulch for the shrubberies. They used to be taken downstream on the Thames by barge to be dumped in landfill sites.

The Queen's Temple

Take the path that leads directly south, following the right fork leading away from the Long Water toward the Queen's Temple. Between the Peter Pan statue and this temple, by Front Walk, are some ancient gnarled sweet chestnut trees, the only ones surviving from Bridgeman's plantings of the 1730s. The Queen's Temple was designed by William Kent (*see* page 9), who worked at Hyde Park after Bridgeman. He was famous for his 'picture' approach to landscape, designing buildings and the settings for them. This temple had been used as a keeper's lodge, but was restored in 1977.

Continue walking south along the path and you come to what was originally a refreshment house designed by Henry Tanner in 1908, when it was decided that 'poorer visitors' might cause trouble if there were no facilities. It remained a tearoom until the 1960s and is now the Serpentine Gallery, a leading art gallery.

The Albert Memorial

From the back of the Serpentine Gallery stroll along the path that leads to the Albert Memorial, a huge monument now gloriously restored. Its intricate decorative inlays of agate, jasper, crystal and other glittering semiprecious stones are much photographed.

Albert, Queen Victoria's cousin and Consort, died from typhoid in 1861. His memorial, built from money raised by public subscription, was erected between 1864 and 1876. It was designed by Sir George Gilbert Scott (1811–78), architect of the fantasy front of St. Pancras railway station, and built by the Lucas firm, who were also builders of railway stations. They often dined their 80 workmen on beef and plum pudding while suffering them to hear speeches on temperance.

The base of the monument, in neoclassical style, is adorned with statuary groups in marble representing the four continents. They can still be seen: for Europe, Britannia rides a bull surrounded by crowned women. The next stage is a frieze of Great Figures, ranging from William Shakespeare to Sir William Chambers, the designer of the Pagoda in Kew Gardens (*see* page 130). Above them is the statue of Prince Albert, 15 feet (4.5 metres) high, seated and grasping a catalogue of his Great Exhibition of 1851, which was held nearby in Hyde Park (*see* page 52). Above him the monument changes to neo-Gothic style.

The map on page 47 shows a worthwhile diversion due east along South Carriage Drive to see the Coalbrookdale Gates from the Great Exhibition. They are intricately decorated with metalwork stags and other ornament.

The Flower Walk

Retrace your steps along the path leading north from the Albert Memorial and go through a gate in the railings to the left. Ahead of you is one of London's best and most carefully planned flower walks. The 500-yard (457-metre) path was laid in 1843 and exotic trees planted along it. They are name-tagged: near the Lancaster Walk entrance, for example, is a maidenhair tree (*Gingko biloba*), a species thought extinct until it was found growing in China in the 18th century; a Lucombe oak, with thick, fissured bark; and an enormous ilex (an evergreen oak). There is also the weeping beech where, in the play, Peter Pan spent a very cold, wet and miserable night.

Today's garden format is a shrubbery of varying depth backing curves of flower beds (50 in all) set in fine green turf. But there are also delightful hollows with evergreen and deciduous azaleas and small, highly colourful Japanese maples. Planting is programmed to maintain interest through the growing season and to offer a continual element of surprise as you walk slowly along and meet the various colour combinations, both complementary and contrasting. The colour range of each bed can be heightened in summer with the greater variety of bedding plants available. In August, for example, you might see beds ranging from a multicoloured mixture of dahlias to one with a cool motif of white and green. There might also be exotics – young banana plants, for example.

Pass through a pair of gates and find Peter Pan's beech overhanging the path. It is unmarked but is easily spotted on the right, with its beaming swollen trunk. Turn right at the bottom and left to Palace Gate where the walk ends. In J. M. Barrie's story *The Little White Bird*, Peter Pan thinks he is a bird. He watches them drink in puddles and tries to do the same: 'When a real bird falls in flop, he spreads out his feathers and pecks them dry, but Peter could not remember what was the thing to do, and he decided, rather sulkily, to go to sleep on the weeping beech in the Baby Walk'. Baby Walk is the Flower Walk.

At the west end of Flower Walk turn left along Snake Walk, a sinuous side path bordered by raised heather beds, camellias, deciduous azaleas, rhododendrons and magnolia trees.

HYDE PARK

LOCATION	About 1½ miles (2.4 kilometres) west of Charing Cross.
TRANSPORT	North side: Queensway, Lancaster Gate and Marble Arch Underground stations (Central Line); south side: Knightsbridge and Hyde Park Corner Underground stations (Piccadilly Line). Buses: Bayswater Road 10; 12; 94; Knightsbridge: 9; 10; 19; 22; 52; 137; Park Lane: 2; 36; 137. There is an underground car park on Park Lane.
ADMISSION	Open daily dawn–dusk. Admission is free.
SEASONAL FEATURES	The Flower Gardens in spring and summer; the Dell in winter and spring; autumn tree colour.
EVENTS	Concerts at the Bandstand on Sundays and Bank Holidays in summer; Speakers' Corner on Sundays. Events booklet (see page 183).
REFRESHMENTS	Serpentine Bar and Restaurant open daily 8:00–20:00 hours or later. Lido café open 09:00–20:00 hours (10:00–16:00 in winter). Refreshment points open daily 09:00–20:00 hours (10:00–16:00 hours in winter).

In 1536, Henry VIII purloined land around the manor of Hyde, which belonged to the Abbots of Westminster, fencing it to make a private park for the royal hunt. During the next century, James I permitted his courtiers access to the enclosure, and a circular drive called The Ring became fashionable. It was daily filled with the chaises (light, horse-drawn carriages) of the wealthy. The ground was opened further by Charles I, but after his execution Cromwell sold it off in three lots. The diarist John Evelyn noted on 11 April 1653: 'I went to take aire in Hyde Park, when every coach was made to pay a shilling and horse sixpence by the sordid fellow who purchased it off the state'. After the monarchy was restored under Charles II, the park was reopened and The Ring became fashionable once again. The diarist Samuel Pepys wrote: 'To Hide Park, where great plenty of gallants. And pleasant it was, only for the dust'. He was wearing his 'painted gloves … all the mode'. This was just before the park was swamped by refugees fleeing the Great Plague of 1655.

In the 1690s William III renovated Kensington Palace and set up court there. However, footpads became a danger on the road leading to it along the south side of the park and, as a deterrent, he had it illuminated at night with 300 flickering oil lamps hung from the branches of the trees alongside. They were the first known street lights. This road was called the Route du Roi, a name that became corrupted to Rotten Row. In the mid-18th century Queen Caroline, wife of George II, deprived Hyde Park of as much as 200 acres (80 hectares) to form the grounds of Kensington Palace (see page 45), but she had the southern part landscaped, creating the Serpentine lake. In 1851 the Great Exhibition, initiated by Queen Victoria and Prince Albert, was held there.

Hyde Park covers an area of 350 acres (142 hectares), and many walks are possible across its wide expanses of grass and trees. The one described here embraces the majority of the most important sights.

THE HYDE PARK WALK

Start and finish Marble Arch. **Time** Allow 1¼ hours.

Marble Arch was erected at Hyde Park's northeast corner in 1851, as the main gateway to the park, but in 1918 it was severed from the park by traffic, and today it is outside the park boundary, isolated on one of the busiest traffic roundabouts in London. Reach it via subways 4 and 5 from Park Lane or from Marble Arch Underground Station, emerging at Exit 3. A recent scheme for an underpass to bury the traffic extends from Marble Arch to Hyde Park Corner, so creating a piazza to rival St. Mark's Square in Venice, with the arch as its centrepiece.

The arch was to have been the main gateway to a remodelled Buckingham Palace and a memorial to the victories in the wars against Napoleon, but when finished it was said to be too narrow for the state coach. When Queen Victoria had the front of the palace rebuilt, it was moved to this spot. Designed in 1827 by John Nash, with decoration by artists such as John Flaxman, Marble Arch is a dream of pure white Italian Carrara marble, styled on the triumphal Arch of Constantine in Rome. It originally carried a statue of George IV rising from horseback without the aid of stirrups, which is now in Trafalgar Square. The arch is hollow and housed a tiny reporting police station in the days before radios. There are gatekeepers' rooms above, unused for many years now, although there have been recent proposals to let them out as an apartment. They have twisting staircases 2 feet (60 centimetres) wide, vaulted brick ceilings, Regency fireplaces, and portholes as windows.

The early 20th-century bronze gates open onto what is believed may have been the site of the Tyburn Tree, the public gallows for two centuries, until they were moved to Newgate in 1783. There is a memorial stone on the floor of the small traffic island at the mouth of the Edgware Road. Condemned prisoners were transported to the gallows by cart, on which they stood for the noose to be put round their necks, then the cart was whipped away. Up to eight unfortunates could be hanged at a time on each of the gallows' three sides. Most were not hardened criminals but impoverished citizens who were down on their luck. The laws of the time were a morass: to take fruit from a neighbour's tree was a minor crime, but to steal fruit already picked was a hanging offence. Hanging days were like public holidays, with crowds of spectators avid for morbid entertainment. As a joke, the highwayman Jonathan Wild picked the chaplain's pocket of a corkscrew, which he held while dying. This part of London is a haunted place.

Cross to Hyde Park via the pedestrian cossings, and enter the park gate.

Speakers' Corner

The area in which you are now standing is Speakers' Corner, the traditional spot where anyone can speak on almost any subject to anyone who will listen – at any time, although

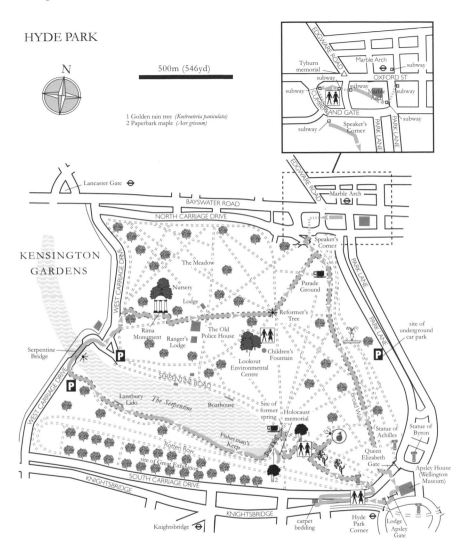

HYDE PARK

N

500m (546yd)

1 Golden rain tree *(Koelreuteria paniculata)*
2 Paperbark maple *(Acer griseum)*

Tyburn memorial
Marble Arch
subway
OXFORD ST
subway
subway
CUMBERLAND GATE
Marble Arch
subway
subway
subway
Speaker's Corner
PARK LANE
PARK LANE

Lancaster Gate
Marble Arch
BAYSWATER ROAD
NORTH CARRIAGE DRIVE
Speaker's Corner
KENSINGTON GARDENS
The Meadow
Parade Ground
WEST CARRIAGE DRIVE
Nursery
Lodge
Reformer's Tree
PARK LANE
site of underground car park
Rima Monument
The Old Police House
Ranger's Lodge
Serpentine Bridge
Children's Fountain
Lookout Environmental Centre
P
P
P
Lansbury Lido
The Serpentine
Boathouse
Site of former spring
Holocaust memorial
Broad Walk
Fisherman's Keep
Rotten Row
Statue of Achilles
Statue of Byron
site of Great Exhibition
SERPENTINE ROAD
SOUTH CARRIAGE DRIVE
Queen Elizabeth Gate
Apsley House (Wellington Museum)
KNIGHTSBRIDGE
KNIGHTSBRIDGE
Knightsbridge
carpet bedding
Hyde Park Corner
Lodge
Apsley Gate

activity is mainly on Sunday mornings. Some maintain that the tradition originated with the right of the condemned to speak before their execution. However, the legal right of assembly here was only established in 1872 as a result of public demonstrations mounted by the Reform League to campaign for a wider vote, established by Edmund Beales. Speakers' Corner remains a showcase for stubborn opinions straight from the mouth (microphones are not allowed) and encourages real audience participation with topics that range from the flatness of the earth to pro-smoking tirades. For anyone who is keen to have their say, the ground rules are: no sedition, treason, blasphemy or obscenities; and no incitement of race hatred.

Park Lane

Stroll south along Broad Walk, the footpath leading to Hyde Park Corner, heading directly away from the mouth of the arch. Park Lane, to your left, is hardly a lane any more. Some of the private houses and mansions built along its east side to face the park were rebuilt as hotels or showrooms, mainly after bombing in World War II, so the façades are now largely 20th century, although one or two old curved bay windows remain. Roughly marking the halfway point between Marble Arch and Hyde Park Corner, just to the left of the path, is *The Joy of Life* fountain, an enthusiastic 4-ton bronze sculpture of 1963 by the sculptor T. Huxley-Jones. It has star-shaped pools surmounted by a nude couple holding hands and was donated by the Constance Fund, which had been set up in 1944.

The 7 July 2005 Memorial

After the fountain, continue walking beneath the splendid avenue of plane trees until a cluster of narrow grey pillars appears on your left. This is the memorial to the 52 victims of the London Underground bombings of 7 July 2005. The 52 columns are of roughly textured stainless steel and were unveiled by the Prince of Wales on 7 July 2009 at a ceremony that was also attended by the Prime Minister, Gordon Brown, and leaders of the Opposition parties. The columns are arranged in four clusters of six, seven, 13 and 26, each group representing the lives lost in each of the separate bomb blasts that day. The pillars are engraved with the date, time and place of the attacks, thus: '7 July 2005 08.50 King's Cross'. From a distance, the columns appear to move in and out of line, inducing a reflective, meditative state of mind.

A plaque on the far side has all the victims' names and often has flowers laid beside it. Friends and relatives sometimes tie ribbons to the pillars. One of the memorial's two designers, Andrew Groarke, said: 'When you see it standing, and see how it holds the light rather than reflecting it, that's a very powerful thing.'

Hyde Park Corner

Follow the path down a shallow slope to the park's southeast corner, commanded by a bronze statue of a naked Achilles, 18 feet (5.5 metres) high and weighing 33 tons, by the Royal Academician Sir Richard Westmacott. It was erected in 1822 as a memorial, paid for by public subscription 'by the women of England', to the victorious Duke of Wellington, whose home was Apsley House, the large neoclassical building – now home to the Wellington Museum – ahead of you. The statue was cast from 22 French cannon captured at Salamanca, Waterloo and other Napoleonic battles. In 1822 there were complaints about the statue's fig leaf, along with calls for more substantial cover, but it is obvious that the statue is underendowed and George Cruikshank, Charles Dickens's cartoonist, was quick to make fun of it. The fig leaf has twice been chipped off, in 1870 and 1961, and the leaf you see now dates from 1963.

The statue of Achilles occupies a small rise, and round it, to the left, are the ornate Queen Elizabeth Gates, closing South Carriage Drive off from Park Lane. The gates, designed by an Italian metalworker, Giuseppe Lund, were erected in 1996 in honour of

Queen Elizabeth, the Queen Mother, and are a magnificent example of intricate filigree work. From the gates, you can look out into Park Lane, where you can see a statue of the English Romantic poet, Lord Byron, erected in the park in 1880 but now isolated on a road island outside. It was carved by Richard Belt from an eccentric lump of granite that was donated by the Greek Government, for Byron was an active participant in the Greek War of Independence against the Turks.

Cross South Carriage Drive to the formal gates beside Apsley House to the right. The classical screen of Apsley Gate was designed by the British architect Decimus Burton (1800–81). The horsemen motif is based on the frieze from the Acropolis in Athens, parts of which are in the British Museum. Turn right, at this point, for a good vista down the wide, sandy, tree-shaded Rotten Row, also known as The Mile. The horses ridden along it are hired from stables around the edge of the park, or from private riding clubs. The Household Cavalry have their modern barracks on the south side of the park, and you often see detachments riding along South Carriage Drive. Ahead of you, the Friends of Hyde Park Information Centre is in the Lodge just inside the Apsley Gates. Walk through the gate beside it onto Hyde Park Corner.

Carpet Bedding

The southeast corner of Hyde Park has been a hotbed of horticulture for a century and a half. The Victorians delighted in the botanical discoveries being made at the ends of their empire, and enthusiastically grew many of the plants newly introduced by botanists, many of them delicate species native to hotter climates, which were propagated in greenhouses for bedding out in the warmer months. Turn right and walk along the pavement until you reach a round concrete structure (an air shaft serving Hyde Park Corner Underground Station) in the grassy bank on the right. Planted on the bank beside it is an example of traditional carpet bedding, in which words or significant dates are sometimes spelt out.

Carpet bedding uses foliage plants that can be close-clipped to create intricate designs. The plants, tightly positioned with formers (wooden frames) while in the greenhouse, might include fleshy-leaved South African crassulas and Mexican echeverias. The displays used to be sponsored, but, curiously in this age of logos, this is no longer the case. In winter these beds are usually planted with wallflowers for spring display.

The Flower Gardens

Re-enter the park via the steps back at the bus stop, cross the South Carriage Drive at the crossing and walk through the gate ahead into the flower gardens. You now join the Diana, Princess of Wales Memorial Walk and the path takes you past two interesting fountains. The first one you come to is a boy with a dolphin, the water jetting unexpectedly not from its mouth but from its nose. It is by a Victorian sculptor, and was first erected in 1862 on a site on Park Lane, was later moved to The Regent's Park, and then came to this spot. The second, to your left, has the mythological Diana, drawing her bow over a bowl supported by four caryatids; this was executed in 1906 by Countess Feodora Gleichen.

The borders on your right are particulary pretty. On the west side, the Flower Gardens give way to a necklace of small rose gardens, a type of planting very much in tune with current fashion. Follow the path left to walk through an impressive long, sinuous, metal-framed pergola, planted with a white rambler, *Gloire de Dijon* and other roses (all name-tagged), and large-flowered hybrid clematis. When the shady path curves to the right, turn sharp right opposite the gate and exit next to the special Caucasian elm (*Zelkova carpinifolia*) ahead of you. Turn left, and just past the toilet block to the left is a young, recently planted, golden rain tree (*Koelreuteria paniculata*), a species from eastern Asia, which carries large, open clusters of yellow flowers in July. Just past this, leave the road and wander to the left, down a grassy bank planted with some magnificent trees, many of them labelled. There is, for example, a magnificent weeping beech, its contorted branches forming a tent. It is worth penetrating beneath its pendulous branches when it is in leaf, to see the unusual sculpturing of its branches.

About halfway down the slope to the right, a small stand of young silver birch trees surrounds a moving memorial to the Holocaust, composed in 1985 simply of two natural boulders set in raked gravel, ringed by silver birch trees. The inscription is a quotation from The Book of Lamentations: 'For these I weep, streams of tears flow from my eyes because of the destruction of my people'.

The Dell

Turn right up the path beside the Holocaust Memorial, which leads back up the slope, and you are now walking through the Dell. This is an attractive hollow with, to your left, a cascade and a pool fed by spillage from the Serpentine lake which lies unseen, banked up behind the bridge-like parapet above. The planting, set in smooth grass, is mainly for foliage effect with, for example, spiky yucca, tall reeds, cypress and other evergreens, and a magnolia. Behind you, at the exit of the stream, is a swamp cypress (*Taxodium distichum*), with a stand of gunnera, looking like a giant rhubarb, nearby. Other interesting species here include a strawberry tree (*Arbutus unedo*) up the bank and a Caucasian elm (*Zelkova carpinifolia*), with toothed leaves and peeling bark. This is a rich corner of the park, worth a visit in winter when the different shapes of the bare trees create picturesque patterns. In early spring the grass is alight with snowdrops and other bulbs, and the magnolia is in magnificent flower.

The couple of colossal lumps of Cornish granite halfway up the hollow are not prehistoric but are the remains of an 1861 drinking fountain. At the top of the slope to your left is a memorial recording the fact that spring water was once tapped at this spot to serve the monks of Westminster Abbey.

The Serpentine

At the top of the slope make a U-turn to the left, past the Dell café-restaurant, which is marvellously placed with a view along the Serpentine. There are outside tables beside the water for warm days in summer or winter. Walk south across the bridge-like parapet, from where you can look down for another perspective into the Dell and admire more trees, among them a paper-bark maple (*Acer griseum*).

The path from the Dell restaurant bends right to hug the south bank of the Serpentine. This 32-acre (13-hectare) lake was created from the old River Westbourne and a chain of small ponds, probably by the architect and landscape gardener, William Kent (*see* page 9) for Queen Caroline, wife of George II. It was extended to form the Long Water of what is now Kensington Gardens, making some 40 acres (16 hectares) of water in all. The spoil that was dug out was used to build up the banks of the Dell and Fisherman's Keep – the part of the Serpentine now to your right – where people may still fish (with a licence from the Park authorities). The depth of the Serpentine is variable but can be up to 20 feet (6 metres) in places. It was opened on May Day 1731, with George II and his family in two yachts, perhaps accompanied by the pair of tortoises sent by the Doge of Genoa to mark the event. The lake was the site of another great gala in 1814, a reenactment of the Battle of Trafalgar of 1805. It was, however, rather a smelly lake for the first part of its life, partly because sewage was carried into it by the River Westbourne. Its murky image was further endorsed by its occasional use as a venue for suicides. Harriet Westbrook, the deserted and pregnant first wife of the poet, Percy Bysshe Shelley, drowned herself in its waters in December 1816. Today, the lake is much cleaner and certainly more cheerful – usually full of high-prowed boats painted an attractive, dusky aquamarine blue. They can be hired from the boathouse that is visible on the opposite side of the lake.

The Great Exhibition
To the south, opposite Rutland Gate, was the site of the Great Exhibition of 1851. It was held in a great hall of glass and iron, like a gigantic greenhouse, big enough for tall trees – and their accompanying birds – to be enclosed within it. When Queen Victoria asked the Duke of Wellington what could be done about the pigeon and sparrow nuisance, he uttered the immortal answer: 'Sparrowhawks, Madam'. When the Great Exhibition was over, the hall was moved to Crystal Palace Park. The entire area south of Rotten Row is now occupied by sports pitches and courts and a children's playground.

Diana, Princess of Wales Memorial Fountain
Temporarily leave the Diana, Princess of Wales Memorial walk to enter the Lansbury Lido, a 20th-century creation named after George Lansbury, a pioneer of the Labour Party. Note the shower for bathers. Bear left beyond it to view the Diana, Princess of Wales Memorial Fountain, one of the royal parks' most popular sites with around a million visitors each year. Opened by the Queen on 6 July 2004, the memorial is constructed in a circular shape from 545 pieces of Cornish granite. The sections have varying surfaces, which mean the water makes different patterns as it flows over the stone. The effect is calming, even meditative, despite the number of visitors. There are little bridges to cross the stream and children love to cool their feet in the water in hot weather. It is open, spacious and welcoming, full of light: all qualities which some would ascribe to the figure it remembers and who lived not far from here, in Kensington Palace.

The Serpentine Bridge
This was a Regency addition of 1826 by Sir John and George Rennie, sons of the famous John Rennie (1761–1821) who built the first Waterloo Bridge and updated the Southwark and London Bridges that stood at the time (they have since been replaced).

Whatever the weather, and at any time of day, there is a splendid, nostalgic view from this bridge down the Serpentine across to the towers of Westminster Abbey and the Victoria Tower of the Houses of Parliament. This is a classic scene, framed by trees and with water in the foreground, perhaps broken by those elegant, high-prowed rowing boats.

The Nursery

Cross the bridge, follow the West Carriage Drive past the car park, and then take the first turning to the right, beside what looks like a plantation. This is, in fact, the nursery area, where, hidden away behind the shrubs and trees, 12 great greenhouses produce 500,000 plants a year for bedding out in the royal parks and government gardens, and for indoor displays. The tally includes 2,000 varieties of 200 different species (ten different shades of begonia, for example). Along the path to your left, built into the boundary shrubbery of the Nursery, is the Rima Monument, comemorating the Anglo-American naturalist and writer, W. H. Hudson (1841–1922). It takes the shape of a formal pond and an emerald green lawn, at the back of which is a memorial stone carved in 1925 by the American-born sculptor, Jacob Epstein (1880–1959). It shows Rima, a goddess in Hudson's book *Green Mansions*, with an eagle and other symbolic birds. It is difficult now to understand what all the fuss was about, but when the statue was first unveiled there was public outcry, spurred on by some of the newspapers of the day; it was tarred and feathered on two occasions.

The Ranger's Lodge

Facing the Rima Monument, follow the path eastward (right) to drop down a dip and then climb toward a group of buildings. To the left is a quaint house, a typical keeper's lodge, while to the right is the Old Police House, still a working police station, and beyond it, the old Ranger's House, now the headquarters of the Royal Parks Management. On its far side is a relic, a handsome red double postbox. The police share this building with the Royal Parks, with the police on the ground floor and the Royal Parks upstairs. Officers will proudly tell you that they always win the annual gardening competition. With many large trees, this part of the park looks for all the world like a settlement in the New Forest.

In front of the Old Police House is a signpost; follow the sign pointing to the Reformer's Tree. This path leads northeast through ancient woodland and to the north is the Meadow, an area of grass left to grow tall, which encourages many butterflies. Shire horses once pulled haycarts here, collecting up to 250 bales a day; most of the hay was sold to riding stables, some went to the 16 police horses that were then based in Hyde Park. Times have changed. Following a merger between the Royal Parks Police and the Metropolitan Police in 2004, there are no longer police horses stabled in Hyde Park.

To your right you see a coppice which is a protected area for birds and conceals the Lookout Environmental Centre for local schools, a joint venture between the park agencies and the Royal Society for the Protection of Birds (R.S.P.B.). In front of the coppice is the Children's Fountain, erected in 1981, following an enormous party for 180,000 children in celebration of the Year of the Child in 1979. A detour to the fountain is great fun for children, since it squirts water in unexpected directions.

Continue along the path, keeping the copse concealing the Lookout Centre to your right, and you come to a point where several paths meet. It is called the Reformer's Tree because an oak tree that once grew on this spot was a rallying point for the Reform League and other protest groups – huge crowds used to assemble around it. Today a lamppost marks the point where it grew. There are magnificent open views from this spot across an expanse of treeless ground called the Parade Ground, where Elizabeth I reviewed her troops; during the Civil War this open space was the front line in Cromwell's chain of defence, and bristled with his troops. The left-hand path takes you back to Speakers' Corner and Marble Arch, where the walk ends.

THE REGENT'S PARK

LOCATION	About 1½ miles (2.4 kilometres) north of Charing Cross.
TRANSPORT	Southeast side: Regent's Park Underground Station (Bakerloo Line) and Great Portland Street Underground Station (Hammersmith and City, Metropolitan, and Circle lines). Southwest side: Baker Street Underground Station (Jubilee, Metropolitan, Hammersmith and City, and Circle lines); Marylebone Station (overground terminus). Northeast side and Primrose Hill: Camden Town Underground Station (Northern Line). Buses 18, 27, 30, 205, 453. There is meter parking on Chester Road.
ADMISSION	Open daily 05:00 hours–dusk. Admission is free.
SEASONAL FEATURES	Avenue Gardens and Queen Mary's Rose Garden in spring and summer; spring blossom; autumn tree colour.
EVENTS	Open-air theatre; music on the Bandstand and in Queen Mary's Rose Garden in summer; birdwatch walks and talks. Events booklet (*see* page 183).
REFRESHMENTS	Garden Café open daily 10:00–21:00 hours (to 16:00 in winter); Honest Sausage open 08:00–19:00 hours (08:00–16:00 in winter).

In the 18th century a relic of the Middlesex Forest, an old royal hunting ground to the north of London, was being let out as farmland, but by chance the leases came to an end in 1811, the year when the Prince of Wales (the future King George IV) took the title of Prince Regent. The architect John Nash (1752–1835) seized the opportunity. Until then, he had had a humdrum career, including a spell of bankruptcy following failed property speculation in Bloomsbury Square, and he was nearly 60. There were rumours that his wife was the Prince Regent's mistress, but the two men got on well, sharing an interest in architecture.

Nash proposed a courageous plan to honour the prince – and change the face of London. A triumphal route was to link Whitehall via Regent Street to the farmland, which, renamed The Regent's Park, was to become a 'garden city' of large houses in their own grounds, a foretaste of the Victorian suburb. Terraces, squares and open spaces were designed together, all part of one plan. Nash, working with Decimus Burton and other assistants, based the almost circular park on two ring roads, the outer faced by terraces of breathtaking beauty clad in stucco. The north side of the park was left open so that people might enjoy 'the many beautiful views toward the villages of Hampstead and Highgate'. The lake was dug by 1830, and the park was opened to the public in 1835. The Prince Regent was delighted: 'It will quite eclipse Napoleon,' he said. The grand plan was never completed, however. Apart from the great terraces, there are only fragments, such as Park Crescent, with its sweeps of Ionic columns, which was finished by the early 1820s (and is now separated from the park by traffic). Another is Park Square, with its little doll's-house Greek Doric lodges. Within the park only eight of the planned 26 villas were built, and few of those remain. The Prince Regent's own retreat was never started.

As for the park, although it was laid out on more or less flat ground it is marvellously varied, with vast expanses of open grass planted with statuesque trees at one extreme, and highly detailed and intricate flower gardens at the other. Water plays an important part, with a lake to match any in London and a splendid complement of waterfowl. To the north of the park is Primrose Hill, a 50-acre (20-hectare) public open space managed by Regent's Park staff. No primroses grow in the grass, but the area is scattered with some stately trees and it is a marvellous place for a brisk walk. There is a panoramic view over London from the brow of the hill 219 feet (65 metres) above sea level.

THE REGENT'S PARK WALK

Start Avenue Gate. **Finish** York Gate. **Time** Allow 1½ hours.

Opposite Avenue Gardens, where the walk begins, are Park Square Gardens, where horse chestnuts are in flower in late spring. As you enter the gate into The Regent's Park, you see the broad Avenue, bordered by hedging, stretching ahead, but instead of proceeding along it, turn right, and then immediately left at the stone fountain just ahead of you. Your gaze is immediately arrested by a vista of brilliantly colourful formal gardens and the sight of many fountains playing. On the other side of the garden, a similar scheme of flower beds and fountains is repeated.

These are the Avenue Gardens, perhaps the most handsome formal gardens to be seen anywhere. They were first laid out in 1864 by the great Victorian garden designer William Nesfield (*see* page 10), with strong spring and summer bedding backed by alleys formed by hedging and trees, set with stone vases and shallow tazzas (planters shaped like wine cups) spilling flowers. But little of his original design and even less of its splendour lasted long into the 20th century. Walk up the path ahead to admire the restoration work, which started in 1993. It has involved replacing the original paths and boundaries and major planting, including the four rows of a selected form of small-leaved lime trees (*Tilia cordata* 'Green Spire') on the central avenue of trees to your left, and tulip trees on the outer. Your route is clearly marked by more of these green spines.

The new scheme includes stonework, as did the original: there were 32 tazzas or vases. You see that some, such as the Lion Tazza on the left, in the gardens have been restored, but most have needed the casting of new moulds, and around eight have been or are being restored as fountains, not part of the original scheme. Sponsors are invited to finance this stonework. A highlight of these formal gardens was the cable frieze beds halfway up. The name comes from the rope-like pattern of the low evergreen hedges.

A Grand Terrace

Cross Chester Road and veer right across the grass to view Cumberland Terrace, built in 1826–8, across the Outer Circle Road. It is 800 feet (244 metres) long, and is adorned with Ionic columns topped with rooftop statues. At the centre is a classical pediment with white Empire females in elaborate poses against a blue background. At the end of World War II, this was damaged, but it had been restored by 1980, and converted into apartments. The amount of leaves on the trees determines how much of the terrace you can see, but any glimpse will be rewarding.

London Zoo

Cross the grass in a northwesterly direction, heading for the line of trees opposite, which flank the Broad Walk. When you reach it, turn right and you soon have a splendid view of Cumberland Terrace to your right. Continue and you soon reach a handsome Victorian Gothic drinking fountain, a gift in 1869 of Sir Cowasjee Jehangir of Bombay. The designer is unknown. To one side there is a sacred humped cow under a palm tree and, as well as a fulsome inscription, a plaque honouring Queen Victoria. Drinking fountains were a popular Victorian commemoration. In the days before cafés, a drink of water was the only alternative to visiting an inn or a pub, with all the temptations they offered.

Retrace your steps to the edge of the belt of trees around the fountain, and take the first path to the right leading southwest across a large expanse of open grass. The southern border of London Zoo can be seen to the right. The Zoological Society of London moved in 1828 from the Tower of London into buildings designed by Decimus Burton, on the northern edge of The Regent's Park. Some of the original buildings, including the giraffe house, remain, but there are also some startling 20th-century creations to be glimpsed rising above the walls. Passersby can certainly hear the animals, and on a hot day their odours will also be unmistakable. To the north of the zoo is the Regent's Canal, which formed the edge of the park's grand design.

The park north of the path is given over to facilities for sports. Several hundred teams might be registered every year, and there are usually golf and tennis schools.

The Lake

As you reach the sports pavilion halfway across, keep to its left, rejoin the main path and turn left at the second crossroads. The belt of trees to your left marks the bank of the lake, and the path takes you to its western end. At the head of the lake the path narrows to cross a bridge to the small Duck Island. Ahead, a second bridge leads off the island to the opposite bank, where there is a round children's boating pond with blue-topped pedalos. To the right, beyond a children's playground, you can just glimpse the grounds of Winfield House, built in 1937 for Barbara Hutton, who was then the heir to the Woolworth's stores. When her marriage to film star Cary Grant ended in 1945, she gave the house to the U.S.A. as the American ambassador's residence. Its garden, which extends into the park, is one of its few remaining private areas. Above the trees to the west rises the golden roof and minaret of the Central London Mosque, built in the 1980s.

Retrace your route back over the two bridges across the lake and bear right to follow an arm of the Y-shaped lake, 22 acres (9 hectares) in area, one of Nash's creations. In the boatyard to the right, handsome, high-prowed wooden rowing boats are for hire. This lake

THE REGENT'S PARK

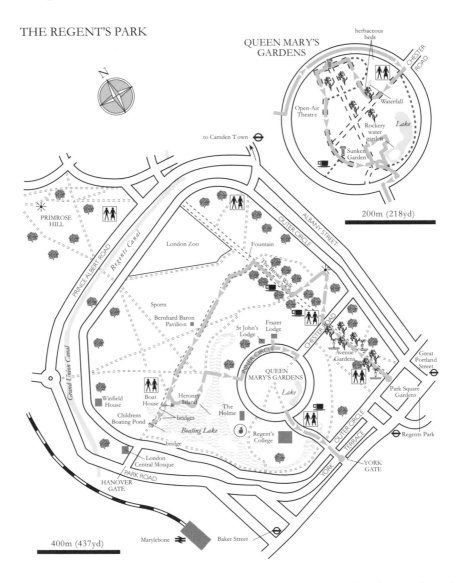

QUEEN MARY'S
GARDENS

herbaceous
beds

CHESTER ROAD

Waterfall

Open-Air
Theatre

Rockery
water
garden

Lake

Sunken
Garden

200m (218yd)

to Camden Town

PRIMROSE
HILL

London Zoo

Fountain

OUTER CIRCLE

ALBANY STREET

The Broad Walk

Sports

Bernhard Baron
Pavilion

St John's
Lodge

Frazer
Lodge

CHESTER ROAD

Avenue
Gardens

INNER CIRCLE

QUEEN
MARY'S
GARDENS

Lake

Great
Portland
Street

Park Square
Gardens

PRINCE ALBERT ROAD

Regents Canal

Grand Union Canal

Winfield
House

Boat
House

Heronry
Island

The
Holme

Boating Lake

Childrens
Boating Pond

bridges

bridge

Regent's
College

OUTER CIRCLE

TERRACE

Regents Park

London
Central Mosque

PARK ROAD

HANOVER
GATE

YORK

YORK
GATE

400m (437yd)

Marylebone

Baker Street

64

was the scene of a disaster in January 1867, when 41 skaters drowned after the ice collapsed. Several park lakes were made shallower as a result, and new regulations subsequently forbade skating in London parks on ice less than 5 inches (13 centimetres) thick. Across the water and through the trees you may be able to catch a glimpse of Hanover Terrace, with a pediment of white figures against blue, as they are on Cumberland Terrace. Sussex Place to its south has unusual octagonal domes; it was designed by John Nash in 1822 when he was also designing Brighton Pavilion for the Regent's father, George III.

Continue past Heronry Island, the name a reminder (if you need one) that the lake is bursting with waterfowl – by now you will have heard the squeakings and gruntings and clatterings of ducks. The Holme can be seen across the water, an essay in cream. Built in 1818, it was the first villa Decimus Burton designed, at the age of 18, for Nash's scheme, and the first of the villas to be built. Its garden is occasionally open to the public; consult the notice boards dotted around the park.

Cross the water by the next bridge you come to. It is a substantial bridge with stone piers at each end, separating the bird sanctuary to the left from the Boating Lake to the right. On the opposite side of this bridge is a bird identification board. The lake accommodates an outstanding collection of waterfowl, including 45 different duck, some familiar from other parks, others – the canvas-backed duck, for example – less so. The bar-headed goose, its white head cut by dark stripes running from the nape of its neck, is among the most handsome of the geese with its elegant, classic plumage. Alongside this board there is sometimes a handwritten list of recent sightings of wild birds – the spotted flycatcher, the garden warbler, and so on, all summer migrants, perhaps dropping by to rest.

Secret Gardens

Turn left to follow the Inner Circle road, and pass St. John's Lodge, originally designed by Decimus Burton, but later extended. The house and grounds together give an idea of how Nash's original settlement could have looked. Lord Bute lived in this house in late Victorian times, describing it as 'terra incognita to a great many Londoners ... almost a country house yet only a shilling cab fare from Piccadilly Circus'. It is now in government use.

Continue past the low, single-storey Fraser Lodge and turn left down a narrow alley, arched with widely spaced, wisteria-covered iron pergola hoops, with flower beds to each side. This is the entrance to Lodge Garden, a delightful secret garden created for an owner of St. John's Lodge as a place of meditation. At the end of the alley a stone urn, brimful of plants, is a memorial to the London *Evening Standard* journalist Anne Sharpley (1928–89) who loved this place. To enter the garden, turn left and you will see an immaculate lawn with beds edged with lavender, always busy with bees in summer. The garden curves in quadrants around a pool with a fountain and, at its centre, a statue of a boy and a girl frolicking. If you look closely, however, you see that the girl is a mermaid, with fins growing from her thighs; the boy is Hyras, a favourite of Hercules. The statue was sculpted in 1933 by the Royal Academician, H. A. Pegram. To the left is the impressive façade of St. John's Lodge, fronted by a handsome ironwork screen. On top of the pillars to each side, figures of boys, called 'armorini', display the coat of arms of Lord Bute. To the right, an ironwork gateway beckons you on.

This gateway leads to another garden, which some regard as the real hidden delight of this urban haven. It is a secluded, round garden, encircled by a ring of pleached, interlacing lime trees and flower beds, with perfumed roses in summer, lavender edging, and trimmed box topiary balls. In a recess facing the gateway is a blue-painted seat in memory of Nicholas Baker, who died not so long ago aged 16, and who loved the quiet of these gardens. They are at their most nostalgic when the first falls of autumn leaves drift across the grass.

There is a recent addition, following the original design. A gap in the lime trees to the north leads to a second, new, round garden, its limes only newly planted and still quite thin. To the left, at the end of the alley, is a statue of a shepherdess carrying a lamb, with an inscription reading 'To All Protectors of the Defenceless'. It was sculpted in 1932 by C. A. Howell, and protests against cruelty to animals.

Queen Mary's Gardens

Continue around the Inner Circle and turn right by the 1933 gateway at Chester Road to enter the central gardens. For this area, Nash had originally planned a temple dedicated to British greats. For nearly a century, until 1932, the beds here were planted by the Royal Botanic Society. Nowadays, however, as you see to your left and ahead, a great deal of the area is occupied by a most marvellous rose garden, where rambling varieties hang in swags between pillars wreathed in climbers, set in beds of large- and cluster-flowered species. The garden is named for Queen Mary, wife of George V and a keen gardener. It has a collection of perhaps 30,000 roses of almost 400 different varieties, including the greatest modern cultivars. All are labelled, which is a boon to beginners, and among those with appropriate names 'Ice Cream' is vanilla white and 'Greta Garbo' is (of course) a deep, lipstick red. There are some interesting trees to spot, too, such as the manna ash (*Fraxinus ornus*), a tree from central Europe, with showy heads of white, scented flowers.

To the right of the Chester Road path, follow a curved path which climbs gently into a superb herbaceous border, perhaps the best in London. This is another of The Regent's Park's secret gardens. You pass many cordalines, which look like small palm trees, as well as dark strawberry trees, acacia and yuccas. Toward the end, on the right, you can see a red maple, before you emerge by a small waterfall and pond. Follow the path up and to the left to find the Triton Fountain, with a sculpture of the sea god by William McMillan, which was erected in 1950. The route circles anti-clockwise to the Open-Air Theatre, opened in 1932. Programmes for the summer season are displayed on notice boards, and the theory is that London rain falls mainly in the afternoon, the sky clearing for the evenings.

Toward the central crossing of the garden paths is a small sunken garden found by turning sharp left before the garden café, and then right. It has a bedding display surrounding a statue of a boy with a frog. The display changes several times a year. Almost opposite is a rockery water garden with a cascade and island planted with alpines and with a majestic bronze eagle to one side. There is a swamp cypress (*Taxodium distichum*) growing by the water on its south bank.

Leave the gardens by the massive gilded gateway toward York Gate; it was presented by the artist Sigismund Goetze in 1935. The red-brick building on the right, dating from 1913, was built on the site of a Nash villa, and was until very recently Bedford College of London University, the first university college for women. It is now called Regent's College and houses various American colleges. Cross York Bridge to see, opposite, York Terrace. This is the longest of the Nash terraces, with massive Corinthian pillars (with leafy tops to the columns) decorating the centre block and with pavilions at each end. Cross the Outer Circle Road to York Gate, where the walk ends.

KENWOOD AND HAMPSTEAD HEATH

LOCATION	About 2⅓ miles (3.7 kilometres) northwest of Charing Cross.
TRANSPORT	Highgate Underground Station (Northern Line) is half an hour's walk; the 210 bus from South Grove, Highgate Village, stops near West Gate. Hampstead Underground Station (Northern Line) is 45 minutes' walk away. Bus: 210 from Finsbury Park, Archway, Golders Green and Brent Cross Underground stations. 603 from Hampstead and Swiss Cottage Underground stations. H3 from East Finchley and Golders Green Underground stations. There is a car park alongside the West Gate.
ADMISSION	Open daily 08:00 hours–dusk. Admission is free.
SEASONAL FEATURES	Spring blossom; the Lime Walk in June and July; autumn tree colour.
EVENTS	Summer concerts beside Concert Lake; monthly walks on the estate; regular talks.
REFRESHMENTS	Brew House Restaurant open daily 10:00-18:00 hours.

Most Londoners regard Kenwood as part of Hampstead Heath, and at one time the Kenwood Estate extended from Kentish Town in the south to Highgate, covering an area of 1,600 acres (650 hectares). For almost two centuries, however, the house and around 200 acres (80 hectares) of surrounding parkland were the private property of the Earls of Mansfield, and were closed off from the surrounding heath and common. The mansion we see today we owe to William Murray, Chief Justice to George III and the 1st Earl of Mansfield. In 1754 he bought an older house on the site for its fresh air and magnificent views south across London, and ten years later called in Robert Adam to improve it. William Murray also started to landscape the grounds, but in the 1790s his successor employed Humphry Repton to carry out further improvements.

Between 1889 and 1928, most of the former grazing lands of the larger estate were gradually broken up. In 1922 the 6th Earl sold off 120 acres (49 hectares) for public use and these were added to the existing open space of Hampstead Heath. In 1925, Lord Iveagh (one of the Guinness dynasty) bought the by then derelict Kenwood House and restored it in 18th-century style, filling it with paintings by Gainsborough, Turner, Rembrandt and other great English and Dutch artists. On his death in 1927 he bequeathed the house, its contents, and the remaining 75 acres (30 hectares) of the surrounding land to the public, through London County Council, stipulating that 'the atmosphere of a gentleman's private park should be preserved'. The estate has remained in public ownership ever since –

subsequently administered by the Greater London Council and, when that was abolished, by English Heritage, which has carried out careful restoration work.

Today, Adam's remodelled Kenwood House and its surrounding gardens and woods occupy 112 acres (45 hectares) at the northeastern edge of Hampstead Heath. From the terrace on the south side of the house, wide lawns sweep majestically down to the lakes, where the Sham Bridge perfectly complements the landscape. Originally devised either by William Murray or by Robert Adam, it was despised by Humphry Repton, but it survived to be rebuilt many times. It makes a perfect setting for the summer concerts, which were inaugurated in 1951 and are performed on a stage behind the Concert lake.

Our short walk focuses on the landscaped gardens, the lakes and the woods behind them. About 30 per cent of the area of these grounds are officially designated an S.S.S.I. (Site of Special Scientific Interest), and large areas are dedicated to conservation. They contain ancient woodlands with many rare and exceptionally old trees, and areas of wetland with rare wild flowers, ferns and mosses.

On the southern side the landscaped grounds merge with the wilder acres of Hampstead Heath. Strictly speaking, the heath is outside the scope of the walks in this book – it is not a park – but the two are so closely linked that it seems almost *de rigueur* to extend the Kenwood walk into a trek across the heath's wider expanses. The map on page 70 gives two ideas for walks of about 2 miles (3 kilometres).

The first walk extends the route from Hampstead Station, crosses the heath and continues through South Wood to Kenwood House. Keeping to the leftward paths after entering Ken Wood (South Wood) will take you past the old farmhouse and dairy of the Home Farm to the west gate, where the Kenwood walk begins. This route gives a good view of the heath's prized natural, undulating wilderness of open grass, scrub and woodland, set with pools and ponds, perched above London and with some magnificent views across the city to the Surrey Hills in the south. Hampstead Heath was rescued from builders in the 19th century (Highgate Common, which ran alongside, disappeared completely) and since then has always had a forceful protection society, heavy with well-known local residents. Their predecessors vigorously campaigned to extend the heath and, as a result, Parliament Hill, then occupied by farmland, was bought in 1886 and Golders Hill was added in 1899. The Kenwood Estate was the last addition, in the 1920s.

The second of the Hampstead Heath options continues the main walk through the gate to the east of Kenwood House terrace, then southward, across the newly planted Wild Flower Meadow, around Highgate Ponds – the string of lakes along the heath's eastern edge – and across Parliament Hill to Hampstead. Each of the ponds has a different use and atmosphere: the Men's and Ladies' ponds are for bathing, there is a pond for model boats and a bird sanctuary pond to the south of it. From Parliament Hill, 320 feet (97.6 metres) high, there is a good view of the Highgate roof line and out across London beyond (there is a view board on the spot to help identify landmarks).

Together, Kenwood and Hampstead Heath cover a vast area, with much to do and to discover, and there are rich possibilities for many alternative future walks – including formal monthly walks and talks led by the Head Ranger.

THE KENWOOD WALK

Start and finish West Gate. **Time** Allow 1 hour.

The walk begins at the West Lodge Gate, which once opened onto the main carriage entrance to Kenwood House. There is another gate on the eastern side of the house, and it, too, is overlooked by its own charming octagonal lodge. Both were designed by Humphry Repton. Walk down the long, curving gravel path. The trees to the left mark the boundary of North Wood, and Kenwood House is screened from view by the shrubbery on the right. There are a number of splendid oaks in the wood here, and on a knoll (reached by taking the path that leaves the car park to the left of the drive) you will see a quartet of superb beech trees which miraculously escaped damage in the great storms of 1987 and 1989 that decimated much of southeast England's woodland.

The front entrance of the house comes suddenly into view as you round the last bend in the path. The 2nd Earl of Mansfield diverted Hampstead Lane away from the front of the house, re-routing it around North Wood, and he had the drives laid out specifically with the intention of giving visitors this surprise view of the impressive north front. Pause for a while to appreciate its simple Ionic portico of giant columns, with a single medallion in the triangular pediment above. The Half Moon Lawn in front of the house was laid over the old road. Scenes from *Notting Hill*, the 1999 film starring Hugh Grant and Julia Roberts, were filmed on this lawn.

The Ivy Tunnel

Take a sharp right turn along the path leading into the shrubbery. To the left of the path is a monument to peace – a metal column impressed with Japanese characters that translate as 'May Peace Prevail on Earth' – which is a legacy from the former Greater London Council. A short distance ahead you pass through a hooped tunnel clad with ivy which is quite low (perhaps Lord Mansfield was not a tall man) and popular with children. When you emerge, look to the right to see a young paper-bark maple (*Acer griseum*), a tree originating from China, with orange-hued bark that peels off in patches. Just ahead and to the right is a raised recess with seating, overlooked by a huge old oak. This is the spot where there once stood a 'humble little summer house of rough wood', in which Dr. Johnson used to sit and talk with Mrs. Thrale. It was moved from her Streatham house in 1968, but was burned down by vandals in 1993.

The area to the left is called the Flower Garden – oddly, it seems, since rhododendrons in island beds are the only flowers to be seen. However, this was the site of a fenced flower garden, created by Humphry Repton, which was grassed over in the 1960s. Follow the path around the end of the lawn and leftward, passing a couple of rhododendron roundels and a sculpture by Barbara Hepworth entitled *Monolith-Empyrean (The Heavens)*, and turn left. A shingle path leads through an avenue of limes, which perfume the air in June and July, to the terrace along the south front of the house. It is generously provided with commemorative seats.

KENWOOD AND HAMPSTEAD HEATH

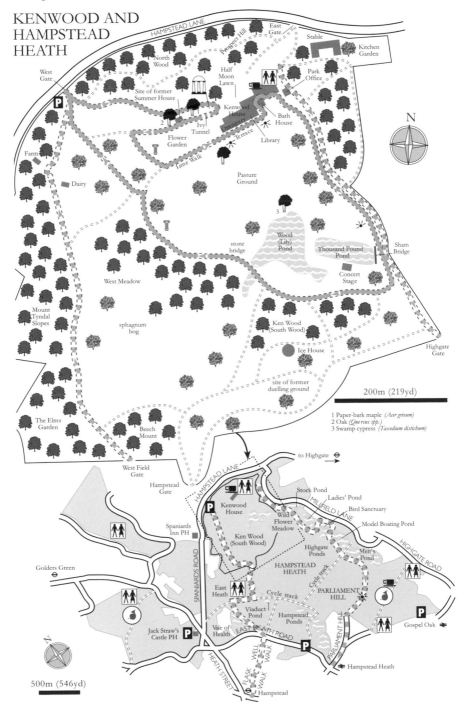

1 Paper-bark maple *(Acer grieum)*
2 Oak *(Quercus spp.)*
3 Swamp cypress *(Taxodium distichum)*

200m (219yd)

500m (546yd)

The 'Oyster Shell'

The South Front of the house is a perfect Adam composition, enhanced by the Orangery to the left and the Library to the right. The Orangery was already built in Adam's day, but he remodelled it to match the Library that he built on the other side of the house. As you reach the terrace, your eye will be drawn to the magnificent vista to the south – as typical of the 18th century as is the house. This sweeps down the steep bank in the foreground, past a splendid magnolia tree, across lawns planted with fine trees to two lakes, and there are glimpses through the foliage of the London skyline beyond. This landscaped area between the house and the water has been described as 'a gigantic oyster shell beside a lake'. This is a man-made view, the trees originally placed and planted to a tight plan, but it is easy to forget that although landscape designers like Humphry Repton could plant sizeable trees while designing their idealized paradise, they would never see the results in their full-grown glory.

Stroll along the terrace, where, in the past, the path was surfaced with a cork preparation to deaden the noise of footsteps when concerts are held in the Orangery. From here, the handsome white bridge at the left edge of the left-hand lake catches the eye. It is, in fact, a fake – only measuring about 2 feet (61 centimetres) wide, a *trompe l'œil* of flat, painted wood, which was placed to add a focus to the view. It is a typical 18th-century conceit, possibly added by William Murray himself.

Walk on past the library (the interior is counted the best Adam room to be seen anywhere), and look for a small white door labelled 'Bath House'. If it is open, turn to go through it and walk down the narrow steps; if it is locked, walk further on and down the steps on the left to the café, turn left at the bottom, and walk to the end of the yard. The steps from the terrace door lead down to the 18th-century Bath House, a small, round building housing a chilly-looking white marble plunge bath. The buried bath at Greenwich Park (*see* page 79) must have been rather like this.

The Lakes

Walk through the yard, full of café tables in summer, which is overlooked by outbuildings that were once stables and other service areas. Return to the terrace via the steps to the right, turn left at the top and follow the path, leading along the eastern edge of the oyster shell. You pass some magnificent old oaks and a chestnut tree planted in Repton's time.

As you approach the lake the Sham Bridge can now be seen for what it is. Look back, as you reach it, for a magnificent view of the house, standing proud at the top of the slope. Such views were part of Repton's original concept. Woods, water and lawns, paths and drives were arranged in a composition devised so that the house would be shown to its best advantage from every point of view.

The lake ahead of you has several names. It was originally called Thousand Pound Pond – a name apparently inspired by the cost of the excavation when it was created as a reservoir in the 18th century. Today, however, it is most often referred to as the Concert Pond, since on summer evenings open-air concerts are held on a stage behind this lake, the audience dotting themselves down the grassy slopes across the water. The lake is well populated with carp and rudd. Its partner is traditionally called Wood Pond, but has come to be known as Lily Pond after the water lilies that flower on its surface in summer. It was formed from a number of medieval ponds in the mid-18th century, and was later enlarged. It has an island which has become a refuge for wildlife, and amphibians and all manner of invertebrate life thrive in it because it has no predatory fish. Along its north bank, a stately swamp cypress (*Taxodium distichum*) with feathery leaves grows. This North American tree was very popular a couple of centuries ago.

Ken Wood

Walk behind the bridge and bear right along the path through Ken Wood (also called South Wood). In the past, these ancient woodlands were set out in 'quarters': islands of trees separated by paths to give quiet and secluded walks. This was an 18th-century idea, and its purpose was to give visitors an opportunity to stroll through safe, idealized wilderness. A similar idea was realized in the enclosures behind Holland House (*see* page 37). Ken Wood is a marvellous wildlife wood. The oaks and beeches are statuesque, and among them are plenty of trunks and boughs that lie rotting, creating a good environment for beetles and other insects, which then attract birds. Ken Wood is a breeding area for 40 bird species, and an important resting point for migrant birds.

Keep right along the paths through the wood and you skirt the southern banks of the lakes. Look right now and again to catch glimpses of the house through the trees. Eventually, the paths lead to a short bridge at the west end of Wood (Lily) Pond. Walk up the rise. The sculpture to the right, by Henry Moore, is entitled *Two-Piece Reclining Figure*. When you reach the west end of the terrace across the front of the house, take a left-hand path back to the West Gate, where the walk ends.

GREENWICH PARK

LOCATION	About 6 miles (9.5 kilometres) east of Charing Cross.
TRANSPORT	Greenwich, Maze Hill or Blackheath stations (overground trains from London Bridge; 15 minutes' walk from Blackheath Station). Island Gardens D.L.R. Station on the Isle of Dogs, then to the Greenwich bank via the foot tunnel. Buses 53, 129, 177, 180, 188, 286. Boats (about 45 minutes) from Charing Cross Pier. There is a car park within the park.
ADMISSION	Open daily 06:00–dusk. Admission is free.
SEASONAL FEATURES	The Flower Garden has azaleas in spring; bedding plants and perennials in summer and autumn.
EVENTS	Band concerts and children's workshops in summer; cricket, rugby and hockey to watch in season.
REFRESHMENTS	Pavilion Tea House open 09:00–20:00 hours (to 16:00 hours in winter); Observatory Café open daily 09:00–20:00 hours (weekends only in winter).

Greenwich Park, beside the River Thames, is one of the most dramatic open spaces in London; and the Palladian and English baroque buildings by two of the most notable British architects, Inigo Jones (1573–1652) and Christopher Wren (1632–1723), on its riverside are a masterpiece. There is a good view of the architecture from a small garden (created in the 1890s) on the Isle of Dogs near Island Gardens D.L.R. Station. This viewpoint, favoured by Wren, can be reached by foot tunnel under the river from the Greenwich side; its entrance is near Greenwich Pier and the *Cutty Sark* tea clipper.

In 1433 the Duke of Gloucester, uncle of Henry VI, fenced in 200 acres (88 hectares) and built a lodge, Bella Court, on the banks of the Thames. The Tudors felt at home there and rebuilt the lodge as a favourite palace. Henry VIII and his daughters Mary and Elizabeth were all born there, and Henry married two of his wives there. Elizabeth I used the palace when she became queen, arriving on her gilded royal barge (it was at Greenwich that Sir Walter Raleigh reputedly flung his cloak over a puddle in her path so that her feet wouldn't get wet). Around 1620, James I surrounded Bella Court park with a brick wall, some of which remains. Greenwich Park occupies the area within this enclosure.

James I did not much like Bella Court, however, and settled it on his queen, Anne of Denmark. And it was for Anne that in 1616 Inigo Jones began to build Queen's House (also known then as the House of Delights) behind the palace; it was England's first Palladian villa, although it was not to be finished for some years. It is worth making a diversion, before or after exploring the park, to admire this jewel of a building. If you stand between the buildings of the Royal Naval College (entered from King William Walk) you have a framed view of it with the Old Royal Observatory on the brow of the hill behind. In

1614 Inigo Jones wrote of this unaffected Palladian style: 'Ye outward ornaments oft to be solid, proporsionable according to the rulles, masculine and unaffected ...'.

The old palace was vandalized by Oliver Cromwell's 'Roundhead' soldiers, and when the monarchy was restored in 1660 Charles II ordered it to be demolished and a new palace built to complement the Queen's House. However, the project stalled when the money ran out, and, since William and Mary preferred the then country setting of Kensington Palace (*see* page 45) when they took the throne, the Greenwich site was turned over to a Royal Naval Hospital (to match Chelsea's military hospital) and Wren given the job of designing it. He worked without fees, so it is said; and the English baroque architect, Sir John Vanbrugh, who lived nearby, later also played a role. The need to keep the view of the river from Queen's House explains why Wren's design for the hospital was essentially two buildings. In 1873 they became the Royal Naval College and remained so until the navy departed in 1998 and the buildings were converted for the University of Greenwich. The ornately painted interiors can be visited in the afternoons.

The Queen's House has also had changes of tenants. In the early 19th century two side blocks were added, joined by colonnades, to make a school for naval orphans. Today the whole assemblage houses the National Maritime Museum.

The park has seen many changes since it was laid out. Cromwell's troops cut down many of the park trees, but Charles II energetically set about restoring them, with the aid of the French landscape designer, André Le Nôtre, who was most famous for his work at the Palace of Versailles outside Paris, which combined Italian influences in its terraces with Dutch-style formal avenues and canals. Large numbers of trees were planted, including 300 elms in 1664, to surround a formal terrace at the brow of the hill. Avenues of sweet (edible) chestnut were also planted and some of these trees are still alive. The buildings of the Old Royal Observatory, founded in 1675 by Charles II, are also in the park.

THE GREENWICH PARK WALK

Start *and finish* St Mary's Gate. **Time** Allow 2 hours.

Before beginning the walk, stop to admire the nicely gilded ironwork of St. Mary's Gate, and, to the left, the statue of William IV, king for seven years before Victoria, holding a jutting telescope. He was known as the 'sailor king' because of his naval background, serving at the first Battle of Cape St. Vincent, Portugal, in 1780 when he was only 15, and later in the West Indies. Just inside the gate, turn immediately right onto a path that leads off the tarmac road called the Avenue. Past St. Mary's Lodge, now a café, you will see a small scented herb garden, which is at its fragrant peak in June and July. Ahead the ground rises, but the flat ground before the rise was the scene of tilting, archery and midsummer bonfires in Tudor times. Later, it became the setting for riotous May Day and October fairs (described by Charles Dickens in *Sketches by Boz*) until they were banned in 1857. Broad, grassy steps are cut into the slope. There seem to have been a dozen originally and they may well have been terracing, part of Le Nôtre's scheme. Running up and down them was part of the fun for children at those fairs.

After the Knot Garden, take the left-hand path and stay on it to cross the Avenue and climb diagonally up the steep hill ahead toward the dome of the Old Royal Observatory which rises above the treetops. When you reach the top, walk over to the statue of General James Wolfe (1727–59), which commands the highest point of the park, 165 feet (50 metres) above sea level. It was donated by the Canadian government in 1930 and commemorates his 1759 victory against the French at the Heights of Abraham in Quebec, which won Canada for the British. Wolfe lived in Macartney House (*see* page 79). Parts of the statue's pedestal remain holed and chipped by shrapnel from World War II – there were anti-aircraft gun emplacements in the Flower Garden (*see* page 78). The statue faces a superb view north, across the river to the City and East London, and a panorama board identifies what you can see, including the ever-visible Canary Wharf Tower, the dome of Wren's St. Paul's Cathedral, Tower Bridge and the O2 Arena (formerly the Millennium Dome).

The Old Royal Observatory

From the Wolfe statue cross to the complex of linked buildings surrounding a courtyard which lie just to the west (left). Charles II encouraged science, and in Greenwich Park, because of its position clear of the 'Great Smoake' of London, he set up his Royal Observatory in Flamsteed House. A fortified tower called Greenwich Castle had long stood on the site, acting at various times in Tudor days as a prison, a wine store and a lodge. Henry VIII penned some doggerel there: 'Within this towre/There lieth a flowre/That hath my hart ...'. Flamsteed House was built in place of the tower, in 1675, by Wren 'for the Observator's habitation and a little for pompe'. The red-brick building is charming but not all it seems: what look like stone dressings are, in fact, wood.

John Flamsteed (1646–1719), the first Observator, or Astronomer Royal, was convinced that astronomy and the mapping of the stars would enable longitude to be determined, and hence make proper navigation possible (in the days before radar). Armed with a sextant, two clocks, a 52-foot (16-metre) telescope and a quadrant, he went to work. The calculation of longitude requires a base line to represent zero, and through the iron gates that close off the courtyard can be seen the Greenwich Meridian: a metal strip set into cobbles and continuing up the wall of the Meridian Building adjoining it to the left. This is the Prime Meridian of the World.

To the right of the courtyard gate, a Shepherd 24-hour clock – one of the first electric clocks – keeps Greenwich Mean Time, based on the zero meridian. Set into the wall there are also yardsticks, the official compensated metal measures of 1 yard and 1 foot, and an Ordnance Survey benchmark. This is the height above mean sea level at Newlyn in Cornwall (of all places).

Entrance into the courtyard is free. Every day hundreds of visitors are photographed astride the Meridian, with one foot in the eastern hemisphere and the other in the western. Explore Flamsteed House, opposite the courtyard gates, part of it decorated and furnished much as it was three centuries ago. The Octagon Room is a rare example of an unspoilt Wren interior. Atop the eastern turret is a red time ball on a pole (erected in 1833) which is raised half way at 12:55 and to the top at 12:58, to drop at 13:00 hours precisely. It once enabled departing ships to set their clocks accurately for their long voyages across the oceans of the world. In the courtyard there is also a camera obscura, a device for viewing the scenery in miniature from within a dark room, a precursor of the camera. From the courtyard you can also visit the Meridian Building, which houses original telescopes used by the Astronomer Royal. The Peter Harrison Planetarium lies behind, its giant bronze cone, with a line pointing at the Pole Star, rising like the funnel of a giant liner.

The Formal Avenues and Queen's Oak

From the planetarium, cross Blackheath Avenue to the east (right) and walk toward the Tea House. It is a typical 1930s building, with a restored dovecote on top, and a pleasant lawned garden for fine weather. As the map shows, it is almost at the hub of the park's original formal avenues. By some accounts these reflect Le Nôtre's hand – and by rights they should have converged on Queen's House (as Lover's Walk does), but there is little sign of this. The truth is that Le Nôtre did his designs by letter; he may never have seen the park and was never told that the ground dropped away. His Grand Avenue (the Blackheath Avenue), for example, ends at the Wolfe statue alongside Flamsteed House.

Make a diversion past the Tea House, turning right into Great Cross Avenue. Although the elms that were planted in the park succumbed to old age and the Dutch elm disease epidemic of the 1960s, many of the original sweet chestnut trees planted in these avenues in the 1660s still survive, and a few can be seen along this avenue. Their massive trunks often have curiously netted bark with a spiral twist.

Some of these ancient chestnuts are also to be seen on the way to the Queen's Oak. Return to the Tea House and at the edge of its car park, walk across the grass following a line of trees, with the fenced maintenance area to your left. Just over the rise you come to a huge, dead tree, surrounded by railings. With its iron-grey wood and prostrate form it looks a veritable dinosaur, and in tree terms it is primeval; it is thought to have grown from an acorn in the 12th century. Elizabeth I often picnicked nearby, it is said, and Henry VIII danced around it with Anne Boleyn. It was hollow, nearly 6 feet (1.8 metres) across inside, and in its time had been used as a lockup for offenders against park rules (apparently a doorway and windows were cut in it), but it last bore leaves over a century ago and it tottered over in a storm in 1991. A replacement sapling has been planted alongside.

Vanbrugh Castle

Take the path to the right toward Maze Hill Gate, passing on the left a sunken stone drinking fountain and the steep Lover's Walk, planted with planes and other trees. From the open ground approaching the park wall there is a marvellous view of the watery reach of the River Thames. The brick wall was probably built in the 1620s, although the simple ironwork of Maze Hill Gate probably dates to 1699. Leave the park through the gate to view Vanbrugh Castle. Sir John Vanbrugh (1664–1726) built it for his own use, finishing it in the 1720s. He had an eccentric career as a soldier (he was imprisoned in the Paris Bastille for a time), a playwright, and finally as an architect. Although he was untrained, he became a prominent architect of his age. In 1716 he succeeded Wren as Surveyor of

GREENWICH PARK

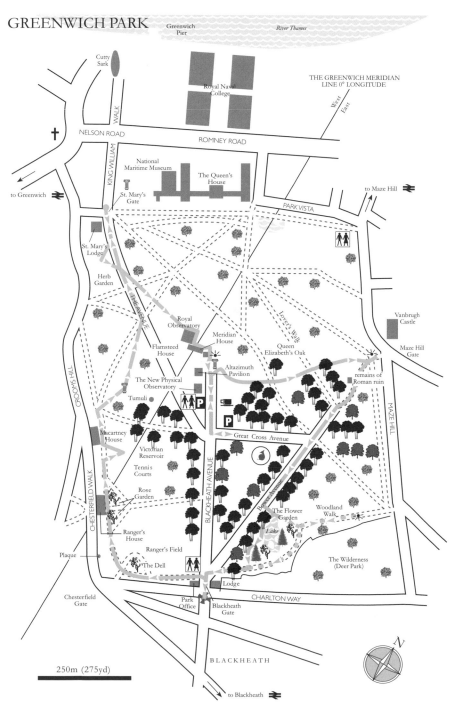

Greenwich
Pier

River Thames

Cutty
Sark

Royal Naval
College

THE GREENWICH MERIDIAN
LINE 0° LONGITUDE

West   East

NELSON ROAD

ROMNEY ROAD

KING WILLIAM WALK

National
Maritime Museum

The Queen's
House

to Greenwich

St. Mary's
Gate

PARK VISTA

to Maze Hill

St. Mary's
Lodge

Herb
Garden

THE AVENUE

Royal
Observatory

Meridian
House

Lover's Walk

Vanbrugh
Castle

CROOMS HILL

Flamsteed
House

Queen
Elizabeth's Oak

Maze Hill
Gate

Altazimuth
Pavilion

The New Physical
Observatory

remains of
Roman ruin

Tumuli

P

MAZE HILL

Macartney
House

P

Great Cross Avenue

Victorian
Reservoir

Tenni s
Courts

BLACKHEATH AVENUE

Rose
Garden

Bower Avenue

Ranger's
House

The Flower
Garden

Woodland
Walk

Plaque

Ranger's Field

Lake

The Dell

The Wilderness
(Deer Park)

Lodge

Chesterfield
Gate

CHESTERFIELD WALK

Park
Office

Blackheath
Gate

CHARLTON WAY

N

250m (275yd)

BLACKHEATH

to Blackheath

Greenwich Hospital. This house was quite unlike anything else he designed. It was an early folly, a brick building with turrets and battlements in places, possibly modelled on the Bastille in Paris. Vanbrugh has the quaint (but perhaps just) epitaph in St. Stephen's Church, Walbrook: 'Lie heavy on him, Earth! for he/Laid many heavy loads on thee.'

Re-enter the park and take the second path from the left; shortly, to the right, inside metal rails, is a boss of tiled flooring, marking the site of a Roman temple. Coins were found when it was excavated in the 1800s.

The Flower Garden

Follow the southward path until you reach Bower Avenue. To the right, near Great Cross Avenue, is a bandstand erected in 1891. To the left you see a gate leading into the Flower Garden, a pretty, quiet park within a park, which also dates from Victorian days. These large, triangular gardens are visually striking, their smooth turf planted with cedars and other ornamental conifers. There are one or two ancient chestnuts to be seen, and notable examples of exotic trees which became popular last century – the tulip tree (*Liriodendron tulipifera*), for example, the paper-bark birch (*Betula papyrifera*), with papery peeling bark; and the Pride of India, or bead tree, introduced in 1763, which carries dense clusters of orange berries that were once used to make necklaces and rosaries. Some trees show truncated tops – they were lopped during World War II to give clear lines of fire for the anti-aircraft gun batteries in the park.

In addition to the banks of azaleas and a variety of magnolias, there are more than 30 flower beds in these gardens, notable for their spring displays of bulbs and later for the dahlias. There is much imagination at work here, evidenced by an autumn bed tight with mingled white, ochre and yellow chrysanthemums, for example. But every year, indeed every season, sees its own changes in planting.

Taking detours along the paths through the beds and curving round the sunken lake will be well rewarded. Ducks nest around the lake, offering visitors the odd experience of being chased by pochard. There are identification boards to the birds on the railings. Alternatively, wander along the diversion to the Deer Enclosure, marked on the map. It lies hidden in the Wilderness, originally created in the 1660s, just prior to the planting of the chestnut avenues, by Sir William Boreman, keeper of the park at the time. The open deer lawn is hidden by a belt of shrubbery; the best viewpoint is down the path nearest to Vanbrugh Gate. The herd of mixed red and fallow deer is about 30 strong.

Blackheath Gate

From the Flower Garden or the Deer Enclosure make your way southwest to the Blackheath Gate, passing, to the left, a fine ancient chestnut with a girth of about 34 feet (10.5 metres), which grows on the edge of the flower gardens. Through Blackheath Gate you can see the open expanse of Blackheath; this was an assembly point for those marching on London, from invading Danes to Wat Tyler and Jack Straw (the historic figure, of course, not the current politician), with their throng of 100,000 peasants in revolt. Here Henry V was greeted on his return from victory at the Battle of Agincourt in France, and John Wesley, the founder of Methodism, preached at this gate in the 1800s. In recent years it has disgorged runners at the start of the annual London Marathon, held in April.

Turn round again to face into the park. Blackheath Avenue, ahead of you, is lined by young horse chestnut trees replacing the original 1700s planting. Walk along the avenue, past the park office, and turn left along the path in front of the toilets. The Ranger's Field to the right is dedicated to cricket, hockey or rugby depending on the season. Follow the path to Chesterfield Gate in the southwest corner past the Dell, an enclosed and sunken rhododendron and azalea garden, noted for its nesting birds and its spring colour. An enormously tall beech tree looms to one side, now pollarded.

The Ranger's House

Turn northward (right) and walk toward the Ranger's House. Look left when you are about half way there. A plaque on the park wall records that below the paving lies a sunken cold bath, all that remains of Montague House, which was once the home of Caroline, queen to George IV while she was Princess of Wales. The house was demolished in 1815, and the bath was discovered in 1890, but in 1983 it was filled in.

The Ranger's House overlooks a large rose garden, another park within a park, resplendent with delicate scent and colour all through the summer. Pass through the gate in the railing surrounding it and follow the path past the house front. The Ranger's House was built of red brick, mainly in the 18th century. The title of Park Ranger was often given to a member of the royal family, and the house came with the job. The house has been restored and is open to the public. It is also home to the Wernher Collection, comprising medieval and Renaissance paintings, pottery, jewellery and sculpture.

Leave the rose garden by the gate on the far side and follow the path ahead. To the right, across the grass you see a giant, grassed mound skirted by bushes and trees. This is the Victorian Reservoir, built to feed water via conduits to drinking fountains and elsewhere. There is a subterranean network of these conduits, some quite wide and paved, but they are not open to the public.

Almost opposite the reservoir, to the left of the path, is the elegant Macartney House, the home of James Wolfe during the years 1727–59, and from where he departed for Quebec in 1759. Just beyond it, at Croomshill Gate, take a detour eastward along the path that leads to a cluster of tumuli, or burial mounds, low humps in turf. Some were excavated in 1784 and glass beads, wool and hair were found. They may be Danish, since a Danish army camped on Blackheath in 1011. To find them, head for the observatory domes. Continue walking down the slope back to St. Mary's Gate, where the walk ends.

VICTORIA EMBANKMENT GARDENS

LOCATION	About 400 yards (366 metres) either side of Charing Cross Station.
TRANSPORT	Charing Cross Station (overground terminus). Embankment Underground Station (Bakerloo, District and Circle lines). Bus 176. There is parking in the South Bank complex on the opposite side of the river.
ADMISSION	Open daily 07:30–dusk. Admission is free.
SEASONAL FEATURES	Spring and summer bedding; autumn tree colour.
EVENTS	Occasional recitals of music, poetry and dance.
REFRESHMENTS	Café open daily 07:30–19:00 hours.

Victoria Embankment Gardens spread along the north bank of the River Thames from Westminster Bridge. This narrow strip of land is beautifully landscaped with curving borders planted with shrubs and fine trees, and close-clipped, verdant lawns pierced by formal flower beds and ornamented with pools, fountains and statuary. The gardens provide a contemplative atmosphere, colour, visual interest, and a respite from the noisy road outside. They were laid out in 1870, as the finishing touch after the completion of the Victoria, Albert and Chelsea embankments along $3^1/2$ miles (5.6 kilometres) of the Thames. In fact, as long ago as 1666, following the Great Fire of London, Sir Christopher Wren first suggested narrowing the River Thames in order to gain extra space for the new city he was proposing. His plan fell by the wayside, however, partly because the required engineering skills were not available in his day.

The Victoria Embankment is a magnificent feat of engineering skill, but most of it lies hidden – indeed, a major reason for its construction was the building of a sewer. The work was controlled by Joseph Bazalgette, and started in 1864 in the face of opposition from wharfingers (wharf owners) and other interests, taking over six years to complete. It is $1^1/2$ miles (2.4 kilometres) long and 37 acres (15 hectares) in area, with a variable width. The tidal mud flats were drained and a wall built against flooding, speeding the flow of the water, which partly explains why the Thames no longer ices over in winter. The area behind the wall was filled in to carry a road, which was then lined with plane trees. Then the Embankment Gardens were laid over 20 acres (8 hectares). They were designed by one Alexander Mackenzie 'to avoid the need for expensive gardening'. Presumably that meant they did not have much in the way of floral plantings, and they were criticized by the architectural press of the time for being too rural. They do have striking flower beds today.

The gardens are crowded with statues and memorials to a mixed bunch of people, ranging from dignitaries of the London County Council to military leaders and figures from the worlds of literature and music. There are memorials outside the gardens, as well as within them – among several facing the river is one commemorating Samuel Plimsoll who died in 1881 and is famed not for the sports shoe (that name was first coined in 1927) but for the safety-loading line and associated shipping law.

These gardens fall into four main sections, each of which has a different character and atmosphere. At the entrance gates, a Westminster City Council notice board outlines the history of the building of the Embankment and of that part of the gardens. With a few exceptions, however, the trees, shrubs and flowers are not labelled, and since the gardens contain some exceptionally fine trees and the borders are planted with unusual foliage and flowering plants, it will make the walk more rewarding to take one of the pocket tree recognition guides listed on page 185.

The walk concentrates on the gardens west of Waterloo Bridge, but an interesting diversion can be made to the east of it. Temple Place Gardens are lushly planted with trees, flowers and shrubs, and they shelter a statue of the philosopher John Stuart Mill (1806–73). Beside them you can see the magnificent spread of the Inner Temple Gardens, the private property of the Inner and Middle Temple, two of the Inns of Court with the exclusive right to license English barristers. For a walk concentrating on these gardens, *see* pages 174–181.

THE VICTORIA EMBANKMENT GARDENS WALK

Start Embankment Underground Station. **Finish** Westminster Underground Station.

Time Allow half an hour.

Take the south exit from Embankment Underground Station and cross the Victoria Embankment road to the riverside alongside Hungerford Bridge. Just to the right of the bridge is a memorial erected in 1899 to Joseph Bazalgette, Chief Engineer in charge of building the Embankment. Turn back beneath the bridge and walk toward Waterloo Bridge, passing a memorial to the 19th-century librettist, W. S. Gilbert, who collaborated with the composer Arthur Sullivan on the still popular Savoy operettas.

The Riverside

The serried lines of stately London plane trees, planted in the 1860s by the Victorians and stoically resistant to pollution from the heavy traffic, are one of the most striking features of the Embankment. However, it is also amply provided with intriguing Victorian street furniture, such as Timothy Butler's lamps along the balustrade, featuring two dolphins entwined around each other, head down, at the base. The benches on this river side of the road have wrought-iron arm rests in the form of an Egyptian figure. They are a sign that you are approaching Cleopatra's Needle. This 86-foot (26-metre) high ancient Egyptian obelisk was presented to the U.K. by the Viceroy of Egypt in 1819. It is dated to 1450BC, and most of the inscription on its sides commemorates Pharaoh Rameses the Great, so it is unconnected with Cleopatra, who ruled at a much later date – the name actually comes from the barge that transported the memorial to the U.K. It is flanked by two sphinxes, which, by rights, should face outward.

The eye is inevitably drawn to the view across the River Thames to the South Bank arts complex, begun for the Festival of Britain in the early 1950s. Along the riverside you pass Charing Cross Pier, from where boats take visitors on trips up and down the Thames; *Queen Mary*, a floating restaurant and pub, used to ferry Glaswegians 'doon the watter' on the Clyde from 1933 to 1977.

Continue ahead toward Waterloo Bridge. Its elegant concrete curves are little more than 65 years old, completed by Giles Gilbert Scott in 1945, but it replaced a span bridge designed by the Scottish civil engineer, John Rennie, and built in 1811–17, soon after the end of the Napoleonic wars. Cross to the north side of the Embankment at the crossing a few yards short of the bridge, which takes you to the entrance to the gardens.

The Gardens

From the gate, the path winds left between borders planted with shrubs and trees, to reveal an exciting vista of vivid green lawns bordered by beds full of interesting colour and texture, interspersed with statues of a dark, almost blackened bronze, standing on pedestals of pure white stone. The trees along the approach to this garden are planes and a few exotics. Look in particular for a pretty Judas tree (*Cercis siliquastrum*), with brilliant pink blossoms in spring. It stands on the left, at the point where the gardens widen.

Follow the path as it meanders through the gardens, bordered by strips of emerald green lawn and curvaceous borders. Those to the right rise slightly and are planted with shrubs and small trees. By contrast, those on the south side contain modern planting schemes, composed of hostas and other foliage plants with decorative leaves, clumps of festuca and other low-growing grasses interspersed with tall fritillaries, and backed by clematis and other climbers.

Soon, to the left, you will see a bust by William Goscombe John, erected in 1903, of Arthur Sullivan (1842–1900), the composer of hymns such as *Onward Christian Soldiers* (1873) and many popular light operas. His plinth is accosted by a lamenting half-naked woman representing music (this was added at the sculptor's own expense); while on one side are a music score, a mask of Pan and a guitar – all in a heap. You have already passed the monument to his librettist, W. S. Gilbert (*see* page 82), between Hungerford and Waterloo bridges. The riverside entrance to the Savoy Hotel is almost opposite Sullivan's memorial, to the right. In a small, hedged garden beside it, a hooped armillary sundial rests on a metal casque commemorating Gilbert and Sullivan's Savoy operas, written mainly between 1871 and 1890. They were staged in the Savoy Theatre by the D'Oyly Carte company (Richard D'Oyly Carte of the Savoy Hotel was the impresario).

VICTORIA EMBANKMENT GARDENS

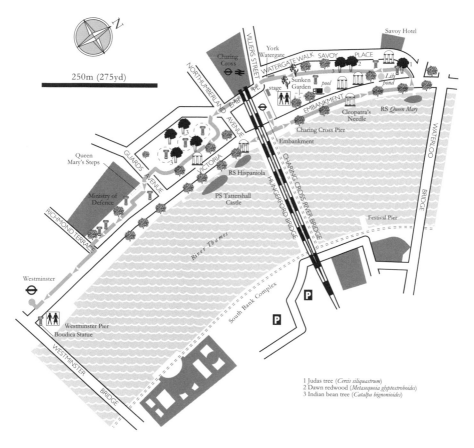

250m (275yd)

Savoy Hotel

Charing Cross

York Watergate

WATERGATE WALK · SAVOY · PLACE

Lily pond

stage

Sunken Garden

pool

EMBANKMENT

Cleopatra's Needle

RS *Queen Mary*

Charing Cross Pier

Embankment

Queen Mary's Steps

RS Hispaniola

PS Tattershall Castle

Festival Pier

Ministry of Defence

River Thames

South Bank Complex

Westminster

Westminster Pier
Boudica Statue

P

P

1 Judas tree (*Cercis siliquastrum*)
2 Dawn redwood (*Metasequoia glyptostroboides*)
3 Indian bean tree (*Catalpa bignonioides*)

There is no escaping the constant noise of the traffic along the Embankment outside these gardens, yet they do possess a serenity, and they are full of pleasant surprises. For example, further along on the left is a lily pond with a little fountain, its surrounding beds planted with dwarf azaleas for spring colour, followed by bedding plants. It was installed in 1915 and is planted with handsome emergent marginal plants, such as flags. With its air of intimate seclusion, this is perhaps the finest garden pond in London. Benches ranged along the gardens are perfectly placed for sitting awhile to admire such gems.

A short distance on, the path is crossed by another leading to gates on either side of the gardens. Guarding the right-hand gate is a statue dated 1880 by Sir Thomas Brock of Robert Raikes. A century before, Raikes had founded the first church Sunday Schools. As if to commend the sanctity of this action, the statue is illuminated after dark.

The centre point of the gardens is marked by two commemorative trees. One, planted in 1971 as first prize in the Britain in Bloom competition, is a rather leafy conifer, a dawn redwood (*Metasequoia glyptostroboides*), called a fossil tree because until its discovery in China in 1941 it was only known from fossils. Beside it is an Indian bean tree (*Catalpa bignonioides*), planted in 1953 for the coronation of Queen Elizabeth II. Behind these trees rises the mighty white monolith of Shell Mex House, home to Penguin Books. Parties are held on the terrace near the clock. The sculpted beds beyond the trees are bright in spring with vivid blue irises. Almost opposite the trees, on the garden wall, is a medallion to Henry Fawcett (1838–84), a blind Cambridge professor and Postmaster General under Gladstone, who was an advocate of votes for women. From 'his grateful countrywomen', the inscription reads. It is flanked by banks of bedding plants, such as wallflowers, and the walls are planted with shrubs and climbers, including some magnificent roses.

A formal pool is the next feature on the southern side of the gardens. Waterlilies float on its surface and flags decorate its margins. It is surrounded by hostas, planted in spreading groups, and ferns grow to one side. Behind it is a memorial by Edwin Lutyens (who designed the Cenotaph in Whitehall, nearby) to Major General Cheylesmore, who was chairman of the London County Council 1912–13. Opposite is a 1909 bronze statue of Sir Wilfrid Lawson, an advocate of temperance in Victorian times.

Toward the Hungerford Bridge end of this garden is a terrace, set with tables from the streetside café in summer. It overlooks a small, sunken garden with a palm as its centrepiece. Opposite is one of the more impressive of the garden's memorials, a massive bronze statue to the Scottish poet, Robert Burns (1759–96) on a granite plinth. It is by Sir John Steell, a Scottish sculptor of note, and was unveiled in 1844. Burns died in 1796, having written 'Auld Lang Syne', among many other familiar poems and ballads, and there is often an aging wreath lying in front of this memorial from the last Burns' Night. Another writer lived close by. Look through the trees to the left of the statue for the roof-top house of J. M. Barrie (1860–1937), author of *Peter Pan*, above a crest in the wall.

The Water Gate

A small Australian war memorial marks the point where the paths divide and the gardens open out, edged on the river side with a wide border magnificently planted with bedding plants and even banana palms (*Musa* spp.) in summer. On the west side, beneath steps that ascend to a gate at street level, is the York Water Gate. This was built in 1626 by master mason Nicholas Stone, but some believe that it was designed by Inigo Jones, or his assistant, Balthasar Gerbier. It marks the line of the old river bank – when it was built it stood at the edge of the Thames. In those days, the usual way of journeying between the City of London and Westminster, Chelsea and other such places was by boat, rowed by watermen, and this water gate was the landing stage for York House, one of the mansions that used to line the Strand behind. This house was owned by George Villiers (1592–1628), the handsome 1st Duke of Buckingham, who was a favourite of

Charles I. The mansion site was sold off for building plots in 1672, but the gate remained. It is decorated with lions, and the family coat of arms is on the landward side. The motto, in Latin, translates as 'The Cross is the Touchstone of Faith'.

Opposite the water gate, surrounded by a hedge and topiary in tubs, is a small stage for dance, poetry readings and music during summer lunchtimes and evenings, with seats for spectators. Leave these gardens by the gate to the right of this enclosure. Turn left and then right through Embankment Place.

The Embankment Gardens Extensions

Hungerford Bridge dates from 1863, but now carries trains to and from Terry Farrell's soaring 1990 Charing Cross Station. Cross beneath, by Embankment Place, to reach Northumberland Avenue and go through the wrought-iron gate into the central extension of the Embankment Gardens.

This part of the gardens is very different in style, wider and more open, with more formal plantings and large areas of grass pierced by flower beds. From the gate, follow the path that encircles the river side of the garden. The centrepiece of the first circular lawn is a statue of General Sir James Outram (1808–63). Lie on the grass here, and you can feel the vibration of the District Line trains below. Moving on to the next circular lawn, pause to admire two particularly fine Indian bean trees (*Catalpa bignonioides*), one of which has several supports, looking rather as if an elderly member of the National Liberal Club (the white building behind) just popped out for a stroll by the river. A second bean tree graces the next lawn, and opposite that, on the right, is a young silver birch, the millionth tree planted after the great storm of 1987. Make your way past the statue of William Tyndale, who completed the first translation of the Bible into English in 1525, then go through the gate and across Horse Guards Avenue to the western extension of the Embankment Gardens.

This third part of the gardens only has a low security wall and so is completely open to the traffic on the river side; on the north side, the white face of the Ministry of Defence forms a backdrop. The style is entirely different from the previous gardens: ahead of you spreads a smooth lawn from which rise handsome plane trees – no beds, borders, shrubs or flowers, but with two or three statues on plinths. The first, on the northern side, is of General Gordon, who was killed in the siege of Khartoum in Egypt in 1885.

Beyond this statue, to the right, an ancient terrace shows the line of the old river bank. It is flanked by curving steps, onto which Tudor royalty once stepped from the royal barge. This terrace was designed in 1691 by Sir Christopher Wren for Queen Mary, wife of William III. The wall behind it is the old river wall of the Whitehall Palace, built by the Tudor king, Henry VIII.

The statues in the central lawn are of two 20th-century lords: Trenchard and Portal of the R.A.F. A winged statue at the far end of these gardens is a memorial consisting of an oriental mythological beast on top of a plinth. The beast is a fabled lion called a *chinthe* in Burmese, the symbol of the Chindits, who fought behind Japanese lines in

Burma in World War II. You might very well see someone standing here in memory of what is still relatively recent history.

The Chindit monument faces the Whitehall police headquarters, with a quaint Victorian 'POLICE' blue lamp standard in front. Note the splendid Battle of Britain memorial opposite, beside the river, which was unveiled 'in the presence of survivors of the Few' by the Prince of Wales on 18 September 2005. Past that is Westminster Bridge, adorned with a statue of Boudicca (Boadicea) and her daughters, who battled against the Roman occupation of Britain. On the right is Westminster Underground Station, where the walk ends.

VICTORIA TOWER GARDENS AND THE TRADESCANT GARDEN

LOCATION	About ⅔ mile (1.1 kilometres) south of Charing Cross. Victoria Tower Gardens lie alongside Millbank, next to the House of Lords. The Tradescant Garden is in the Garden Museum on the opposite bank of the river.
TRANSPORT	Westminster Underground Station (District and Circle lines) is five minutes' walk from Victoria Tower Gardens. Lambeth North Underground Station (Bakerloo Line), and Vauxhall Station (Underground trains on the Victoria Line and overground trains from Waterloo) are ten minutes' walk from the Garden Museum. Buses pass Victoria Tower Gardens; 77, 507, C10 stop south of Lambeth Bridge.
ADMISSION	Victoria Tower Gardens open daily 09:30–dusk. Admission is free. The Garden Museum opens daily 10:30–17:00 hours, but is closed on the first Monday of every month. Admission to the Museum and Tradescant Garden is £6.00.
SEASONAL FEATURES	Spring bulbs and crown fritillaries; summer colour in the Tradescant Garden.
EVENTS	Exhibitions, lectures and courses in the Garden Museum.
REFRESHMENTS	Café in the Garden Museum, same hours as the museum.

Victoria Tower Gardens spread along the Thames Embankment from Victoria Tower on the south side of the Houses of Parliament to Lambeth Bridge. These riverside gardens have little in the way of colourful flower beds, but they offer pleasant views across the river, a shady haven from stuffy offices on hot days, and benches for visitors to London wanting a place to rest after seeing the sights. These gardens have an apparent link with Embankment Gardens (*see* page 80), but they are older, having been laid out shortly after the rebuilding of the Houses of Parliament following a fire in 1834. Parliament's Victoria Tower does, indeed, tower over these gardens.

This walk is unusual in that it crosses the River Thames, spanning two boroughs to visit the small Church of St. Mary-at-Lambeth, beside Lambeth Palace. This church, rebuilt several times since its foundation, looks much younger than its pre-Domesday Survey date. In the churchyard are buried John Tradescant (1570–1638), gardener to Charles I, and his plant-collector son (1608–62), and the church, now deconsecrated, contains the Garden Museum. In 1979 the present building was saved from demolition by the Tradescant Trust.

The gardens of Lambeth Palace, the official residence of the Archbishop of Canterbury, spread eastward from Lambeth Palace, whose entrance is beside St. Mary's. They are occasionally open to the public (*see* page 184), so a walk of even greater interest might be devised by combining this short walk with an official tour of the palace grounds. When, as is usual, they are not open, an alternative is to extend the walk with an enjoyable stroll around the pretty Archbishop's Park, whose entrance is on Lambeth Road, on the south side of the Garden Museum. This little park was part of the Lambeth Palace gardens until late in the 19th century, when the archbishops presented it to the Borough Council for the use of the people of Lambeth, especially children, who had traditionally been allowed to play in their gardens. On the little green hill here it is common to see news broadcasts being filmed because the Houses of Parliament can be framed in the background.

THE VICTORIA TOWER GARDENS WALK

Start Victoria Tower gate. **Finish** Westminster Bridge. **Time** Allow 1 hour.

The walk begins at the gateway in the northwest of the gardens, beside the Victoria Tower, but if you approach from Parliament Square or Abingdon Street, look out for an interesting sculpture in College Gardens, directly opposite the gateway into Victoria Tower Gardens: *Two Knife Edge Bronze* by Henry Moore (1898–1986).

Ahead as you enter the gardens is a memorial to Emmeline Pankhurst (1857–1928), a leading member of the suffragette movement, who, in 1918, after a long struggle, gained for women aged over 30 the right to vote in general elections to the British Parliament. She fought for women's suffrage by forceful means, and after one skirmish in 1902 she became the last person to be held in the cell at the foot of Big Ben. The memorial, by A. Walker R.A., was erected in 1930. Beside it there is a plaque to her daughter, Dame Christabel Pankhurst (1880–1956), who was among the approximately 1,000 women who went to prison for the cause. On the other plaque the letters 'W.S.P.U.' stand for the Women's Social and Political Union, founded by Emmeline Pankhurst and her daughters in 1903. The crest is the Holloway Brooch, designed by Sylvia Pankhurst and given to suffragettes after imprisonment. It shows the portcullis of the House of Commons and a convict's arrow.

Turn right and follow the path leftward round the shrubbery to reach a replica of Rodin's heroic sculpture, *The Burghers of Calais*, of 1915. In 1347, after the English King Edward III, determined to subjugate Calais, had unsuccessfully besieged the city for eight months, six citizens of the town offered him their lives if he would spare their fellows. Edward's Flemish Queen, Philippa of Hainault, argued their cause and their lives were spared. News reporters are also regularly filmed on this green, perhaps when the other green across the river is full. Look over the river wall and note the yellow security buoys around the Houses of Parliament. From the sculpture, turn right and right again to walk along the riverside path. There are some handsome plane trees alongside the river, and shaded benches beneath them have a view across the water to St. Thomas's Hospital and Lambeth Palace.

Toward the southern end of the lawn is the extraordinary Buxton Memorial by S. Teolon, first erected in 1865 in Parliament Square by Charles Buxton M.P., in memory of those, including his father, who had been active in the fight against slavery. It was moved to this spot in 1957. It takes the form of a small edifice, a complete essay in the ornate neo-Gothic style. It is circular, with bunches of red granite pillars supporting intricately carved, gargoyle-like

Kenwood House: *The tranquil lawns of Kenwood House, which dates from the early 17th century*

Kenwood House: *View through the ivy tunnel to Kenwood Lake*

Greenwich Park: *The Shepherd Gate 24-hour clock and standard lengths on the wall of the Royal Observatory, Greenwich*

Victoria Embankment Gardens: *A popular lunchtime haunt for office workers, these gardens boast many statues – this one is of the English Radical and MP Sir Wilfred Lawson (1829–1906)*

Victoria Tower Gardens: *The secret garden at the Garden Museum is one of London's hidden treasures*

Green Park: *This avenue shows some splendid examples of the pollution-tolerant London plane tree* (Platanus hispanica), *which is almost as much a symbol of the city as Big Ben*

The Regent's Park: *A small waterfall, tucked away near the Chester Road entrance of the park*

figures. Above them rises a bizarrely patterned and coloured conical cap. Following its restoration, the memorial was unveiled on 27 March 2007 to commemorate the 200th anniversary of the Act that abolished the transatlantic slave trade. Note also the mosaic patterns that are set into the white stone. Within the shelter of the pillars, four lion or leopard heads once spouted water into stone basins.

Lambeth Bridge

From the gardens there is a fine view of Lambeth Bridge, built in 1932 to replace a Victorian suspension bridge. It has elegant curves and is handsomely painted red and grey, with ornamental street lights set at intervals. Lambeth Pier juts out on the opposite bank and has its own pleasant café. In the late 17th century, the diarist John Evelyn was able to walk across the ice at this point to dine at Lambeth Palace. There seem to have been ice-age winters three or four centuries ago, and the freeze-up was aided when the giant bastions of old London Bridge impeded the river's flow. That was also before the Embankment had been reclaimed (*see* page 80). The narrowing of the river as a result of this engineering speeded the flow of the water.

At the Lambeth Bridge end of the gardens is a small children's playground, overlooked by two guardian rams carved in stone on top of the encircling wall. Beside it, steps lead up to an ornate gate, which opens onto the bridge. Leave the gardens by this gate, and walk across the bridge.

On the opposite side is Lambeth Palace, the official residence of the Archbishops of Canterbury. You can admire the brick Tudor gatehouse of the palace, dated 1501. Alongside stands the Church of St. Mary-at-Lambeth. Most of this building dates from the 1850s, but the tower was built in the 14th century and the foundations go back to 1032. The church and its small churchyard house the Garden Museum. Cross Lambeth Palace Road and enter the churchyard between pillars appropriately capped with delicate wrought-iron ivy leaves. Turn left into the porch of the church.

The Tradescants and The Garden Museum

The Museum honours the two John Tradescants, father and son, gardeners and plant collectors. The elder John was gardener to several aristocratic families, such as the earls and marquesses of Salisbury at Hatfield House in Hertfordshire, and George Villiers, Duke of Buckingham. He was the first of a line of men who were both garden designers and horticulturists. He went on expeditions to Europe in search of plants that were new to Britain or unusual, introducing pomegranates, oleanders, figs and brooms. In 1618 he joined an expedition to Muscovy (Russia) and some claim that he brought back to Britain the European larch (*Larix decidua*), which came to be grown both for its timber and for medicinal turpentine. Two years later he sailed for Algiers as a volunteer 'shott' on an expedition to quell pirates, but also in search of the small, delicious Algiers apricot, which he brought back, along with lilacs.

John Tradescant the elder became so famous in the field that he was sent plants from the new colonies. In 1617 he became a member of the Virginia Trading Company, a source of exotic plants new to Britain. Through routes such as this, plants such as tradescantia

VICTORIA TOWER GARDENS

N

250m (275yd)

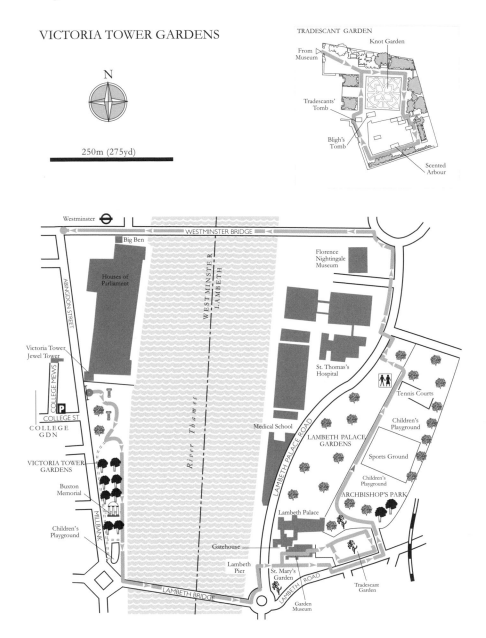

TRADESCANT GARDEN

Knot Garden

From
Museum

Tradescants'
Tomb

Bligh's
Tomb

Scented
Arbour

Westminster

WESTMINSTER BRIDGE

Big Ben

Florence
Nightingale
Museum

Houses of
Parliament

WESTMINSTER
LAMBETH

St. Thomas's
Hospital

Victoria Tower
Jewel Tower

COLLEGE MEWS

P

COLLEGE ST

COLLEGE
GDN

Medical School

Tennis Courts

Children's
Playground

River Thames

LAMBETH PALACE ROAD

LAMBETH PALACE
GARDENS

Sports Ground

VICTORIA TOWER
GARDENS

Buxton
Memorial

Children's
Playground

ARCHBISHOP'S PARK

Children's
Playground

MILLBANK

Lambeth Palace

Gatehouse

Lambeth
Pier

St. Mary's
Garden

LAMBETH ROAD

Tradescant
Garden

LAMBETH BRIDGE

Garden
Museum

(*Tradescantia virginiana*), Virginia creeper (*Parthenocissus quinquefolia*), and the black walnut (*Juglans nigra*) reached Britain from North America, and the scarlet runner bean from the West Indies. He never visited America, but in 1637 he sent his son John on the first of three trips. After his death, his son returned from Virginia with 200 new species, including the swamp cypress (*Taxodium distichum*), a tree now seen in many parks. He made two other journeys in 1642 and 1657, from which he brought back the tulip tree (*Liriodendron tulipifera*) and rock bells (*Aquilegia canadensis*), which grow in the knot garden behind this church.

Father and son had their home nearby, where they collected curiosities and opened what was virtually the first public museum, known as the Ark, which became the kernel of the Ashmolean Museum in Oxford. They are buried in the churchyard here, and although some elements of their work – at Hatfield House, for example – remain or have been restored, this church was the obvious base for the first museum of garden history, which was formally opened in 1983. The museum has displays on the history and development of gardens, and among the exhibits is a fine collection of garden tools, ranging from a 17th-century watering pot to early lawn mowers, one dated 1832. Six Archbishops of Canterbury are buried in the church (look for their memorials). The church also has a very good bookshop specializing, of course, in horticultural titles.

The Tradescant Garden

Leave the church through the door at the back, which leads into the living part of the museum – the garden. Late-flowering plants were less usual in the Tradescants' day, so the flowering season of this period garden is concentrated in early summer. The plants here all have name-tags and a map is available in the museum.

The highlight is the knot garden, ahead of you on the right. It is about 33 feet (10 metres) square and was laid out by the Marchioness of Salisbury to a traditional 17th-century geometric design, with the flower beds marked by low clipped hedges of miniature box (*Buxus sempervivens* 'Suffruticosa'). At the centre there is a sculptured, striped holly (*Ilex aquifolium* 'Golden King'). An original knot garden would probably have had only a few different favourite plants growing within its hedges, perhaps just one type in each bed, but in this garden the beds (and the beds surrounding the knot garden) are full of plants that the Tradescants would have known or themselves grown. Some are native species that they found growing wild in the countryside; others were brought to Britain from abroad, although some of these had already been familiar for centuries. The striped holly, for example, is said to have been first recorded growing in Britain in AD995, Mediterranean lavender (*Lavandula angustifolia*) in 1265, and hollyhocks (*Alcea rosea*), which originate in China, in 1300; the apothecary's rose (*Rosa gallica officinalis*), from southern Europe, was first recorded in AD900, and the crown fritillary (*Fritillaria imperialis*) was brought from Turkey in 1590 – in the knot there are four groups of this majestic plant, which is in flower early in the season.

In a bed by the fountain ahead of you is a strawberry tree (*Arbutus unedo*), native to the mild west coast of Ireland and the Mediterranean; it was recorded growing in England before 1548. Before moving on, note the sundial high up on the garden's north wall.

Turn right and right again at the end of the path, and walk along the scented arbour. Near one of the bower seats is the attractive smoke bush (*Cotinus coggyria*) brought from southern Europe in 1629, and so called because its feathery white fronds give it a misty appearance.

The Tombs

Turn right at the end of the scented arbour. Facing you is the fine tomb of the two Tradescants, a feature of this unusual garden. It was erected in 1638, and is decorated with scenes showing the dangers they met on their travels. Nearby is the tomb of Captain William Bligh (*c.*1754–*c.*1817), who also lived nearby and was captain of *The Bounty* in 1787. This ill-fated expedition set out to collect breadfruit seedlings from islands in the Pacific to grow in the young British colonies in the Caribbean. After the ship's crew mutinied, Bligh was cast adrift in an open boat with 17 men, and navigated 3,618 miles (5,822 kilometres) to Timor, near Java.

This being a London church, there are, of course, many others buried here. If you sit on the seat on the opposite side of the knot from these tombs, you rest your feet on a memorial slab to the Evans family, whose youngest members were John, aged 3, and his sister Ann, aged 16 months. They were victims of diseases that were rampant in the days before modern medicine, which has a debt to many of the plants that the Tradescants and others of their kind so enthusiastically collected.

Archbishop's Park

Return through the church and turn left into Lambeth Road. After about two or three minutes, just before the railway bridge, turn left along a cutting leading to Archbishop's Park. There are many fine trees in this park, which was for a long time part of Lambeth Palace Gardens. Facing you as you enter the park are two Indian bean trees (*Catalpa bignonioides*), and the northern end of the park is shaded by the spreading canopies of immensely tall London planes. Following the park's tradition as a recreation area for local children, there are children's playgrounds at either end, and sports pitches in the centre.

Turn left along a path heavily shaded by overhanging limes and a variety of other trees, which circumnavigates a cluster of rose beds. As the path bends right, the walls and towers of historic Lambeth Palace appear. The Archbishops of Canterbury have had an official residence on this site since about 1200, but the present palace is largely the result of rebuilding in 1828–34 in neo-Gothic style. Beyond the palace appears the red-brick tower of St. Thomas's Hospital Medical School, built in 1871.

Follow the path along the shrubbery and past a small flower garden at the north end of the park, and turn left onto Lambeth Palace Road. Turn right after crossing the road and walk along by St. Thomas's Hospital, eventually turning left onto Westminster Bridge, where the walk ends.

GREEN PARK

LOCATION	About ⅔ mile (1.1 kilometres) west of Charing Cross.
TRANSPORT	Green Park Underground Station (Jubilee, Piccadilly, and Victoria lines) and Hyde Park Corner Underground Station (Piccadilly Line). Victoria Station (overground terminus, underground trains on the Victoria, District and Circle lines, and bus terminus) is ten minutes' walk away. Buses along Piccadilly are: 8, 9, 19, 14, 22, 38.
ADMISSION	Open daily 05:00-12:00 hours. Admission is free.
SEASONAL FEATURES	Spring bulbs; autumn colour.
EVENTS	Gun salutes on special occasions, such as the Trooping of the Colour.
REFRESHMENTS	Kiosk at Ritz Corner and Canada Gate open daily approximately 09:00-20:00 hours (10:00–16:00 in winter). Café in St. James's Park (*see* page 99). Refreshments also in the hotels along Piccadilly and around Hyde Park Corner.

Green Park is aptly named – apart from deep drifts of colourful springtime bulbs and the autumn golds and russets of its closely planted trees, the greens of its leaves and grass are its dominant colours. Although it has no flower beds, this is an attractive park all year round, and it is much loved as a haven of tranquillity, despite its location between the traffic lanes of Piccadilly and Constitution Hill.

The peaceful atmosphere of Green Park today makes it hard to believe its hidden history of violence and raucous revelry. Before the 1660s, the area covered by the park was meadowland, rather swampy in places – the Tyburn stream, which arose in Hampstead, flowed south to St. James's Park lake, via Marble Arch, Piccadilly and Green Park. The meadows were acquired by Henry VIII, along with the land on which he established the Court of St. James's Palace in Westminster, and it was enclosed for grazing and hunting. After the king's death it was fortified by forces loyal to Mary I, who clashed with opponents of the queen's marriage to Philip II of Spain. And during the Civil War it was fortified again by Parliamentarians intent on threatening Charles I, in residence in the Palace of St. James. In 1667 Charles II turned some 36 acres (16 hectares) of this land into a formal park. A network of paths was laid across it, trees were planted, and a deer enclosure was built near Hyde Park Corner. At that time it was called Upper St. James's Park.

In those days, the park was at the very edge of London, and its proximity to the main route west – the road that is now Piccadilly – attracted highwaymen. It also became a convenient venue for duelling. In 1771 a duel between a Viscount Ligonier and one Count Alfieri ended with the latter wounded, but staggering off to the theatre, muttering darkly.

In the 18th century Green Park was handy for military parades and fireworks. It was here that George II staged his Royal Fireworks of 1749, celebrating the peace treaty which ended

93

the War of the Austrian Succession, the last war to be led by an English monarch. George Frederick Handel (1685–1759) composed music especially for the occasion, employing 40 trumpets and 20 French horns, plus oboes, bassoons and drums, augmented by 100 cannon. A magnificently decorated Temple of Peace – a pastiche of a Doric temple – was built of wood, 410 feet (125.5 metres) long and 114 feet (35 metres) high, with a stage for the 100 musicians (a print of the time shows it standing in a virtually treeless park). But at 20:30 hours on 27 April, when the first of the rockets were set off and the cannons roared, the building caught fire. Two arches collapsed and a girl in flames had to be stripped to her stays. However, the display continued and the king stayed until midnight.

Later, in 1814, a Temple of Concord in the form of a great, revolving 'Gothick' fort was built there to celebrate a centenary of Hanoverian rule and victory over Napoleon – but the temple was mysteriously burned down one night, and the park severely vandalized the next day by a crowd cheated of its entertainment.

In the 19th century, the park became a popular ballooning ground. A balloon ascent marked the coronation of George IV in 1821. There were inevitably disasters, however; on one occasion a man attempted a lift while mounted on his horse; the balloons failed, and horse and rider fell to the ground. The coronation of Queen Victoria in 1838 was marked by firework displays all over London, including a brilliant one in Green Park.

Today, Green Park is more popular as a venue for quiet walks and lunching. The charm of this small park lies in its trees, of which there are about 950 in its 53 acres (21.5 hectares). When the park was first laid out, the trees in the waterlogged dip, toward the Mall, were mainly willows and poplars. On the higher ground, toward Hyde Park Corner and Piccadilly, oak and ash predominated. Over the centuries, a greater variety of trees has been planted. Although rarities are lacking among the Green Park trees, there are many venerable London planes, and fine forest trees, such as chestnut, lime, poplar and oak. They are not name-tagged, however, so it is advisable to take with you on this walk one of the tree identification guides listed on page 185.

THE GREEN PARK WALK

Start The Ritz entrance. **Finish** Hyde Park Corner or Green Park. **Time** Allow 1 hour.

The gate beside the entrance to the underpass to Green Park Underground Station, beneath Piccadilly, is overshadowed by the Ritz Hotel, built in 1906. It was the first steel-framed building and a precursor of today's skyscrapers, but it was disguised as a grand French-style château. Some of its rooms have a restful view onto the park. Proceed through the gate and take the path to the right, parallel with Piccadilly, heading west. You may have to skirt underground work due to finish in 2011.

The ground swells away to the west, its rolling grassland set with trees. They are plane trees (*Platanus x hybrida*) in the main, with limes (*Tilia* spp.) and smaller hawthorns (*Crataegus monogyna*), planted in loose groups. But there is a scatter of others, such as the unusual black poplar (*Populus nigra*), its trunk often carrying burrs, or warts, of bark. Although it is a very different shape, this tree is a close relative of the familiar tall, thin Lombardy poplar. There

GREEN PARK

The Ritz
Hotel

Clarence
House

The Ritz
entrance gate

Spencer
House

Lancaster
House

Green Park

site of former
bandstand

ST JAMES'S PARK

Queen Victoria
memorial

Canada Gate

Naval & Military Club

PICCADILLY

The Constance
Fund fountain

CONSTITUTION HILL

Buckingham Palace

subway

subway

subway

Constitution Arch

250m (275yd)

1 Indian Bean-tree (*Catalpa bignonioides*)

Apsley House
(Wellington Museum)

HYDE PARK CORNER

Hyde Park Corner

are also silver maples (*Acer saccharinum*), with finely cut leaves that are silvery below – in North America this tree is a source of maple syrup; and silver lime (*Tilia tomentosa*), so called because the undersides of the leaves are silvery white. Young walnuts (*Juglans regia*) and other trees have also been planted out in some of the open spaces.

There is usually little to see in the way of flowers in this part of the park for most of the year, but in spring, flares of naturalized daffodils and other bulbs bloom in the grass along the Piccadilly railings and beside Queen's Walk in the east. Some of the trees bear blossom in spring, and there is red and gold leaf colour in autumn. The park remains attractive in winter after the leaves have gone, when the spidery branches of the empty trees are starkly silhouetted against the sky.

The Devonshire Gate

Follow the path running parallel to Piccadilly for a short way. There is a street market along Piccadilly at the weekends, when artists and other stallholders sell pictures and crafts from pitches along the railings. After a short stroll, you come to a fine, ornate gate on the right, with no road in front of it on the park side, only rough grass. This is the Devonshire Gate. Its stone pillars have vermiculate rustication (that is, a 'worm-eaten', antique look), and are still etched black, a legacy of the days before smokeless zones were introduced. This gateway was moved here in 1921 after a stay at Devonshire House, the Devonshire family mansion in Piccadilly (by the corner of Berkeley Street), which has since been demolished. Before that it was at Chiswick House – the sphinxes that surmount the pillars are a Chiswick motif. Notice that the ironwork is touched with gilt, and that the coat of arms (three stags' heads) is inscribed with the royal motto.

Through the railings you can see a splendid house on the north side of Piccadilly. This is the Naval & Military Club – known as 'the In and Out' from the traffic notices posted prominently at the entrance to its driveway. In Victorian times this was the residence of Lord Palmerston (1784–1865), the Prime Minister. Green Park was first opened to the public in 1826, and at that time visitors were confined to walking on the paths only, as they still are in the countryside. Lord Palmerston – at that time still to become Prime Minister – was among those who argued against legal trespass, and in favour of allowing people to walk on the grass. He asserted that the grass should be 'walked on freely and without restraint by the people young and old for whose enjoyment the parks are maintained'. From this gateway, the Broad Walk stretches south. At this point, either exercise your right to walk down it on the grass, or take one of the paths that border it to left and right.

The grassy Broad Walk is the main avenue descending gently north–south through the centre of the park, lined by a double row of youngish plane trees. It was created to provide a vista from Piccadilly to the Queen Victoria Memorial in front of Buckingham Palace. As you walk down it, however, look to the right (west), to contemplate magnificent treed vistas.

Queen's Walk

Near the bottom, the Broad Walk is crossed by a path. Turn left here, and immediately to your left, and labelled, is a sweet chestnut tree (*Castanea sativa*). These familiar trees are named after the town of Castania, in Thessaly, Greece, where they grew in abundance. During World War II chestnut wood was used for trackways to enable military vehicles to cross the sandy beaches of Normandy.

Turn left and walk past the chestnut, taking the path up past the site of the old bandstand marked by a handsome lamp standard. Cut across the grass to the right to Queen's Walk, which leads from Ritz Corner in the north to The Mall, opposite St. James's Park in the south. It was laid out in 1730, the creation of Charles Bridgeman (*see page 9*) for Queen Caroline, wife of George II, specifically as a place for her to walk with the royal family in spring. The Queen's Library, a small summer house for resting and reading, stood just off the walk until it was burned down during the celebrations of 1749.

In 1790, Queen's Walk became a fashionable promenade, competing with St. James's Park. From the Ritz down to Lancaster House, it was lined with fine mansions, some of which you can still see. Note Spencer House – the fourth grand house up from the Mall, recognizable by the sculptured figures standing on the pediment. It was the private residence of the

Spencers, the family of Diana, Princess of Wales, until 1927. It was designed in Palladian style in 1752–4 by John Vardy, assistant to William Kent (*see* page 9), and is the finest building in this area. Its main façade, which fronts onto the park, is so designed that the shadows strengthen its features. Notice the odd wings decorating the central round window. The house is open to the public on Sundays (except during January and August).

Stroll down to the southern end of Queen's Walk. Behind the railings on the right, great drifts of daffodils bloom in spring. To the left, as you reach The Mall, is Lancaster House, built in warm Bath stone. Note Milkmaid's Passage on its left. It was begun in 1825 by Benjamin Dean Wyatt, and completed by the Greek Revival architect, Sir Robert Smirke in 1841. Queen Victoria was often a guest in this magnificent house, owned by the dukes of Sutherland.

By comparison with St. James's Park, which you can see across The Mall, Green Park is abruptly rural, with none of the sophistication of man-made lakes and water birds of its neighbour. It has its remote spots where people scarcely ever walk. And it also has handsome, old-fashioned lamp standards and benches.

Turn right at the bottom of Queen's Walk along the path leading westward by The Mall. A pool of water once collected in this dip, and trees grow more thickly. You can see across to Buckingham Palace, and through the stone balustrade to the left you glimpse the flower beds surrounding the Queen Victoria Memorial (*see* page 103). No house existed here when Green Park was first laid out; Charles II resided in St. James's Palace, part of which still stands in the Mall. Buckingham House, the core of the present palace, was built in 1702–5 for the 1st Duke of Buckingham. In the 1820s, George IV, having rejected a proposal by Sir John Soane to build a palace in Green Park, commissioned the architect John Nash, who rebuilt part of Buckingham House as the present palace.

Constitution Hill

Continue past the ornate Canada Gate. Across the grass to the right (northwest) a stone memorial is set in the grass. It is the modern Canadian Memorial, unveiled in 1994, an unusual and impressive creation taking the form of a pair of smooth, polished red granite wedges, angled one to the other, with maple leaves etched into the stone, their veins glinting with brass. On occasions, water is set to flow gently down their upper surfaces.

Continue walking west. To your left, across a horse ride, is Constitution Hill. The name is said to originate with Charles II's frequent and perhaps rather dangerous constitutionals among his subjects, accompanied by his favourite spaniels. The wall on the opposite side of the road surrounds the gardens of Buckingham Palace. There have been one or two incidents along this route. Sir Robert Peel, twice Prime Minister, was thrown from his horse along this road in 1850 and died soon after. And Queen Victoria was shot at here in 1840, and again in 1842 and 1849. A different assailant was identified each time; all three were arrested and found guilty but insane.

From this side of the park, instead of following a path, head off in a northwesterly direction across the grass and through the trees toward the Constance Fund Fountain, which is marked on the map (page 95). In this park, the paths are really for navigating from; it is far more pleasant to walk across the grass. There is a wooden keeper's hut, keeping itself to itself in the centre of an open space. You may have this part of the park almost to yourself, and it feels as remote as anywhere can be in London. Few people walk here, simply because it is not on the way to anywhere.

Close to Hyde Park Corner, you come across the Constance Fund Fountain. It looks like an ornamental fountain, but is, in fact, a drinking fountain (now dry) with ornate twisting iron-work branches below, supporting a curvaceous nymph with a leash in her hand and a grey-hound bounding across her feet. Created by E. J. Clack in 1954, it is a gift of the Constance Fund, a private charity commemorating the wife of Sigismund Goetze, an artist who was quite well known in inter-war London, and who died in 1939.

Hyde Park Corner

From the Constance Fund Fountain, take the path that leads to the top of Constitution Hill and cross at the lights. Hyde Park Corner is at the top of a slight rise. It was fortified as a gun battery at the beginning of the Civil War in 1642. In 1750 it was described as 'one of the finest eminences in nature, commanding a vast extent of variegated country bounded by distant hills'; one such hill was Wimbledon. There were attempts in the past to turn this spot into a ceremonial western entry to the heart of London, but they all failed. The Regency architect Robert Adam was one of several notable people who had grand plans for the area.

The island houses a handful of notable military monuments. Ahead of you is Constitution Arch (also called Wellington Arch). Designed in 1828 by Decimus Burton, it was intended as a gateway to Hyde Park. It had on top a colossal equestrian statue of the Duke of Wellington, victor of the Battle of Waterloo of 1815 against the French army under Napoleon, but in 1883 the arch was moved to its present position to ease traffic congestion and the statue of Wellington was sent to the military at Aldershot. In 1912 the Arch was crowned with its statue of Victory riding a quadriga, a four-horse chariot, by Adrian Jones. A visit to the top is a must, since it is rewarded by a rare view into the gardens of Buckingham Palace, where the staff tennis court is clearly visible.

Walk through the Arch and follow the path to the right, passing a memorial to Royal Artillery soldiers who fought in the two world wars – a naked David resting on a gigantic sword, a symbol of the machine-gun slaying of tens of thousands during World War I.

Between the two memorials is a statue of the Duke of Wellington, hero of Waterloo in 1815. At the corners of the plinth are detailed figures wearing the regalia of four regiments of his time. Wellington is astride his famous horse, Copenhagen (1808–36). They face Apsley House, isolated by traffic since its neighbour was destroyed by the building of the access road into Park Lane. Its address is Number 1, London. It was built in the 1770s, and was later enlarged and encased with stone when it became the Duke of Wellington's residence. Finally, beyond *David* is the unusual New Zealand war memorial, looking like a piece from the Turner Prize. Retrace your steps into Green Park at the traffic lights and take the left-hand path to bring you back to Green Park Station where the walk ends.

ST. JAMES'S PARK

LOCATION	About 400 yards (366 metres) southwest of Charing Cross.
TRANSPORT	St. James's Park Underground Station (District and Circle lines) is five minutes' walk from the park on the south side; Westminster Underground Station (District and Circle lines) is about five minutes' walk from the park's south-eastern corner. Charing Cross Station (Northern, Bakerloo and Jubilee Underground lines and overground terminus) is about 15 minutes' walk from the northeast corner; and Victoria Station (Victoria and District and Circle Underground lines and overground terminus) is about 15 minutes' walk from the southwest corner. Many bus routes pass along Victoria Street and Whitehall, to the south and west. Parking in the area is difficult.
ADMISSION	Open 05:00 hours–midnight. Admission is free.
SEASONAL FEATURES	Spring blossom; rose beds and Nash flower beds in summer; autumn tree colour.
EVENTS	Bands give concerts on the band stand from May to August.
REFRESHMENTS	Inn the Park open Mon–Fri 08:00–23:00 hours, Sat–Sun 09:00–22:00.

St. James's is a magnificent park, strong on birds and strong on people, and since it is only a few minutes' walk from the Houses of Parliament, there is always a chance of seeing a famous political face taking the air among the civil servants. This park has also long been highly popular with English and foreign visitors to London. During the 20th century it has also been used as the setting for spy stories involving envelopes containing secrets left on benches, and similar plots.

St. James's is the oldest of the eight royal parks. It came into being in the 1530s, when Henry VIII enclosed a park for deer coursing and other palace amusements on marshy land attached to the leper hospice of St. James. It was a convenient distance from his three palaces: Whitehall (burnt down in 1698); Westminster (where the Houses of Parliament now stand); and St. James (part of which remains).

Charles II (1660–85) introduced dramatic changes to the park, creating a more formal area between Whitehall and St. James's. He had much admired the Palace of Versailles, outside Paris during his exile in France, and the name of the renowned French landscape designer André le Nôtre (1613–1700) has been linked with St. James's Park. However, a contemporary visitor from Switzerland wrote that Le Nôtre 'was of the opinion that the natural simplicity and in some places wild character had something more grand than he could impart to it, and persuaded the King not to touch it'. Nevertheless, free radiating alleys were planted, and a straight canal 100 feet (30 metres) broad was excavated, with an island for water birds.

99

Samuel Pepys recorded in his diary, on 15 July 1666, that he 'lay down upon the grass by the canalle and slept awhile'.

The park was then a fashionable venue, but was less so by the start of the 18th century. Queen Anne, in an attempt to restore its cachet, introduced stricter regulations: no walking on the grass; no clogs; nothing to be sold (in those days milk was often sold directly from a cow grazing on whatever grass was available); and no linen dried. Later in the century, Queen Caroline, wife of George II, asked the Prime Minister, Sir Robert Walpole, how much it would cost to restrict its use to royals. 'Only three crowns, Madam,' he replied. A crown was a coin (there were four crowns to £1), but Walpole meant the kingdoms of England, Ireland and Scotland. Later in the century, the park had its own breed of muggers, called mohocks; and it had become a haunt of prostitutes, as James Boswell discovered and recorded.

The original formal layout of the park was undone when John Nash (1752–1835), who had upgraded Buckingham House into Buckingham Palace in the 1820s, redesigned St. James's Park, turning the canal into a more natural-looking lake surrounded by the winding paths and lawns, skilfully broken by clumps of trees, that typify its style today.

THE ST. JAMES'S PARK WALK

Start and finish Storey's Gate Lodge. **Time** Allow 1 hour.

The walk begins at the headquarters of the Parks Police, with its quaint blue lantern. Follow the path leading northward to the lake. Either side of this path and elsewhere in this park there are some magnificent plane trees, almost cathedral-like in scale and with massive, buttressed trunks, like rainforest trees. They are numbered, since there are Tree Protection Orders on them, and named as London planes (*Platanus x hispanica*). When you reach the lakeside, notice the great, sprawling fig tree. The grass alongside it (so reads the notice) is for the enjoyment of wildlife, not humans.

The Lake

Follow the path around the eastern edge of the lake. Nash's water feature is very different from the original formal canal, although the map shows that the north bank retains something of the original straight edge. In fact, this wing of the lake was once a 'decoy' – a set of rectangular pools amid swampy ground, dug to attract wild duck, which could be netted for the table. The lake is on average 5 feet (1.5 metres) deep, which was shallow enough to drain and erect huts for government staff during World War II.

St. James's Park is famous for its pelicans. They have resided in the park for centuries, the first having been given to Charles II in 1684 by the Russian ambassador. They like this first bay and they can often be seen camped out, collapsed on the rocks in the middle of the water, looking like piles of washing awaiting laundering. There is, at the time of writing, a population of four pelicans here. The park has always been a home for birds, some of them exotic. Apart from the pelicans, the diarist, John Evelyn (1620–1706) noted storks, swans, geese and cranes. James I had a menagerie, complete with crocodiles and an 'ellefant' which was fed with a gallon of wine a day. He also kept 'outlandish fowl' and had an aviary.

Walk on until you see a rustic cottage to the left. Nash's new lake embraced Duck Island, which is now narrowly joined to the bank and hidden away on it are artesian wells that feed St. James's Park, including the pumps for the fountains and for aerating the lakes both of this park and of Kensington Gardens. In 1837 the Ornithological Society of London built a house on the island for a birdkeeper – the quaint Duck Island Cottage, its cottagey garden bright with flowers (they are name-tagged). The pelicans are fed on the lawn here at 14:30 hours every day. They enjoy 12lbs (5.4 kilograms) of fresh fish, plus a vitamin supplement, and it is fun to watch this spectacle. Duck Island Cottage is now the address of the London Historic Parks and Gardens Trust, an organization that is active in restoration, but also arranges lectures and entertaining visits for members. Tours of Duck Island take place three times a year, between October and January, outside of the breeding season.

Horse Guards Parade

Follow the path past the top of the lake toward the Guards Memorial – prominent to your right – its figures cast in metal from German guns captured in World War I. To the right, you look across Horse Guards Parade, a large military parade ground. The surrounding buildings make it one of the most dramatic open spaces in London, and it is the venue for the Trooping of the Colour ceremony, held on a Saturday early in June. Just before the path passes the wood-clad Inn the Park, a café with a view out over the water to the sprawling willows of Duck Island, note a tall maidenhair tree (*Ginko biloba*) in the first flower bed. Inn the Park is the latest of a number of cafés on this pleasant spot; the first was established at the end of the 17th century, during the reign of William and Mary.

The Rock Garden

The path from the Guards Memorial runs left past flower beds and an unusual rock garden feature and cascade; it is unusual because the plants that are grown on it are not the conventional alpine and rockery flowers but ordinary garden varieties. There is a fountain jet in the lake off Duck Island to the left – although it is not always switched on – while the path is lined with benches, where civil servants munch sandwiches at lunchtimes, and seemingly every day tourists from all over the world sit and rest. This is a place to hear languages you have never heard before.

The Mall

Continue along the lakeside. To the right, at the point where the path diverts from the water, is a picturesque beech tree with a twisted trunk. Here you will also see more of those statuesque plane trees.

Leave the waterside path where it forks to the right for Marlborough Gate, opposite St. James's Palace, to view The Mall. The walk passes a circle of flagstones where, in summer, an awning is erected for daily concerts by military guards' bands. These popular concerts are held at lunchtimes and in the evenings. Visit at the end of the summer and you will see the scatters of mauve autumn crocuses that appear in the grass by the gate. They are not strictly crocuses, but colchicums (they flower without leaves appearing).

ST JAMES'S PARK

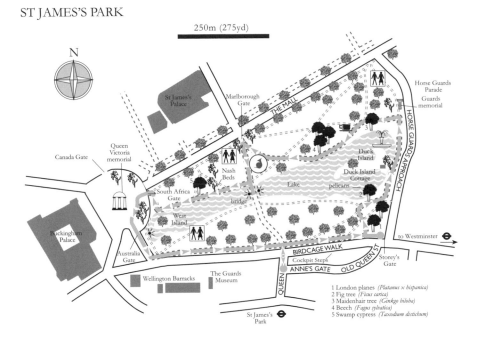

250m (275yd)

N

1 London planes *(Platanus x hispanica)*
2 Fig tree *(Ficus carica)*
3 Maidenhair tree *(Ginkgo biloba)*
4 Beech *(Fagus sylvatica)*
5 Swamp cypress *(Taxodium distichum)*

St. James's Park is bounded along its north side by The Mall. It was a fashionable walk in the days of Charles II, and takes its name from the game of Paille Maille or Pell Mell that people played here in those days. This was a game which seems to have resembled croquet in some ways: a ball was hit down an alley floored with crushed cockle shells, the aim being to drive it through a goal (perhaps an iron ring hung at the end of the alley). Today's wide Mall, however, lined by young plane trees, was laid down in the early 20th century and was designed by Sir Aston Webb as a ceremonial route between Admiralty Arch and the Queen Victoria Memorial in front of Buckingham Palace. The old line of the walk runs parallel to it on the northern side. Notice the ceremonial flagpoles, and the unusual design of the lamp standards – eggs held by iron banding – rather art deco in style. The tarmac here is not the usual black, but red, composed of chippings of Northumberland granite.

The Bridge

Return along the path to the northern lakeside and onto the bridge that crosses the lake. This is a blue, slim-line 1950s replacement of a Victorian iron suspension bridge which, in 1857, had replaced John Nash's original bridge. It offers a marvellous view back down the lake to Duck Island, with the roofscape and domes of the official buildings beyond looking more Moscow than London. Return to the lake shore and turn left. Many waterfowl can be seen: crested duck; great crested grebe; shelduck; teals of many kinds; Bahama and other pintails; chiloe wigeon; and many others, including ten different types of geese, and black and white (mute) swans. There are usually about 1,000 birds which are forcibly resident because they have had their flight feathers clipped, plus countless wild birds. During the breeding season in May and early June, tawny owls can be heard calling from Duck Island at dusk.

The Nash Beds

Continue walking west along the lake path until you see three flower beds to the right. Take a detour to them. Although they are relatively new, they are of key interest because they are based on garden principles set out by John Nash in 1826. They contain small trees, shrubs, climbers, flowers and bulbs, all ranked and planted so that they have a natural look, and the edges of the beds are made to curve against the grass. The flower colours and foliage are carefully positioned, and plantings include sweet pea, wild geraniums, dwarf chrysanthemums, hollyhocks, and various flowers that belong to the daisy family. Many are pleasantly scented. These Nash beds are, in fact, semi-formal in appearance, but planted with a cottage-garden mixture of flowers.

Continue up the side path running to the right (north) of these beds, passing a number of rose beds to the right. These were dedicated in 1980 to Queen Elizabeth the Queen Mother on her 80th birthday. Her personal choice of roses included 'Korrasia', 'Congratulations', 'Just Joey', 'Blessings' and 'Young Venturer'.

The Horseshoe Fountain

Return along the path to the northern lakeshore and continue walking west toward the end of the lake. Note the tall swamp cypress at the end of the Nash beds, at the lake edge, by a large willow; look for its telltale knobbly roots protruding from the bank at the lake's edge. Water aeration devices can be seen in one or two places; this lake is quite shallow and keeping it from becoming stagnant is something of a problem. At the end of the park, in front of Buckingham Palace, is a high wall looking like a quay with a horseshoe-shaped fountain at its centre, now sadly dry. Apparently, the lake did extend up to it at one time. There is some attractive bedding, including various hostas (foliage plants) and a tall variety of the cottage garden flower, London pride.

Queen Victoria Memorial

If you have never looked closely at the Queen Victoria Memorial facing Buckingham Palace, it is worth a short detour. It is a good, solid, sentimental edifice, exhibiting some highly skilled work. It consists of a colossal white marble statue of Queen Victoria carved by Thomas Brock from a single block of stone. The queen faces down The Mall toward Admiralty Arch, and is accompanied by female allegories of Charity, Truth and Justice; below her, around the edge of the memorial, there are bronze groups representing peace, agriculture, architecture and other achievements of her reign. Fountains spout below figures, while at the pinnacle of it all is a golden gilded Victory.

As for Buckingham Palace, in 1829 George IV employed John Nash to improve it, but in fact he rebuilt what had been Buckingham House as a royal palace. St. James's Palace was set aside for use for court ceremonies. Queen Victoria made the palace her main home. Almost all that you can see from the front, however, is of a later date, for the façade was added in 1912. The palace's real front faces its gardens. Before leaving the memorial, stop to admire the handsome gates encircling it: Canada Gate (1906) leading into Green Park, bearing the coats of arms of various Canadian provinces, and the gates – actually just two white pillars now – leading into the Mall.

Birdcage Walk

Now return to the lake to complete the circuit along its south side, or along Birdcage Walk with its lines of plane trees. James I and Charles II had aviaries here – hence the name – and diarist John Evelyn noted many 'curious kinds of poultry'. The late Regency barracks of the Brigade of Guards (the body guard) can be seen on the opposite side of Birdcage Walk. Further along, you see the 1883 statue, opposite Queen Anne's Gate, that is known as *The Greek Boy* for reasons now forgotten. It is also worth taking a detour from the walk by ascending the slope and turning left into Queen Anne's Gate, with its rows of what are in all probability the best-preserved early 18th-century houses in London. They are built of mellow, dark brick, with porches and torch extinguishers. Follow Queen Anne's Gate to the end, go left into Dartmouth Street and down the secretive cockpit steps. There was once a cockpit here; cock fights (called 'mains') were very popular. The biographer, James Boswell (1740–95) wrote: 'I then went to the Cockpit, which is a circular room in the middle of which the cocks fight ... nicely cut and armed with silver heels (spurs) ... one pair fought three quarters of an hour ... the uproar and noise of the betting is prodigious ...'. At the bottom of the cockpit steps turn right and continue back to Storey's Gate, where the walk ends.

BATTERSEA PARK

LOCATION	About 2⅓ miles (4 kilometres) west of Charing Cross.
TRANSPORT	East and southeast sides: Sloane Square Underground Station (District and Circle lines) is about 20 minutes' walk away; Battersea Park Station (overground trains from Clapham Junction and Victoria) and Queenstown Road Station (overground trains from Clapham Junction and Waterloo) are five minutes' walk away; 137 and 137a buses stop on Queenstown Road. West side: 19, 39, 44, 45, and 49 buses stop on Battersea Bridge Road. South side: 44 and 344 buses stop on Battersea Park Road. There are car parks with metered parking within the park.
ADMISSION	Open daily 08:00–dusk. Admission is free.
SEASONAL FEATURES	The Old English Garden, the Herb Garden and the Subtropical Garden in spring and summer; autumn tree colour.
EVENTS	Many events throughout the year (*see* page 184); Easter Parade; regular sporting events.
REFRESHMENTS	La Gondola al Parco open daily 10:00–18:00 hours or until 22:30 hours for sporting events.

Battersea Park is a relatively recent park, created in Victorian days. Before that, the land now occupied by the park and its surrounding streets was an area commonly flooded by the River Thames. There were market gardening plots in places, where 'Battersea bunches' (bunches of asparagus) were grown. Otherwise, Battersea Fields had a reputation as an unruly playground, with a weekly fair and, on Sundays, donkey-racing, fortune tellers, drinking booths and much besides. It was often a place of violence. In 1829, the Duke of Wellington rode out of town over wooden Battersea Bridge to fight a duel with the Earl of Winchilsea on this open land. A 19th-century city missionary described it as '... a place out of Hell that surpassed Sodom and Gomorrah in ungodliness and abomination'.

Eventually, in the mid-1800s, the Victorian authorities decided to do something about Battersea Fields. They made plans to create a park there, and purchased 320 acres (130 hectares) of land. Regulations were drawn up: '... all persons found trespassing with Horses, Donkeys, Cockshies, Barrows on a Sunday will be taken into custody.' The land was drained and earth was brought from the excavations of the Victoria Docks at Canning Town to raise the level, of which 198 acres (80 hectares) were to become the park, and 120 acres (49 hectares) were sold to a builder, Thomas Cubitt, to erect mansion blocks overlooking the park along the roads south and west of it. The ground was landscaped to an original plan by James Pennethorne, who had worked at The Regent's Park under John Nash (*see* page 61). There were plans to hold the Great Exhibition of 1851 in this park, but it could not be finished in time, and it eventually opened as a public open space in 1858. In 1860 the lake was dug out, and its waters were made to cascade spectacularly down huge, artificial rocks positioned at the lakeside. This was followed by the construction of great banks of earth on the south side to create a subtropical garden. When it was planted in 1864 this garden was considered the horticultural wonder of Europe. There was also considerable planting of the planes and other trees that we see here today. Toward the end of the 19th century the park became extremely fashionable, and the drives were filled with carriages and bicycles.

The Festival of Britain was held in 1951, six years after the end of World War II (and a century after the Great Exhibition), to perk up people's spirits. The main exhibition celebrating Britain's achievements and expectations was held at the South Bank, where the Royal Festival Hall remains, but the fun side was located in Battersea Park. This consisted of the Grand Vista with its waterworks, a funfair, shops and stalls, restaurants and beer gardens, and even The Far Tottering and Oyster Creek Railway, after cartoons by Ronald Searle (1920–). There was plenty of brightly coloured paint – red, blue, white and gold. Many thousands of bulbs were planted, including 20,000 yellow tulips.

Battersea Park has always been a local authority park. In 1889, the Metropolitan Board of Works, which had been responsible for building it, handed it over to the new London County Council; the Greater London Council assumed responsibility in 1965, and Wandsworth Borough Council in 1986. Today, the park is maintained and run with considerable care and, despite today's necessary financial cutbacks, with devotion and love. Its 200 acres (81 hectares) host an extraordinary number of events: sports and children's events; circuses, ballet, and theatre; regular classic and custom car meetings; numerous festivals; and the annual Easter Parade and fairs. Yet it remains a place where you can get away from crowds and enjoy the greenery, the flowers and the birds.

THE BATTERSEA PARK WALK

Start and finish Albert Gate. **Time** Allow 1¼ hours.

The fine ironwork gates and railings touched with gilding that comprise the Albert Gate dated originally from 1901–2, and were inspired by the Arts and Crafts Movement, but they were cannibalized during World War II and replaced in 1986. Before entering the park, walk up Albert Bridge Road toward the River Thames and Albert Bridge, with its delicate lattice of ironwork hung with hundreds of light bulbs – it is one of the classic sights of London between dusk and midnight, when it is illuminated. This Victorian suspension bridge bounces to the traffic, and on the south side there is a replica of a notice put there in Victorian times, requesting marching troops to break step for fear of damaging the structure. There are fine views along the river.

Return to Albert Gate and pass through it. Just inside three of Battersea Park's four gates there are typical park-keepers' lodges, fronted by neat lawns and flower beds. The garden of the one beside Albert Gate is bright with bluebells in spring, with bedding plants later in the season. Pause to read the notice board here, which relates the park's history. Veer left past the Lodge, take the path to the right, and turn left into a walled compound which has the atmosphere of a tiny rural village. The park offices are ahead on the left, and to the right of them is the large Herb Garden with an interesting collection of culinary and medicinal herbs, planted in themes, such as 'Herbs for men's health'.

Leaving the Herb Garden, cross the North Carriage Drive to stand at the top of the West Carriage Drive. Perhaps you can identify a 'champion tree' – one of a list of the tallest or biggest trees in London published by Alan Mitchell, the author of numerous books on trees. There is one at the northern end of the car park beside the West Carriage Drive. It is a North American black walnut (*Juglans nigra*), 110 feet (33.5 metres) high, with more leaflets than the native walnut and producing a very hard, ridged nut.

The planting of many of the trees in Battersea Park was planned by John Gibson, who became the park's first curator in 1856. In general, he avoided rigidly straight lines, following, on the large scale, the 'gardenesque' style which was popular for parks at the time, with serpentine or wavy lines. He planted many honey locusts and planes down this west side of the park.

The Old English Garden

Now walk east along North Carriage drive for about 200 yards (180 metres), and turn right into the walled garden. This was created in 1912 on the site of a small botanic garden. It is a delightfully intimate, quiet, sunny place with dwarf box hedges, wooden pergolas and seats all around. At the centre is a small pool stocked with goldfish and lilies.

Take time to stroll round this pretty garden, then leave it by the south gateway, and turn left along a winding woodland path through fenced enclosures planted with shrubs and trees. Shaded serpentine paths like this were originally a device to give some seclusion in what is public space. Toward the end of the path to the left you see an unexpected statue of a dog, an anti-vivisection memorial. Follow the path to its right and turn right at the end, passing on the left a small white house. This is a house and temple for the monks who look after the Peace Pagoda (*see* page 108).

At the end of the path, bear left and walk onto open ground studded with flower beds and, to left and right, water features. These were part of a Grand Vista, a sequence of shallow rectangular pools and fountains devised in 1950 or thereabouts by the cartoonist Osbert Lancaster (1908–86). To the left you will see a couple of eccentric colonnade erections by the artist John Piper (1903–92). They are what remain of a colourful period in the park's history, when the area stretching from this point to East Carriage Drive was a 37-acre (15-hectare) pleasure ground, part of the Festival of Britain celebrations of 1951. The pleasure ground was planned to continue for six months, but eventually it remained open for a year. At the northeast corner was a funfair with a big dipper, and although this was scaled down, it did not close until 1974. It explains the puzzling foundations you can still see in some places. The fountains in the large pool to your right often play during the weekends in summer. To the left of the fountains is 'the dance tent', a raised, circular grass mound decorated with colourful narrow beds that reflect the shape of a striped dance marquee that stood here during the festival.

BATTERSEA PARK

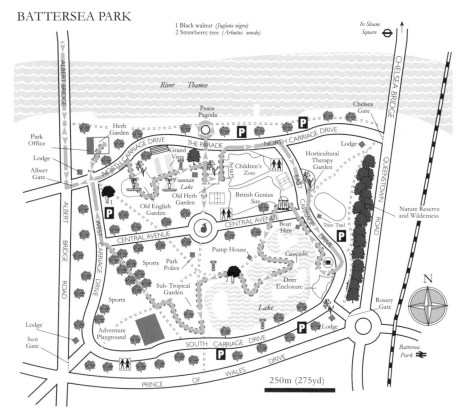

1 Black walnut *(Juglans nigra)*
2 Strawberry tree *(Arbutus unedo)*

The Peace Pagoda

Take the white path beyond the Piper colonnades and turn left at the line of stones. The shrubbery to your left conceals a grotto, which is another relic of the funfair. As you skirt it, the wooden Peace Pagoda with its four gilded Buddhas comes into view. It was a gift to London from the Japanese Buddhist Order Nipponzan Myohoji, and was erected in 1984–5, when the park was under the management of the Greater London Council. It is built of Canadian Douglas fir, and its architecture is based on ancient Indian and Japanese Buddhist designs.

The Children's Zoo

Take the left path that goes south from the Peace Pagoda toward the bandstand, a 1988 replica of the original Victorian structure, erected as one of the improvements effected by Wandsworth Council. Drop down three steps and up two steps to the left into the Lavender Garden. Turn left when you come to the aviary you can see ahead. It is part of the Children's Zoo, which also originated at the 1951 Festival of Britain as a temporary feature. It remained and was expanded until, in the late 1980s, the animal houses were at last rebuilt. The inhabitants include monkeys, pygmy goats, miniature Shetland ponies, ring-tailed lemurs, meerkats and the bizarrely-named Kune Kune pigs – pronounced 'cooney cooney' and meaning 'fat and round' in Maori. Kune Kune pigs did not arrive in the U.K. from New Zealand until 1992, after two British animal lovers, who had worked in New Zealand, heard that the population was under threat. They imported a small group to start a breeding programme in the U.K.

Turn right again when you reach the North Carriage Drive, passing the entrance to the zoo. Just beyond to the right is a drive leading to a large open space known as the British Genius site. It is used for funfairs, circuses, outdoor festivals and other activities.

Horticultural Therapy Garden and the Pump House

Continue along North Carriage Drive and veer right along the East Carriage Drive. To the left, just past the tennis courts, is the Horticultural Therapy Garden, laid out as a demonstration garden for disabled people during the 1970s and full of 'ideas for making gardening easier'. Pass through the gate and stroll through it.

You emerge from the garden facing a small leftward-leading path, which runs past the Millenium Arena athletics track, but you should turn right and then left along the East Carriage Drive. To your left is an outdoor fitness circuit. Beyond it, stretching away to the left, is the nature reserve, a wilderness area of thicket, boggy patches and pools, which was established to encourage British woodland plants, insects and birds. The cream towers of Battersea Power Station, between which Pink Floyd famously suspended a giant pig for their 1976 album, 'Animals', are visible through the trees.

Ahead of you to the right is a small grassy hill enclosed by a fence. Cross the East Carriage Drive and follow the path around it. This is the deer enclosure, which dates from 1888, but has been empty since at least 2006.

By now you should have reached the lakeshore. Turn right and stroll up to the waterside café (an example of 1930s architecture), from where there is a good view across to the rocky cascade signposted by a palm tree. Sadly, the cascade, a feature of the Victorian park, has been dry and silent since 2004, pending funding for restoration work.

Following the lakeside path westward, you passed a boat-hire yard. Take a detour northward, across Central Avenue, and walk across the grass to the War Memorial you can see to your right, surrounded by a neatly trimmed hedge. It was unveiled in 1922. The model for the soldier to the right, as you face the three figures – the one clasping the hand of the figure in front – was the soldier-poet Robert Graves (1895–1985), who was a friend of the sculptor, Eric Kennington; the other two figures may be modelled on the war poets Wilfred Owen and Siegfried Sassoon.

Stroll across the grass to the lakeshore beyond the boat-hire yard, turn right, and walk past the stretch of lake which is set aside for fishing (carp, roach and perch), up to the elegant, Italianate brick Pump House. It was built in 1861 to house a massive steam engine which pumped water from a well to a cast-iron tank at the top of the tower to feed the cascades and the lake. The lake was later fed directly from the Thames. The Pump House was restored in 1992 and now houses displays about the park and a small art gallery.

The Lake

Retrace your steps from the Pump House, and stroll along the lake's northwest shore. The lake was a key feature of the Victorian park, just as it is today. It covers 16 acres (7 hectares) and is only 3 feet (0.9 metres) deep. Many waterbirds, including herons, live on the lake and nest on its islands.

Unwelcome pressure has been put on this ornamental feature in recent years – too much dirty water taken directly from the Thames; algal clouding, partly the result of the shallowness of the lake and lack of water movement; too many waterfowl (500 Canada geese alone); and some 1.5 tons more fish stocks than the lake should support – and regular dredging was not enough to prevent rapid resilting. In the 1990s, however, the park won three years of funding under the European 'LIFE' programme. This has paid for a new 300-foot (91-metre) borehole for clean water, the installation of water aerators, exchanges of fish, and the replanting of the banks with 13,000 shrubs, trees and herbaceous plants. Under the advice of the Wildfowl Trust at Slimbridge, Gloucestershire, ecological control, including culling, has reduced the numbers of Canada geese to the recommended number of about 30. However, the balance is a dynamic one. Pinioned (captive) black swans have lived on Battersea Park Lake since the 1880s, but they recently disappeared, perhaps taken by the park's 40 foxes, whose numbers are also controlled. The swans now in residence are feral. They have beaks of an intense red, and when they fly you can see their white wing flash.

Follow the lakeside path, which meanders alongside the silent cascade to a rustic-style bridge, dating from 1920, with new planting on the nearby watersides. The path winds past the south side of the Pump House, past a tranquil stretch of lake, and then forks. Take the right fork. As you round the bend, look left, between the path and the water's edge, for a spreading hybrid strawberry tree (*Arbutus unedo*) with dark green leaves and dusky red bark. It is another of Alan Mitchell's 'champion' trees (*see* page 107). In the Mediterranean it produces dimpled red fruit, but they are not much like strawberries.

Around a couple of bends, to the right, is a group of three standing figures by Henry Moore (1898–1986). It is the relic of an outdoor sculpture exhibition staged in Battersea Park in 1948, the first time such an exhibition was held in a public park. Pieces were exhibited by other famous sculptors, such as Matisse and Epstein. A work by Moore's contemporary, Barbara Hepworth, also remains on the south shore of the lake.

The Sub-Tropical Gardens

Take the right-hand path into a fenced lawn planted with trees. This area was the site of the Sub-Tropical Gardens, which were a major feature of the Victorian park and aimed to challenge Kew Gardens. Curving banks were built up to give warm, sheltered conditions, and these remain, covered with trees. With its winding paths and sweeps of open lawn, this is a very attractive place. There are evergreen oaks, weeping ash and one or two palms still to be seen, but the original plantings, including tree ferns, tender bananas (*Musa ensete*) from Abyssinia, *Begonia rex* from Assam, *Wiganda caracasana* from Mexico, black-leaved perillas from the Far East, and the castor oil plant (*Ricinus communis*) from tropical Africa, have long since disappeared.

The Sub-Tropical Gardens were among several extravagant displays which made Battersea Park world famous in the 19th century. This park was one of the first places where carpet bedding was tried out, in the 1850s. In this type of bedding, dwarf rosette foliage plants, such as 2-inch (5-centimetre) tall alternanthera, and succulents, such as fleshy-leaved echeverias, are used to create a patterned surface that looks like a carpet. An example can be seen in Hyde Park (*see* page 52). As the *Gardener's Chronicle* of 1864 put it, 'It hardly seems possible at first to realise that one is looking upon a group of living plants ...'. Before long, parks and gardens all over the U.K. were experimenting with the idea. It was largely the brainchild of John Gibson, the Superintendent of Battersea Park at the time, who also planted many of the trees to be seen here today. To be effective with carpet bedding gardeners must achieve perfection, so this form of planting is not only tricky and expensive to produce, but also needs constant maintenance. Nevertheless, there are proposals to research and restore an area of this bedding in Battersea Park.

The Sports Pitches

To complete the walk, leave the Sub-Tropical Gardens by the path on the right and take the path that leads through an avenue of flowering cherry trees (a riot of pink and white in spring) diagonally through the sports fields to West Carriage Drive. To the left are all-weather sports pitches and the largest adventure playground in London, designed for children and young people aged from five to 16. Turn right beneath the marvellous ranked plane trees along West Carriage Drive (notice one or two recent sculptures on the lawn to the left) to return to Albert Gate, where the walk ends.

CHELSEA PHYSIC GARDEN

LOCATION	About 2½ miles (4 kilometres) southwest of Charing Cross.
TRANSPORT	Sloane Square Underground Station (District and Circle lines) and Battersea Park and Queenstown Road stations (overground trains from Victoria and Waterloo respectively) are 20 minutes' walk away across Chelsea Bridge. Buses passing nearby are 239 (not Sundays) from Victoria; 11, 19, 22, 49, 319, 345 along King's Road; 137, 137a along Queenstown Road. There is a car park in Battersea Park across Albert Bridge (15 minutes' walk).
SEASONAL FEATURES	January snowdrops; displays of Cistus in June; autumn tree colour. A free map shows current highlights.
EVENTS	Talks and guided tours.
ADMISSION	Open Apr–Oct: Sun 12:00–18:00 hours, Wed, Thu, Fri 12:00–17:00 hours. Admission £8 adult, £5 concessions.
REFRESHMENTS	Tangerine Dream Café open same times as the garden.

This delightful 4-acre (1.6-hectare) secret garden was founded in 1673, when the Society of Apothecaries (the old name for pharmaceutical chemists) established a physic garden by the Thames. 'Physic' was the old term for the art of healing and the medical profession, and the aim of such gardens was to grow a library of healing plants. At that time plants were virtually the only source of medicines, and even today, around 80 per cent of medicines are still plant-based. In time, plants from around the world were being grown, not all of them for medicinal purposes, and the gardens became known as 'botanic gardens'. There are early physic gardens in Oxford and in Pisa, Italy, but only this one retains its original name.

In the 1700s the garden was threatened by the rising cost of upkeep. It was eventually saved by the well-heeled Court Doctor, Sir Hans Sloane, who in 1712 bought the manor of Chelsea. He restored the Physic Garden, then leased it back to the Society, and the rent remains the same to this day, at £5 a year. A key figure of the time was Philip Miller, who, while he was Curator from 1722 to 1770, made Chelsea the world's finest botanic garden. The 1800s saw another decline in the fortunes of the garden, coupled with threats from would-be building speculators, but in 1899 it was taken over by a parish charity, and maintained for private use by university and other students. In 1983 an independent charity was set up and the garden was reopened to visitors.

Apart from the trees, the plants will hardly be the same as were growing here in past centuries. However, many plants on the original lists are still grown, with many later additions bringing the total to around 3,000 species in all. The beds are usually signed with a plaque giving the category of plants that they contain.

THE CHELSEA PHYSIC GARDEN WALK

Start and finish The Students' Gate. **Time** Allow 1 hour.

Enter the gardens through the 300-year-old gate in the warmly aged, red-brick wall in Swan Walk. Hanging just inside is an equally old small bell for summoning apprentice apothecaries to their studies. Ahead is the kiosk where you purchase tickets. To whet the appetite, to the right, close to the entrance gate is a Mediterranean pomegranate (*Punica granatum*), with striking scarlet flowers at the tips of the shoots from June to autumn. Originally from Asia, it has been cultivated around the Mediterranean since ancient times. It often fruits in this garden, where such foreign plants (and trees) grow successfully because it offers a warm microclimate: the soil is well drained, the tall brick walls act rather like storage radiators, retaining the sun's warmth, and there is even heat from traffic along the Chelsea Embankment. These factors combine to raise the temperature up to five degrees higher than elsewhere, and there are often frost-free areas in winter. As a downside, the traffic gives off exhaust pollution, but the plants seem not to suffer.

Useful Plants

The walk circles the Physic Garden anticlockwise, so turn along the path to the right, passing to the left a large bay tree (*Laurus nobilis*) overhanging one of this garden's many strategically placed seats, to reach the celebrated olive tree (*Olea europaea*). The biggest in Britain, at 30 feet (9.0 metres), this stalwart of the Mediterranean climate was planted in 1901 and it sometimes fruits. With the bay tree and the olive, you are in that part of the garden set aside for useful plants. One of the original functions of the garden was to teach trainee apothecaries to 'distinguish good and useful plants from those that bear resemblance to them and are hurtful'. And so, near the olive there are fruit trees and bushes, including, in the sheltered corner by the office, a healthy sweet orange grapefruit (*Citrus paradise*), nicknamed 'Aunt Queenie', which was planted soon after World War II and first bore fruit outside in 1998 – proof of global warming?

Turn left and left again at the end of the fruits. The path passes a bed of dye plants, with species such as indigo (*Indigofera tinctonia*), which is used to treat laryingitis, and madder, whose roots yield a red dye. Woad can also be seen. Its leaves, when steeped, ooze a blue dye that the Celts in Britain used for tattooing; it produces dense clusters of yellow flowers in May. Dyer's greenweed produces a yellow dye. These plants are of historic interest, for the colours they produce have now mainly been replaced by chemical dyes.

Follow the path, and on the right are vegetables and what are termed lesser vegetables. Many are familiar, including allotment-worthy cabbages, but look also for lentil, soya bean, and less familiar native plants, such as Good King Henry (*Chenopodium bonus henricus*). It was one of the wild greens traditionally gathered and perhaps cultivated in Britain, and its seeds have been found in the archaeological layers of Stone Age sites. It used to be sold in the old Covent Garden market, and although it has been generally discounted as a weed, it is now coming back into culinary use. There is dandelion, still gathered today to make a refreshingly bitter green salad. Many of the plants in the end bed of this section will be familiar as herbs used in cooking.

At the end of this path, circle the neat herb bed. You now pass a bed of subsistence (famine) plants to the left. There is an Asian wingnut tree (*Pterocarya fraxinfolia*), which belongs to the same family as the walnut and the American hickory and carries unusual, long-hanging chains of broad-winged nuts. Next is the phamaceutical bed of traditional herbalism plants, used when health was believed to be a balance of the four humours: blood, phlegm, and yellow and black biles. Black bile was said to cause melancholy and could be counteracted with an infusion of lemon balm, for example. Among the wild plants here is *Atrope Belladonne*, better known as deadly nightshade, a poisonous alkaloid which can speed up an abnormally low heart rate and so may be used in treating heart attacks.

Mediterranean Curiosities and Aromatic Plants

Follow the path past the dye plants again and you see a Mediterranean cork oak (*Quercus suber*) to the right, hung with a necklace of corks. For commercial use, the bark of these trees is stripped every seven years or so and bottle corks are punched out of it. The undamaged dusky red underbark then grows another layer of cork bark. Past the cork oak is the cistus bed with crinkled white or pink flowers in spring. Cistus shrubs also feature strongly in many Mediterranean landscapes. Some have highly scented leaves, and it was the smell of the cistus in the Corsican maquis which lingered in Napoleon's memory.

Alongside the propagating greenhouse is a bed of plants that are used for perfumes and aromatherapy. Plant scents, which usually come from oils in the plant, normally attract insects for pollination, but the scents of the cistus and some other plants are in the leaves, making them distasteful to browsing animals. Note the *Rosa Gallica*, opposite the greenhouse. This is the Apothecaries' Rose which was used as medicine and to scent food. Rosary beads were scented to evoke purity.

Rainforest plants and poisons

Turn right at the end of the path and go through the door of the glasshouse to the left. Pass through it to the Tropical Corridor at the back which is of pre-Victorian date and was restored in 1980. As you walk through the glasshouse you become aware of the variety of climates maintained within, from warm temperate to what seems like a rainforest steaminess in the narrow corridor at the back.

Even today, little of the vast variety of rainforest plant life has been screened for medicinal use. Yams grow here, for example; they yielded the first chemical contraceptive agents, which could never have been discovered by chance in a laboratory, and are now chemically synthesized. Another example is the poison bush from southern and western Africa, yielding an arrow poison, but also used by the Zulu as a remedy for gut worms and an antidote for snake bite. Where the air is cooler, cinchona, the plant origin of anti-malarial quinine, grows, along with the coffee bush.

Leave the the smaller glasshouse, turn right and pass the shop. There is a spiny-leaved evergreen kermes oak (*Quercus coccifera*) from the Mediterranean to the left and, as you

CHELSEA PHYSIC GARDEN

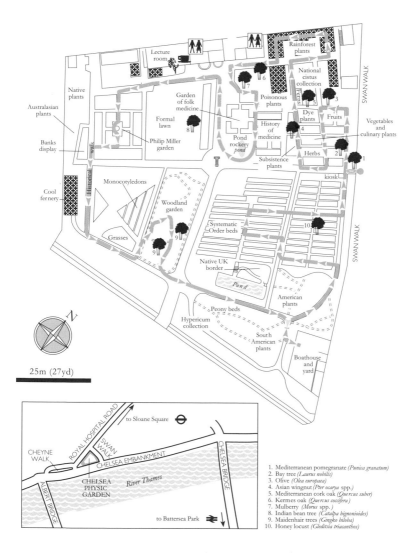

1. Mediterranean pomegranate *(Punica granatum)*
2. Bay tree *(Laurus nobilis)*
3. Olive *(Olea europaea)*
4. Asian wingnut *(Pter ocarya* spp.*)*
5. Mediterranean cork oak *(Quercus suber)*
6. Kermes oak *(Quercus coccifera)*
7. Mulberry *(Morus* spp.*)*
8. Indian bean tree *(Catalpa bignonioides)*
9. Maidenhair trees *(Gingko biloba)*
10. Honey locust *(Gleditsia triacanthos)*

turn left down the path beyond it, you see a black mulberry tree (*Morus nigra*) with sweet-and-sour dark red, raspberry-like fruit. Also spot the Judas tree (*Cercis siliquastrum*), originally from North America, southern Europe and China. In spring it can bear bunches of pink flowers that look like gouts of blood, growing directly on its trunk and branches and on the flowering twigs – an example of what is called cauliflory.

Follow the path left through the garden beds and to your left is a bed of poisonous plants, of the kind that apprentice apothecaries had to learn to recognize. Lily of the Valley is familiar; henbane less so. 'Poisonous in all parts, used in witchcraft' reads its label; the British doctor, Hawley Harvey Crippen, who was hanged in 1910, used it to murder his wife. Some poisonous plants are extremely difficult to distinguish from their harmless relatives – those belonging to the cow parsley (carrot) family are a good example.

The History of Medicine

Further along the path on the left (east) side are the History of Medicine beds, containing plants that first yielded some now familiar manufactured drugs: meadowsweet, for example, which in the 19th century provided the base for aspirin; the autumn-flowering meadow saffron, which has been used in cancer research; and the lilac opium poppy, from whose seed capsules painkilling morphine is extracted. At one time, fields of this poppy were grown in Britain for its seeds, which were added to a tot of gin to create a medicinal tincture known as laudanum.

Research continues into the remedial use of plants, including the use of feverfew for treating migraine, for example. Living plants or dried leaves and stems are scanned by pharmaceutical companies for active chemicals which otherwise could only be fabricated by luck and at enormous expense – the chemical equivalent of finding a needle in a haystack. The Physic Garden is a kind of library of plant chemistry and exchanges plants with organizations all over the world.

Crucial for this exchange in Victorian times (and for the introduction of exotic plants in general) was the discovery made by a Dr. Nathaniel Ward around 1829. He found that plants could survive healthily in a closed glass container (they became known as 'wardian cases'). Exotic plants could be kept safely, almost in suspended animation, in this miniature greenhouse during long sea journeys. Before this, bringing back exotics was a very frustrating business, since most were sure to die on the voyage. Nowadays, with air travel, there is little problem. Wardian cases made it possible for Curator Robert Fortune to introduce thousands of tea plants from China to India, banana plants to Fiji, and Brazilian rubber plants to Malaya in 1876.

The bed with the white weather-record box at its west end is great fun. For many centuries it was believed that God created everything for a purpose and that plants had God-given signs or marks (signatures) which indicated what they would cure. For example, the scarlet pimpernel was used to cure blood disorders, while yellow marigolds were used to treat jaundice, an ailment whose main symptom is yellow skin. Perforate St. John's wort, which is grown in this bed, has perforated leaves, obviously seen as a cure for dagger wounds. Mandrake is also grown in one corner. This Mediterranean plant was held to shriek like a woman giving birth when its forked leg-like roots were pulled up, a sound which would kill anyone who heard it. It was used in love potions, but also as a painkiller in primitive surgery, and the story was probably put about by those who made a living out of collecting it. The garden of folk or world medicine, opposite, grows medicinal plants from around the globe with similar stories.

The Rockery

Follow the path onto the main avenue, then walk round to the right, toward the statue of Sir Hans Sloane in wig and gown. It is a copy of the original by the Dutch-born sculptor Michael Rysbrack (1694–1770), which was in place here in 1748 but is now in the British Museum for safety. Sloane's collection of curiosities founded the British Museum in 1753. Just before the statue to the right is the Pond Rockery, a rockery garden built in 1772 from lava brought from Iceland by the British botanist, Sir Joseph Banks (1743–1820). It was an early attempt at a habitat garden, with plants growing in an environment that imitates their surroundings in the wild, and is now a listed (meaning legally protected) structure.

Now walk back toward the buildings, passing to the left a fine Indian bean tree which carries masses of white flowers in early summer. Turn left and walk past the lecture room. On its south-facing walls there are two plants to highlight because they are linked with Sir Joseph Banks: a lutea, a yellow variety of the Chinese Banksian rose, which flowers in spring; and the glorious ferny-leaved kowhai, New Zealand's national flower, which blooms in April. This is probably a grandchild of the original plant or seeds that Banks brought back from his voyage with Captain Cook in the *Endeavour*.

The Commemorative Beds

Follow the path to the end. Facing you are beds of native British plants, and to the left are the commemorative displays. Turn left into the largest of these, dedicated to Philip Miller (1691–1777), and justly so. As Curator from 1722 he was in charge for nearly half the 18th century, and made this the finest botanic garden in the world at that time, overtaken by Kew only after his retirement in 1770. He wrote the prestigious *Gardener's Dictionary*, published in 1731, and his knowledge of plants was encyclopedic; as well as being versed in medicinal plants he was forever raising unusual plants from seed, or crossing them. His approach was down to earth – he kept melon seeds in his breeches pocket to help them germinate. He propagated the new seed which was sent to the cotton plantations of Georgia in the U.S.A., and he was the first European to grow the Chinese Tree of Heaven (*Ailanthus altissima*).

Stroll through the Philip Miller garden and turn right at the bottom onto the main path through the commemorative beds, called the Historical Walk. Facing you is a smaller garden commemorating Sir Joseph Banks. His name is linked with Australia and the Australasian plants here include the bottlebrushes, whose flowers live up to the name. Banks gave his name to the Banksia genus of plants, with their unusual 'cones'.

Grasses and woodland

So far, the plants on display have been dicotyledons (having two seed leaves). The other great class of plants is the monocotyledons (having one seed leaf), including grasses, irises, lilies and others. Following the path down to the road and round to the left, you can see them growing on the left. In front are grasses with feathery bamboos; there is also a windmill palm, with leaves that look frayed. Beyond them are ranked beds of irises and other monocotyledons.

The Woodland Garden to the right is best explored by taking detours along the narrow, winding paths that cross it. There are snowdrops and hellebores to see in season. On the main path up from the gate that faces the river are two pairs of maidenhair trees, the older pair up the path toward the statue. They have unusual fan-shaped leaves and were common in the time of the dinosaurs. Botanists thought them extinct until, in the 18th century, they were found growing in the gardens of Chinese temples.

The Pond

Turn right out of the Woodland Garden and walk southeast toward the pond. To the right, wild peonies are glorious from April to June, including the rare *Paeonia cambessedesii* from the Mediterranean Balearic Islands, and behind them are specialist collections of hypericums. Among the waterside plants around the pool to the left grows the lovely native flowering rush, with clusters of magnificent dark-veined pink flowers in July and August. It is one of Britain's loveliest wild flowers. There are colonies of great crested and smooth newts, and toads are everywhere here on warm spring evenings, emerging only after the visitors have gone.

Continue along the path to see the Boathouse Yard ahead to the right. This a relic of the days before the Victorians constructed the Embankment (*see* page 80), when the usual way to reach Chelsea from London was by boat rowed by watermen.

The Systematic Order Beds

Return to the pond and turn right. This area of the garden is dedicated to plants from the Americas: South American plants nearest the Boathouse Yard and North American plants beyond them. Behind the pond is a border of plants native to the U.K. Follow the path up into the regular ranks of Systematic Order beds. These follow the geometric layout of the original garden and the many fragrant plants in these beds make pottering a delight. The plants are laid out in family groupings. One idea is to find a plant that you recognize and discover what its (sometimes surprising) relations are. For example, the *Ranunculaceae* (buttercups and their kin) include anemones, hellebores, larkspur and love-in-a-mist. There is a tree of note here in the nearest set of beds: a weeping white mulberry (*Mons alba pendula*).

Following the paths leading north through the beds and then a right turn will bring you back to the Students' Gate, where the walk ends.

RICHMOND PARK

LOCATION	About 7½ miles (12 kilometres) southwest of Charing Cross.
TRANSPORT	Richmond Station (underground trains on the District Line; overground trains from Waterloo). Buses passing Richmond Gate: 371; Petersham Gate: 65, 415, 371; Kingston Gate: 371; Robin Hood Gate: 265; Roehampton Gate: 72, 265, R61; East Sheen Gate 33, 337. There are free car parks.
ADMISSION	Open 07:00–dusk in summer; 07:30–dusk in winter. Admission is free.
SEASONAL FEATURES	Isabella Plantation: camellias and azaleas in spring; heather garden in winter. Pembroke Lodge rose garden in summer; autumn tree colour in the plantations. Beware of deer in spring and early summer (with young) and autumn (the rut).
EVENTS	Children's shows on weekdays; country days in summer; lunchtime light musical recitals at Pembroke Lodge.
REFRESHMENTS	Pembroke Lodge Cafeteria open daily 10:00–17.30 hours (to dusk in winter); Roehampton Café 09:00–17:00 hours.

In 1625 Charles I moved to Richmond Palace, of which traces remain near Twickenham Bridge, to escape a plague gripping London. To satisfy his love of hunting, he purloined nearby land and eventually, in 1637, built a brick wall round it. As a concession to local opposition he kept the tracks and footpaths open, installing gates or ladders where they cut through the wall. This public access was challenged by a daughter of George II, but the threat was defeated when a local brewer won a test case. This right of public access ended the chase, but the park continued as a commercial source of venison and as a preserve for the shooting of hare and pheasant.

It was for the shooting as much as for the timber that plantations were laid; between 1819 and 1824 Sidmouth Wood and Spanker's Hill were among the areas planted with native trees, while in the 1830s, Isabella Plantation was enclosed and planted with oak, beech and sweet chestnut. The shooting ended around 1904, when many of the plantations were opened to the public. During the world wars army camps were set up in the park; much land was ploughed during World War I, but recreational facilities for the public were restored afterwards.

The park today is a wonderfully open place, with sweeps of grass and bracken scattered with often ancient oak trees. It spreads along a terrace of the River Thames, the ground falling away abruptly along most of the park's western edge. There are ponds and lakes in the park, and 15 or so plantations, or planted enclosures, some dating back a century and a half. One of these, Isabella Plantation, is a well-known area of gardened woodland. Tarmac roads cross the park and skirt it inside the perimeter wall, and a fair number of drivers use it as a through route, but there are many footpaths leading away from the roads, past herds of deer. Except for the plantations and the grounds of a private residence or two, most of the park is freely accessible.

Deer are as much a feature of Richmond Park today as when they were introduced around 350 years ago, and they can often be seen grouped in sizeable herds. There are usually about 400 fallow deer and 250 red deer, the latter being the largest wild animal native to Britain, measuring up to about 4 feet (1.2 metres) at the shoulder. The males (stags) have branching antlers which they shed in spring, growing a new, more elaborate set each year. The antlers are not a defence against predators, but, along with bellowing and other activities, they are part of the mating display. Stags can often be seen locked in (rarely damaging) wrestling combat during the autumn rut, when the boss stags seek to claim and keep a harem. The animals become edgy and may attack dogs or people. The females (hinds) are smaller and lack antlers. Calves are born singly in May or June, when the mothers may be aggressive if approached.

Fallow deer were brought to Britain by the Romans for the hunt. A male is a buck, a female is a doe and the young are fawns. Smaller than red deer, they usually have a dappled brown coat with white spots, although this can vary. Fallow does with young can also be aggressive. The number of deer in the park stays fairly constant, the year's births matching deaths from disease and those caused by vehicles and culling. By royal warrant, culling supplies venison not only to the royal household but also to the prime minister, the lord chief justice and other prominent figures.

To some extent, the deer have helped create the Richmond parkland. They graze mainly, but not exclusively, on grass. Grasses survive grazing because the fronds grow from the bottom, whereas a young sapling grows from the tips of the shoots and so is damaged by grazing. When deer are kept in large numbers, no saplings survive, the trees that die and fall are not replaced, and open parkland is the result. Young planted trees must be protected with others in a fenced plantation or with their own guard railings.

Most of the trees in Richmond Park are oaks. Growing in open surroundings they can have a broad shape, the branches spreading low, but many of Richmond's trees are trimmed up to a browse line by deer reaching up for the leaves. It used to be common practice in deer parks to farm unprotected trees (those outside the fenced plantations) by pollarding: the branches at the top of the trunk are cut off and the trunk then puts out a head of new branches, out of reach of the deer. As these thickened they were cut to provide smallwood, which was harvested for fencing poles, charcoal and other uses.

Most pollarding of park trees ended before the beginning the 20th century, so that the branches at the top subsequently thickened. With their head of heavy branches bunched at the top of the trunk, Richmond's pollarded trees are easy to recognize. As pollarded trees were no use for timber they were not usually felled. Some of these old pollarded oaks are, therefore, among the oldest trees to be seen in Richmond Park. Trees with dead, antler-like branches sticking up from a crown of foliage are also common in Richmond Park. Their staghead

St. James's Park: *The famous view across the lake to Duck Island, the rooftops of Whitehall and, beyond, the London Eye*

Battersea Park: *A lush view in this peaceful park*

Chelsea Physic Garden: *A woodland corner of the garden which, although small, contains a number of mini-gardens within its boundary*

Richmond Park: *It's not just picnickers who enjoy resting under the trees in Richmond Park*

The Royal Botanic Gardens, Kew: *The famous Pagoda was completed in 1762 and is 163ft high (nearly 50m)*

Ham House Gardens: *A classical touch in the elegant Knot Garden, with its neat, hypnotic rows of carefully manicured box hedges*

shape occurs when branches are killed by insect attack, fungal disease or drought, and the tree subsequently puts out fresh healthy growth below them.

At 2,470 acres (1,000 hectares) Richmond Park is the largest park in London, and many different walks could be devised. This walk takes in two key features – the most interesting in the park – with a marvellous expedition across the open parkland between them.

THE RICHMOND PARK WALK

Start and finish Richmond Gate. **Time** Allow 3 hours.

Enter the park through Richmond Gate, the stateliest of the park's dozen gates. Inside, turn right and take the path by the railings, parallel to the road. Walk past the gates to Pembroke Lodge Gardens. Very soon you pass – to the left across the road – some old pollard oaks and the edge of Sidmouth Wood plantation, before reaching the stone gate of Pembroke Lodge and its pretty, thatched gatehouse. There is a deer grid across the gateway, so use the foot gate to the left and walk down the drive with bushes on each side until you reach the lawns. At this point you can see Pembroke Lodge in front of you, but for the moment turn sharp right.

King Henry VIII Mound

The right turn takes you into a pretty rose garden; take another right turn to walk around it. The fall of the ground is now on your left, and straight ahead, past the end of the rose garden, is the first of this walk's key features: King Henry VIII's mound. Take the righthand path to reach it. This is a prehistoric burial mound, probably from the Bronze Age. Perched on the brow of the hill, it has magnificent views west, down the curve of the Thames and beyond to Marble Hill House (*see* page 141) and Windsor Castle, some 13 miles (21 kilometres) away. There is more green in this view than houses.

Take the path to the top of the mound. A broken ring of holly bushes encircles it, open to the west for the view. A keyhole shape cut out of the holly gives a view to the east, past Sidmouth Wood to the distant British Telecom Tower and (on a fine day) St. Paul's Cathedral. At the top of the mound is a stone roundel set into the ground, engraved with lines from a poem written in 1744 by James Thomson in which he describes this view.

Pembroke Lodge

Take time to enjoy the view then retrace your steps, passing the rose garden again and keeping to the edge of the fall of ground. You pass some fine oak trees to arrive at the lodge. This is a rather charming 18th-century building, white-painted and with wisteria around the entrance porch. In 1847 Queen Victoria gave it to Lord John Russell, then Prime Minister, as a grace-and-favour home. His grandson, the philosopher Bertrand Russell (1872–1970) lived at Pembroke Lodge between 1876 and 1890. Although it is now a café, the downstairs rooms are little changed, and there is an Adam fireplace in the dining room.

Cross the lodge terraces with their superb view over the River Thames to reach the lawns on the other side, where there are some magnificent, primeval-looking oak trees,

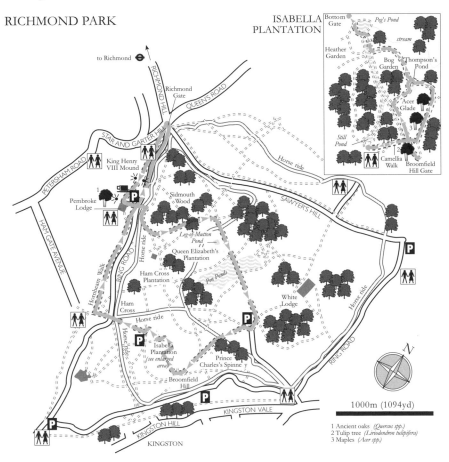

RICHMOND PARK

ISABELLA PLANTATION

1 Ancient oaks *(Quercus spp.)*
2 Tulip tree *(Liriodendron tulipifera)*
3 Maples *(Acer spp.)*

1000m (1094yd)

maybe 300 to 400 years old, botanical dinosaurs with twisted, contorted trunks. There is also a small grave stone of 1907, dedicated to Boy, a pet dog. There are jackdaws in these grounds, and parakeets that have escaped from captivity. More than 100 different bird species have been seen in Richmond Park. Circle the lawns and leave the lodge grounds by the gateway opposite the entrance, which leads to a car park.

The Pen Ponds

Cross the road at the right-hand end of the car park, head toward wooden rails and take the path skirting Sidmouth Wood to the left. Part of the plantation is a bird sanctuary. The rhododendrons that occupy much of the space beneath the trees were originally planted as pheasant cover. They give a showy display in May. Keep hugging the fence to your left. A great silent wood, which hides Queen Elizabeth's Plantation, comes up on the right and at the edge of Sidmouth Wood, by a gnarled oak that could have come straight out of *Lord of the Rings*, there are four paths. Take the third from the left and pass the small Leg of Mutton pond, a watering hole for deer. Steer toward the Pen Ponds at the bottom of the dip, probably named from deer pens. They were dug out in 1746 and are notable for their wildfowl, among them swans, grebe and gadwalls, and also for their fish, which include pike. Fishing permits can be obtained.

Cross the raised causeway between the two Pen Ponds and continue on the path straight ahead for about 500 yards (450 metres) until you reach a car park. On the way, on the skyline to the left, you may catch a glimpse of White Lodge through its surrounding trees. Originally an elegant, stone-clad Palladian building, it now has brick wings and other additions. It was built in 1727, the year of accession of George II, who used it as a hunting lodge, and it later became a self-contained country house for the park's ranger and occasional royals. Since 1955 it has been the home of the Royal Ballet School.

A narrow tarmac road at the top end of the car park is signposted 'Isabella Plantation'. A little way up from the sign take the wide track to the left, cross a horse ride and then walk to the Isabella Plantation, which fills much of the horizon ahead. Take the middle path over the brow of the hill. Follow the plantation's perimeter fence on your right to arrive at the Broomfield Hill Gate.

The Isabella Plantation

Enter the plantation – the second key feature on this walk – through this gate, erected in 1993 and adorned with a handsome nameplate in art-deco style. Most of the tall-trunked oaks, beech and sweet chestnut date from when the plantation was enclosed in 1831. Some of the common, reddish-flowered *Rhododendron ponticum* would have been planted or have seeded itself when a good bottom (thick, low cover) was encouraged for the pheasants. A second wave of planting and shaping began in the 1950s to make the plantation more of a garden, with clearings, ponds and streams (fed by pumps from Pen Ponds). Many different rhododendrons and azaleas were planted, along with exotic trees. For example, on the spur in front of the stream just to the left of Broomfield Hill Gate is a young tulip tree (*Liriodendron tulipifera*).

Just inside the gate to the right is a notice board giving news of things of topical and seasonal interest. In spring there are camellias and magnolias with drifts of daffodils, to be followed by bluebells. By late April and May the azaleas and rhododendrons are in flower, underpinning the fresh young tree foliage. Spindle (*Euonymus*), fothergillas, some deciduous azaleas, guelder roses and rowans with their bright red berries add to the autumn display of the trees in this plantation. In winter there are mahonias, early camellias and rhododendrons, and the bark of trees such as the snake-bark maple (*Acer rufinerve*) to admire, and winter-flowering heathers in the Heather Garden near Peg's Pond.

An attractive stream runs straight ahead (northwest) from the Broomfield Gate, with paths on either side, linked by frequent timber bridges, and banks of azaleas and other flowering shrubs. In summer there is a strong show of Japanese irises, day lilies, tall *Primula floridae* and other flowers along the banks. Some of the azaleas on the right of the central stream are among what are known as the 'Wilson 50' – kurume azaleas which form the core of the National Collection. They were first collected by E. H. Wilson, a plant hunter from Kew Gardens. In his time he discovered 1,000 new ornamental plants, of which 600 species and varieties are still being grown, including 65 rhododendrons.

In early spring glimpses of colour off to the left will make you want to divert along Camellia Walk. It is found by walking down the stream's right-hand side and crossing between two hedges. This leads to Still Pond, hidden on the right, which is shaded by shrubs and trees and rather gloomy. In autumn, a diversion to Acer Glade is a must. It is found by turning right at the entrance. The *Acer* species are the maple family of trees, renowned for their glorious autumn colours. The path from the main stream through Acer Glade leads to Thompson's Pond, set in a wide green lawn fringed by rhododendrons and other flowering shrubs. There are also resident mallards and you may see mandarin duck and the odd heron.

Various emergent aquatics grow along the pond's banks and in its shallows, including some native yellow flags and a handsome stand of greater reedmace (*Typha latifolia*). These are commonly called bulrushes because the Victorian artist, Laurence Alma-Tadema (1836–1912) pictured them in his famous biblical painting of the infant Moses found among the bulrushes. Such is botany.

Thompson's Pond runs off as a stream, crossed by stepping logs, heading in the direction of Peg's Pond. Take the path alongside (this stream is also banked with shrubs) until it swings around the Bog Garden, marked by stepping logs and a stand of gunnera. Keep to the right here. Soon the wood opens out and a marvellous heather garden appears, still vivid in autumn and winter. A short distance further along is Peg's Pond, where you may see black swans. When you have reached the stream, however, you may want to spend some time wandering around this lovely plantation, or just sitting on one of the lengths of cut trunk handily positioned as seating at the foot of the trees.

When you are ready, make your way to Bottom Gate on the western side of Peg's Pond, and follow the path left to the car park for disabled drivers. From there, look for the white sign of Ham Cross in the distance. Make your way across, cross the road and take the path to the right which leads into Hornbeam Walk and back to Pembroke Lodge. The trees along this path have beech-like leaves, but fluted bark. From there follow the path, back to Richmond Gate, where the walk ends.

THE ROYAL BOTANIC GARDENS, KEW

LOCATION	About 7½ miles (12 kilometres) southwest of Charing Cross.
TRANSPORT	Kew Gardens Station (underground District Line; overground North London Line trains). Kew Bridge Station (overground trains from Waterloo) is five minutes' walk via Kew Bridge. Kew Gardens Pier (boats from Westminster Pier) is five minutes' walk. Buses 65, 391.
ADMISSION	Open daily 09:30–18:00 hours in winter, later in summer. Admission £13 adult, £11 concession, child under 17 free.
SEASONAL FEATURES	Camellias and heathers in Jan; Crocus lawn and Rock Garden in Feb; cherry blossom and daffodils in March; Magnolias and spring bedding in April; bluebells and azaleas in May; Rhododendron Dell and Grass Garden in June; the giant waterlily, the Queen's Garden, and summer bedding in July; autumn colour Sep–Nov.
EVENTS	Annual Orchid Festival in the Princess of Wales Conservatory in March.
REFRESHMENTS	The Orangery, Victoria Terrace Café and White Peaks open daily 10:00 hours until 1 hour before the gardens close.

In the 18th century, Kew had become a popular place for aristocratic people to live, away from the smells and diseases of London. In 1728 Queen Caroline, wife of George II, rented Kew Palace and later the Prince of Wales and his wife Augusta lived there. It was Princess Augusta who, in 1759, sowed the seeds of today's botanic gardens by laying out a 9-acre (3.6-hectare) 'exotick' garden, appointing William Aiton as head gardener, and planting an arboretum on the site. In 1767 this was named the Royal Botanic Garden. Meanwhile, Sir William Chambers (1723–96), official architect to Princess Augusta, landscaped the surrounding grounds, dotting them with temples and other follies, including, in 1761, the now-famous Pagoda. At this time, the landscape designer 'Capability' Brown (*see* page 10), was working in the grounds of the adjacent royal residence, Richmond Lodge. His plans of 1764 included the digging out of what is now the Rhododendron Dell.

When Princess Augusta died in 1771, George III merged the two estates. Their botanic importance was underlined when the botanist Sir Joseph Banks (1743–1820) became their unofficial director, beginning a collaboration with William Aiton which lasted for 40 years. The pair sent collectors around the world in search of unusual and useful plants. Kew's bird of paradise flowers may be direct descendants of those first grown in the gardens in 1773. At about this time the flowers commonly called geraniums – which were, in fact, pelargoniums from Africa – were becoming popular.

Kew Gardens declined after Banks died, but in 1840 they were handed over to the government, who appointed another eminent botanist, William Hooker, as director (he was eventually succeeded by his son, Joseph Hooker). This move was largely prompted by the desire to exploit to the full the new crops and medicinal plants to be found in the vast British Empire. Kew was to become a research centre and library for this natural wealth. Just two examples underline its importance. In 1860 the seeds of a plant known as Jesuits' Bark (*Chinchona* spp.) were collected from the slopes of the Andes Mountains in South America, and within five years 1 million trees had been distributed from special greenhouses at Kew, providing quinine to fight malaria. In the 1870s, South American rubber plants (*Ficus* spp.) that had been grown in Kew were sent to the Far East to start the rubber industry. From 1855, Kew also supplied London's parks with new trees from its tree nursery. The last royal touch was when, in 1897, Queen Victoria donated Queen Charlotte's Cottage grounds to be added to the gardens, stipulating that the surrounding land should be kept as a separate arboretum of native British trees, underplanted with bluebells.

Today the Royal Botanic Gardens, Kew – a charity, surviving on a basis of 70 per cent income from government grants and the remainder from admission and other charges – occupy 300 acres (121.5 hectares) planted with 30,000 different species and varieties of plants, growing alongside a host of interesting buildings reflecting their history.

This is a long walk with so much to see that it could well be divided into two or three areas, each to be explored on a different day. The map on page 128 outlines the route of this walk, which takes you to features of special interest, but there is much more to see. Everything is well signposted throughout the gardens, and there are maps on boards at intervals along all the paths. Exploring Kew Gardens could become a regular pleasure.

THE KEW GARDENS WALK

Start and finish The main gate. **Time** Allow 3–4 hours

Enter the gardens through the main gate, but before heading to the left to buy tickets, turn to look at the handsome gateway. It was designed by the architect Decimus Burton (1800–81), and erected in 1848 after the state takeover of the gardens. The double gate is for carriages, with pedestrian entrances on either side, and its polished wrought iron is in Jacobean style, with gilded highlights. The gates were once surmounted by the lion and unicorn that now reside above the Lion and Unicorn gateways in Kew Road.

From this gate stretches the Broad Walk, edged by formal beds with seasonal plantings. You will see that the trees have name tags. Some to the left and right of this walk may be relics of Princess Augusta's arboretum. The glasshouse to the right is by John Nash. It was originally built as part of his improved scheme for Buckingham Palace, but was moved to Kew in 1836. The cylindrical pillars at each end were an addition brought from old Carlton House, which stood at the site of Duke of York's column overlooking The Mall leading to Buckingham Palace. This glasshouse is the oldest at Kew and, compared with the marvels of the Palm House and the Temperate House, it is simple, with a roof of glass tiles. It houses the story of Kew's millennium Seed Bank.

Turn left immediately after the ticket office into the start of Magnolia Walk. Note on your left one of the U.K.'s Heritage Trees, a magnificent Corsican pine (*Pinus nigra*), planted in 1814 and believed to be the oldest in the country. It has been struck by lightning on several occasions and was even hit by a small light aircraft in the early 1900s. Turn right to reach the Orangery of 1761, a beautiful, neoclassical design by Sir William Chambers, with marvellous tree-clad vistas over to the southwest. It is now occupied by a shop and a tearoom, which share the interior with 18th-century French statues of Eros and other classical figures. The terrace edge has a delicate carved timeline introduced in 2009 to celebrate the 250th anniversary of the gardens.

Kew Palace and The Queen's Garden

At the end of the Orangery cross the southward wing of the Broad Walk and bear right across the grass, beyond a splendid Oriental plane (*Platanns orientalis*) which dates from at least 1762, toward a Tompion sundial which marks the location of the White House, a former royal residence that was demolished in 1802. Tompion was a watchmaker, and the sundial has quaint instructions detailing how to set your watch by it. From the sundial bear northward, toward Kew Palace, the red-brick house you can see ahead.

Kew Palace is not so much a palace as an elegant merchant's house, built in attractive Dutch style by one Sam Fortrey in 1631; it was, in fact, once known as the Dutch House. In 1728 the palace was leased by Queen Caroline, wife of George II, for the sum of £100 and a fat deer. It was later used by Caroline's daughter-in-law, Princess Augusta, who laid out her botanic garden nearby, forming the kernel of today's Kew Gardens. The rooms of the palace are furnished much as they were 200 years ago.

The Queen's Garden to the west and north of the house is in 17th-century style. On the western side is a sunken nosegay garden with brick paths, a pleached laburnum walk and a fine well head from Bulstrode Park in Buckinghamshire. By late summer this garden is picturesquely tangled with medicinal and sweetly scented strewing plants (pot pourri is a continuation of this tradition). Delve into the beds to read labels that are enlivened with quotations from old herbals. Caraway, for example, was 'muche put among baked fruit' to help 'digest wind in them, subject thereunto'; while sunflower, its buds 'before they be flowered, boiled and eaten with butter, vinegar and pepper' are 'exceedingly pleasant meate, surpassing the Artichoke in procuring bodily lust ...'.

Walk round to the north side, facing the river, to a replica of a 17th-century geometrical parterre, which was laid out in 1975 and extends all the way from the house to the riverbank wall. There are termini around this garden – pillars topped by sculptured heads – a Roman garden idea that was popularized in the 18th century. By the riverbank wall there is a mount; climb the spiral path to the metal-framed gazebo on the summit, giving pleasant views of the River Thames beyond. The mount is another copy of a popular 17th-century garden feature.

Continue the walk on the path that leads from the mount into the Bee Garden, which lies just beyond the eastern edge of the Queen's Garden. It is to your right as you face the river in the gazebo.

THE BOTANICAL GARDENS, KEW

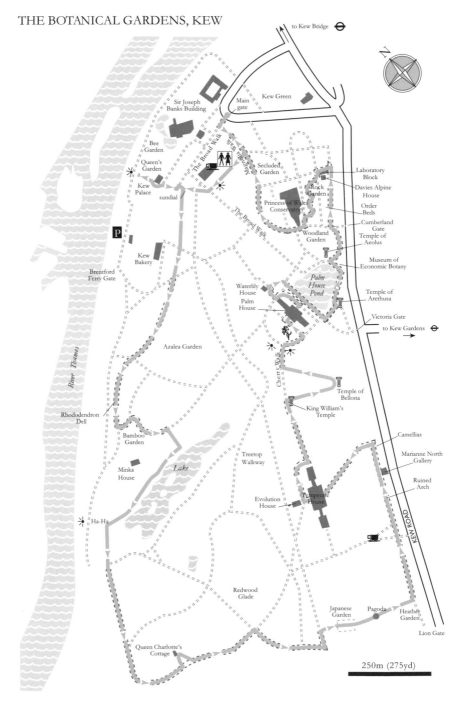

to Kew Bridge

Sir Joseph Banks Building

Main gate

Kew Green

Bee Garden

Queen's Garden

Secluded Garden

Kew Palace

sundial

Rock Garden

Laboratory Block

Davies Alpine House

Princess of Wales Conservatory

Order Beds

Cumberland Gate

Woodland Garden

Temple of Aeolus

Museum of Economic Botany

Kew Bakery

Brentford Ferry Gate

Waterlily House

Palm House

Palm House Pond

Temple of Arethusa

Victoria Gate

to Kew Gardens

Azalea Garden

Cherry Walk

Temple of Bellona

King William's Temple

Rhododendron Dell

Camellias

Bamboo Garden

Marianne North Gallery

Treetop Walkway

Ruined Arch

Minka House

Lake

Evolution House

Temperate House

River Thames

Ha-Ha

KEW ROAD

Redwood Glade

Japanese Garden

Pagoda

Heather Garden

Lion Gate

Queen Charlotte's Cottage

250m (275yd)

The Broad Walk

Museum No. 1

128

The Banks Building

Take the steps to the right of the Bee Garden, which lead down to a fine lawn. To your right is an armillary sundial, with metal hoops representing the equator and the paths of the zodiac. To the left there are waterside gardens and the partly covered Sir Joseph Banks Building. This contains a botanical collection of useful plants from around the globe and an exhibition hall. Banks did much to fire enthusiasm for the exotic. He sailed with Captain James Cook (1728–79) on voyages to the Pacific – a family of Australian plants bears his name – and made several other voyages. In his time, in 1787, *The Bounty*, under Captain William Bligh, set sail to collect breadfruit in the Pacific to plant in the young West Indies colonies. Walk past the armillary sundial and follow the path up and then right.

The Rhododendron Dell and the Bamboo Garden

Cross the Broad Walk, now ahead of you, then cross the grass, veering to the right of the Tompion sundial and rounding a shrubbery. Beyond it you pass the White Café and Shop to the right, and take the path ahead of you. At the first crossroads note the Lilac Garden to your left. It includes the familiar white flowering *Syringa vulgaris*, or common lilac (as the Latin name rather suggests). It is nicknamed 'Edith Cavell', perhaps because it was introduced to the U.K. in 1916 by the French flower breeder Emile Lemoine (1862–1942), who wished to honour her name. Cavell was a British nurse who helped 200 Allied soldiers escape from German-occupied Belgium during World War I. She was executed by the Germans in 1915. Turn right and right again at the next crossroads to head for the Rhododendron Dell.

The Dell, dug out in 1773, appears on 'Capability' Brown's map as a carriageway, and the rhododendrons came later. They were a Victorian craze and the then director, Sir Joseph Hooker, was instrumental in popularizing them; he collected 43 new species of great beauty from Nepal in the years 1847–50. The first blooming starts in the Dell in January, and the rhododendrons are followed by other spectacular flowerings: a carmine magnolia in spring; and from May to late June lilacs, azaleas, late rhododendrons and other magnolias.

Take a left turn into the Dell itself and then right, which eventually brings you to the sign-posted Bamboo Garden path. This garden, with its unusual Minka House, is tucked away in a quieter part of Kew Gardens and it is possible to have it all to yourself. It has a peaceful Eastern atmosphere. Follow the path clockwise past the gently swaying bamboos and through the house. 'Minka' means 'house of the people' and such dwellings used to be common in Japan. Built of wood, with thatched roofs and mud-plastered walls, they were better able to withstand earthquakes than concrete houses. Kew's Minka House was built around 1900 and donated to Kew in 2001 by the Japan Minka Reuse and Recycle Association as part of that year's Japan Festival. Rejoin the original path and turn left, leaving it shortly to walk across the grass to the lake; it is just out of sight on the other side of a rise, but its position is marked by the backs of a line of lakeside benches.

The Lake

Turn right along the lakeside. Although a natural-looking lake was part of many of 'Capability' Brown's landscaping schemes, this one is not his work. It was created about a century later, in 1856–61. It has always been inhabited by unusual birds – pelicans were brought here in 1890; penguins in 1899. You may see black swans, gaudy, purple-chested mandarin duck, orange-headed pochard, and there will certainly be semi-tame black-necked Canada geese. Follow the lakeside path toward the River Thames. The trees on the northwest (right) side of the lake are native to the old world; and those on the southeast side are native to the new world – including monkey puzzle trees (*Araucaria araucana*) from Chile. These were first grown in Britain in the 1790s. A botanist from Kew was served some unfamiliar fruits at dinner while in Chile; he germinated the seeds on the ship home and planted them at Kew. Near the Thames there is a view across to Syon House, and, by the river's edge, a ha-ha dug in 1767.

Pass the top of the lake and at a group of incense cedars (*Calocedrus decurrens*), turn right and climb the grassy bank through the pines to the path where you turn right and then left for Queen Charlotte's Cottage. The path leads deep into the woodland of the Queen's Cottage Grounds and circles Queen Charlotte's Cottage, a thatched picnic lodge built in 1772 and restored in 1996. It stands in a glade, reached by a small side path, and is surrounded by a sea of scented bluebells in late spring. The 37 acres (15 hectares) of land around it were given by Queen Victoria, and much of the area is managed as a nature reserve. Unlike other parts of Kew Gardens, this is an area to explore for yourself, or, perhaps, even to get lost in (an unusual experience so close to the centre of London). Much of it has a parkland feel, perhaps the deliberate result of 'Capability' Brown's natural landscaping.

Return to the main path and follow it through an area planted with conifers from around the world. Detour left at the next junction of paths, and to your right is a glade planted with giant redwoods (*Sequoia* spp).

The Japanese Gateway

Retrace your steps back up to the main path then head straight on for the Pagoda. Follow the shady path, turning left at the Chokushi-Mon Japanese Landscape sign. Keep to this path to find the entrance to the Japanese Garden on your right. The imposing gateway on the mound is a legacy of the Japanese Exhibition of 1910. It is made of Japanese cedar, but for protection a traditional copper roof was substituted for the cedar bark roof. The gateway is decorated with carvings of stylized, polished animals and flowers. Follow the path into the garden which was completed in 1996 and is reminiscent of a Japanese tea garden, with stone-clad paths, stone lanterns, and the slight echo of water dripping into basins from bamboo pipes. A small garden opposite the gateway symbolizes activity and takes the form of water in motion in the landscape; the water is represented by raked gravel, and massive boulders symbolize mountains. A haiku is carved in stone on the left-hand side of the mound.

The Pagoda

Stroll across the grass, past summer-flowering karume azaleas, to the Pagoda, which you can see from the Japanese Garden. The Pagoda is one of Kew's most famous buildings. William Chambers had it built in 1761 for Princess Augusta, as a feature for visitors to discover as they promenaded around the garden. By 1763 there were 30 floors in all. At ten storeys rising 163 feet (nearly 50 metres), the Pagoda is still impressive, although it is now shorn of its chinoiserie decoration of a gilt topknot and gilt dragons at the roof angles. It was one of the first manifestations of the Chinese style in Britain, and some maintain that Chambers adopted it in his efforts to outdo his rival, the naturalistic landscape designer 'Capability' Brown.

Continue across the grass and you soon see the Lion Gate at the end of the path to the right. Turn left, passing to your left the Heather Garden, and further along the path you glimpse the Pavilion Restaurant, set back from the path to your left. Walk on, through the Ruined Arch of stone and well-used brick. This is a mock ruin, and, like the Pagoda, it is one of the 'discoveries' erected by Sir William Chambers in 1759.

Beyond it, the path passes a charming art gallery. Its walls are crowded with 832 detailed oil paintings by a Victorian woman, Marianne North, who travelled widely to paint the plant life and scenery of several countries, including Australia. Next to it is the modern Shirley Sherwood Gallery of Botanical Art, named after the botanist and Kew trustee. Continue, and ahead, to the right of the path, stand sturdy plantings of camellias, which flower in late winter, and an elegant group of Japanese acers (*Acer palmatum*).

The Temperate House

The path crosses a grove of young acers, a brilliant sight when the leaves change colour in autumn, and you arrive at the Temperate House. This is the most elegant of the glasshouses at Kew. It was designed by Decimus Burton in 1860, but was completed years later. It is the world's largest greenhouse, containing suites of plants from subtropical and arid regions, arranged geographically. Some are endangered in their homeland (sometimes by competition from foreign plants introduced by settlers) and are being grown at Kew as a library, with an eye to their eventual reintroduction in their native habitats.

Don't miss the broad-trunked Chilean wine palm (*Jubaea chilensis*), raised from seed in 1846. It is now the world's largest greenhouse plant, almost 60 feet (18.2 metres) tall, and threatening the roof.

Wander at will, enjoying the dappled light, the sound of water and the birdsong (yes, some birds do make their way in). It is also worth climbing the spiral stairways for a 'jungle roof' walk, although a much higher walk in this vein awaits you. Return to the central area, leave the Temperate House by the west door and go across to the Evolution House, an interesting aluminium and glass construction of 1952, once the Australian House. It offers a walk through geological time, from apparently lifeless bubbling mud, and bacterial flats of 500 million years ago, past sulphur springs, to a coal-age swamp loud with frog croaks. The exhibition ends at the appearance of the first flowering plants, of which some specimens on show are live. Follow the signs to the Treetop Walkway, its rusty trunk-like pillars soon looming ahead, blending in well with their real-life neighbours. You should begin with a visit to the Rhizotron on the left. A rhizotron is an underground laboratory for examining plant roots and takes its name from the Greek word for root, *rhiza*. Then, either take the lift or climb the 118 steps to the walkway, 59-feet (18 metres) above you in the tree canopy. Do not be alarmed by the rattling sound – a tourist has not dropped their keys; what you hear is coins tumbling down a 'fund-raising' drainpipe placed at the very top.

A visit to the Walkway is a must whatever the time of year. In the summer and autumn you can experience the full richness of the tree canopies; in the winter and spring you can enjoy unimpeded views to the Wembley Arch and the brown-brick tower of Kew Bridge Steam Museum. Further around are superb views of the Temperate House and, just above it on the horizon, the B.B.C. television tower at Crystal Palace.

On leaving the Treetop Walkway retrace your steps to the Evolution House and turn left along Holly Walk. When a green opens to your right you will see King Edward's Temple. Walk into this secret garden and circle through the Mediterranean Garden on your left, with its gnarled cork oak (*Quercus suber*) trunk. Now visit King William's Temple, another of Sir William Chambers' 'discoveries'. Inside are wall plaques celebrating famous British military victories. Look back, before you enter, to admire the impressive architectural set-piece of the Temperate House, with the Pagoda to the left.

Leave the temple from the right and then carry on straight over the crossroads into the Cherry Walk, planted with flowering cherries, among the treasures discovered by the first European botanists to visit Japan. Ahead of you is the Palm House; walk along the path to the entrance halfway along its western side. The roses here are donated by David Austin Roses.

The Palm House

This glasshouse was built as the focus of Kew Gardens, and William Nesfield laid out magnificent vistas from the Rose Garden outside. The Syon Vista runs past the lake to the river, although Syon House is obscured by trees. The Pagoda Vista leads the eye to Kew's famous Pagoda, surrounded by trees.

The Palm House is a magnificent Victorian creation, 360 feet (110 metres) long, 100 feet (30.5 metres) wide and 62 feet (18 metres) high, a magical construction of wrought iron and glass. Its shape is rather like an upturned ship, and in fact it was beam-built in a similar way. It was designed by the architect Decimus Burton, working with the engineer Richard Turner. The first iron rib was raised, cannily, in 1845, only months after the repeal of the glass tax levied on windows of any kind. Its original green-tinted glass was later replaced when it was realized that the vegetation did not need to be shaded. The Palm House opened in 1848, housing plants from the tropical rainforests to amaze visitors. It suffered badly from condensation, however, and in 1984 had to be closed and almost completely restored.

To the hypnotic background hiss of humidifiers there is much to admire. On the right as you enter the central area is the enormous palm *Attalea butyracea*, the largest plant in the Palm House. A native of South America, its leaves are used for thatching houses and making mats, baskets and brooms. Wander up each of the corridors to see ebony, mahogany and rubber plants, the wonderfully named ylang-ylang – Malaysia's perfume tree whose oil is used for scent – and the lovely red flowers of *Malesia's Tinospora glabra*, which look like hanging caterpillars. A circular staircase leads up to a roof walkway for a canopy view of this jungle. Since heat rises, it is really torrid at the top, with water dripping from the glass roof onto viewers. You can cool off in the marine display in the basement.

When you have explored the Palm House, exit through the small door in the northwest wing and walk across to the Waterlily House, the small building directly ahead, also the work of Richard Turner and built in 1852. It houses lovely bluish, lilac and white lotus blooms from Egypt and Asia. The names are poetic: Nymphaea Foxfire, Pink Flamingo.

Leave the Waterlily House and stroll to the Palm House Pond. Formal beds rather in the Italian style popular in the 1800s front the east side of the Palm House. Note the Queen's Beasts ranged along the Palm House, carved in stone for the coronation of Elizabeth II in 1953, among them the lions of England and of Mortimer, and the dragon of Wales. Walk to the end of these beasts.

The Palm House Pond has as its centrepiece a fountain and a statue of 1826 depicting Hercules and Achelous, a river god, which is apparently favoured as a perch by prospecting herons when the visitors have gone home. On the bank grow a couple of swamp cypresses (*Taxodium distichum*) from the southern U.S.A. Stroll clockwise around the banks and you see, standing guard alongside steps down to the water, a pair of kylins which probably date from the 18th century. They are Chinese mythological beasts, looking rather like lions, of the kind seen in the Imperial Palace in Beijing. Almost opposite, across the path, is another of Chambers' temples, dedicated to Arethusa. She was the Greek nymph who turned into a spring of water. In this temple is a record of the names of the staff of Kew Gardens who died in the two world wars.

The Specialist Gardens

The path to the right on the east end of the pond was temporarily closed as this book went to press, while the building you see to the left, the former Museum of Economic Botany, was being restored. This building once displayed curious fruits and botanical specimens brought for the first time from the ends of the Empire. Its exhibition was boosted when the East India Company made over its plant collections to Kew Gardens soon after the Indian Mutiny in 1857. Temporarily, you must now retrace your steps round the pond and follow the path to Cumberland Gate. Turn left after the beasts and take the path past the kylins. Note the Sessile oak (*Quercus petraea*) grown from an acorn brought from Verdun in 1917 and planted in 1919. The building ahead of you houses the Plants and People Exhibition which explores how man has used plants around the world. Flanking the museum are two swamp cypresses, with their tell-tale protruding knobbly roots. Turn right after museum, passing a small fountain. Soon, on the left, you come to the delicate, round Temple of Aeolus (the Winds). Atop quite a high mound and partly obscured by bushes and trees, it is another of the features built by Sir William Chambers when working for Princess Augusta.

Turn left opposite Cumberland Gate and you have to your left the Woodland Garden. A compromise between formality and informality, it is often voted Kew's most attractive area. It is not hidden in gloomy shadow, but is full of woodland plants in sun-dappled settings. There are often drifts of colour – spectacular, shade-tolerant white or pinkish *Trillium* spp., wood lilies from North America, for example, and the Himalayan blue poppy (*Mecanopsis* spp.), the Christmas rose, and other hellebores also grow here. Sprinklers are often active in this garden to keep the ground moist, a reminder that the soil underlying Kew is poor for plants in many ways. Sprinklers may need to be turned on even quite soon after rain.

Turn right to walk through the Order Beds. These echo the style of the old physic gardens, planted up to teach apprentice apothecaries to recognize medicinal (and poisonous) plants and their look-alikes and relatives. It is interesting to pick out a flower familiar to you and see what its close relations are. There is a bed of poppies, for example, from the red variety sometimes seen in grain fields to white and lilac version, and the yellow long-horned poppy of Mediterranean beaches.

The Order Beds are backed by a laboratory block, where, at the beginning of World War II, rose hips were found to be a valuable source of vitamin C. Schoolchildren collected them from the hedgerows as part of the war effort. Follow the brick and wood arbour almost to the end, then turn left into the Rock Garden. It was laid out in the 1880s, using rubble from the demolished White House which stood opposite Kew Palace, but it now has outcrops of Sussex sandstone, a cascade, streams bordered by marsh plants such as the marsh marigold and brooklime, and peaty gullies for bog plants. There are charming corners busy with bees, and in some places plants spread informally across the bare gravel. Pass through the space-age Davies Alpine House – Kew's smallest glasshouse – which opened on 11 March 2006.

The Princess of Wales Conservatory

Turn left into the Princess of Wales Conservatory, a must on any visit to Kew Gardens. It houses plants from ten climate zones, ranging from cacti native to hot, dry deserts to plants from humid tropical rainforests, It is a superbly designed building, full of little walkways taking you gently up to different areas. You pass through various doors into each climate zone and it is interesting to feel the humidity level of the air change as you do so. Watch out for little blasts of steam from hidden pipes! Eventually you come to the pond at the bottom which has a Sacred Lotus, a symbol of the Buddhist religion because it shows our potential for enlightenment – how we can grow from the mud of suffering to an awakened state, symbolized by the flower. When Indians place their palms together in the traditional *namaste* greeting, they are making a lotus bud shape with their hands. Below these zone rooms, down a slope, is an aquarium.

The Secluded Garden

From the Princess of Wales Conservatory, turn left and discover on your right, over a green bank, the unexpected Secluded Garden. It makes a delightful end to the walk, and you may be glad to rest awhile beside its unusual spiral, plated fountain, or in the small summer house – cool with water and with handsome wooden seating – that contains the bird of paradise (*Strelitzia reginae*). When you are rested, turn right and right again on Magnolia Walk to the main gate, where the walk ends.

HAM HOUSE GARDENS

LOCATION	About 9 miles (14.5 kilometres) west of Charing Cross.
TRANSPORT	Richmond Station (overground and District Line Underground). Buses 65, 371, (walk past the German school at Petersham). St. Margaret's Station (overground trains from Richmond) is 1 mile (1.6 kilometres) walk away, crossing the Thames via a ferry. There is free parking at the foot of the drive.
ADMISSION	Open Mon–Wed, Sat, Sun 11:00–17:00 hours (closes 16:00 in winter). Admission £3.30 adult £2 child.
SEASONAL FEATURES	Seasonal interest through the year.
EVENTS	Summer concerts in the gardens.
REFRESHMENTS	Garden Tearoom open Mon–Thu, Sat, Sun 10:30–18:00 hours. Orangery Restaurant open Mar–Oct from 12:30 for lunch.

Ham House is an outstanding Jacobean mansion that was built in the early 17th century in what was at the time fast becoming a very fashionable purlieu, less than 10 miles (16 kilometres) from the centre of London and with convenient river transport. The house was built in 1610 for Sir Thomas Vavasour, but was remodelled in the 1630s by William Murray, later to become the Earl of Dysart. On his death it passed to his daughter, Elizabeth Dysart, described as a woman 'restless in her ambition, profuse in her expense and of a most ravenous covetousness'. Elizabeth was married to the 1st Duke of Lauderdale, one of the Cabal (key members of the court of Charles II), and, in keeping with their status, the couple extended and luxuriously refurnished the house. Much of the magnificent interior we see today is their work.

The house remained in the ownership of the Dysart family for several generations, until Sir Lyonel Tollemache (a Dysart cousin) made it over to the National Trust in 1948. By then it was in a rather sorry state. The gardens had run to seed and there remained only tangles of sycamore and rampant rhododendrons, not to mention unfilled bomb craters from World War II. Only traces remained of the splendours that the ambitious Lauderdales had created within the grounds – a Prince's palace (in the view of the diarist John Evelyn) with 'Parterres, Flower Gardens, Orangeries, Groves, Avenues, Courts, Statues, Perspectives, Fountains, Aviaries'.

Gifts and donations made it possible, in 1975, to begin restoring the gardens to their former glory of three centuries ago, as part of the National Trust's contributions to European Architectural Heritage Year. A 1671 survey plan made by the Lauderdales' garden designers, John Slezer and Jan Wyck, provided the guide for the restoration, and basically much of what what has been recreated here is a simplified form of a Dutch garden (known at the time as the 'New Mode').

THE HAM HOUSE GARDENS WALK

Start and finish The Main Gate. **Time** Allow 1¼ hours.

Today, the main approach to Ham House is along an avenue of young lime and other trees, the youngest at the Ham Street end. Between this avenue and the River Thames to your left is the North Meadow. If you look straight ahead you can see the Star & Garter home for the disabled on the brow of Richmond Hill. A second avenue of trees leads from the main gate at the front of the house to the river bank. This was originally a main avenue because (tides willing) a barge rowed by watermen would have been a customary method of travelling from central London. There are some old lime trees in this avenue, although one or two young ones now fill gaps in the procession. Turn right to face the house and walk up to the gate.

The Main Gate

Begin the walk by looking at the iron gates and stone piers of the main gateway to the house, just on the right of the avenue of trees. They were designed by Sir William Bruce, a cousin of the Dysarts, and erected in 1671. The piers were made with stone brought from Lauderdale quarries on the Firth of Forth in Scotland. Celia Fiennes, that doughty explorer of Britain in the late 17th century, noted that iron gates such as this should be 'painted proper. Blew with gilt tops'. And the ironwork is again dark blue – not black – today. The urns date from 1671 and the carved pineapples on the pedestals along the edge of the ha-ha, or ditch, from 1799. They are fashioned from Coade stone, an artificial stone made in the 18th century to a very profitable and highly secret recipe in workshops in Fulham. Statuary was made up of pieces fired like pottery in a kiln; clay, flint and ground glass (to melt and bind the mixture) were among the constituents. The railings date from the 20th century.

Look to left and right of the gate and you see that the boundary of the estate this side of the house – the northern edge of the gravel walk – is also marked by a ha-ha. This was a device for embracing the view, creating a way of bringing it into the garden vista without the intrusion of a fence to keep out deer, grazing cattle, or even peasants, perhaps. Wild flowers grow on the slopes of the ha-ha and wild grasses are usually also left to grow tall and seed. This is a modern ecological vogue.

The Entrance Forecourt

Walk through the gates, and into the forecourt beside the front door. Until the 1975 restorations tall shrubs all but obscured the 22 hollow heads cast in lead set in niches in the curving walls. Today the heads look very dramatic when they catch the angled sun. Originally, the walls extended further and housed 38 busts in all; the others are now placed in niches decorating the front of the house. Portraying Charles I, Charles II, and many Roman emperors and their wives, they look well against the damson-coloured brick.

'Two carv'd wainscot benches' referred to in a bill of 1674 are in the 'cloisters' (the covered areas) to each side of the entrance to the house. The armrests sport charming cherubs, reclining curled. The central figure of the entrance forecourt is a Coade stone river god ('Old Father

HAM HOUSE GARDENS

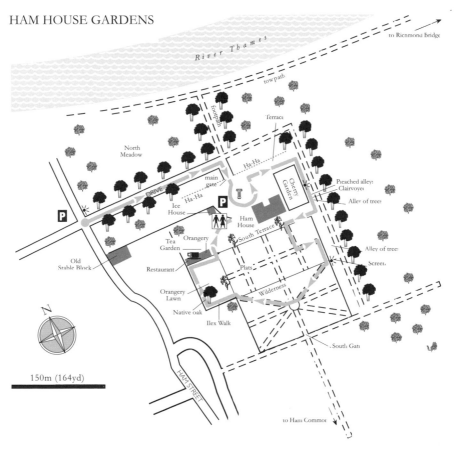

Thames', some call him) placed in this spot in 1799; he better looks the part when dampened by the modern lawn sprinkler. There is a similar figure, but in bronze, at Somerset House in London; in this forecourt he faces away, bottom toward the front door. The topiary in this forecourt was planted by the National Trust: the clipped drums of bay, cones of yew, Portuguese laurel, and low box edging hedges reflect the late-19th century fashion.

Before moving on, stand back and look at the house. It was a favourite of Charles II, who was a frequent visitor, and it remains an authentic period piece. Although the bays on this north face look Victorian, they date from 1610.

Turn and walk back along the eastern side of the forecourt, and turn right along the wide gravel terrace that leads to the Cherry Garden. Ahead, beyond the boundary wall where an avenue of lime trees now runs, there once stretched a 'Melancholy Walk'. Running along the east side of the gardens, it was planted with trees in quincunx order – that is, in fives to a right-angle and diagonal pattern, so that the line patterns changed as you walked. It was a trick designed to aid contemplation, an old meaning of the word 'melancholy' in this context.

The Melancholy Walk originally ended in mounds, or viewing platforms, and the one at this end also had a 'banqueting house', or garden house, where light refreshments might be taken. It was a two-storey building, according to a mason's bill of 1672. Through the railings you can see Ham Polo Ground, where Prince Charles played in his younger years.

The Cherry Garden

Turn right into the Cherry Garden, which was restored in 1976 from the 1671 plans, although perhaps to a less elaborate design than the original. You enter a vaulted corridor of pleached hornbeam (to pleach is to interlace tree branches). Hornbeam often keeps its dead leaves in winter, so offering all-year protection. It is underplanted with box hedges. There is another, similar corridor of pleached hornbeam on the opposite side of the Cherry Garden by the house.

Between the two there is now a geometrical knot garden of diamond-shaped box-edged beds filled with clipped Dutch lavender (which is alive with skipper butterflies and buzzing bees in summer) and silvery dwarf cotton lavender, of acid hue. The rows of trimmed round heads create, in a similar way to the Melancholy Walk, changing patterns as you walk by, and the whole display is accented with cones of box, much as embroidery can be sprigged with French knots. Note the gravel paths of this knot garden.

Early garden plans have shown 40 morello cherry trees growing here. It seems the garden was abandoned following the labour shortage after World War I. In the film *Young Victoria* (2009), Queen Victoria (played by Emily Blunt) proposes to Prince Albert (played by Rupert Lee) here. On the south side is a sundial, with four o'clock represented by the old-fashioned 'IIII' instead of 'IV'.

Walk to the end of the pleached hornbeam corridor and leave the Cherry Garden, passing to the right a trimmed alley leading to a side door to the house. You emerge on to a long terrace which runs along the south side of the house.

The South Terrace

This broad terrace ends at a railed break in the brick wall, which gives a view out toward Richmond Hill to the east. This architectural device, called a clairvoyee (literally, an 'opening to a view') predated the ha-ha, which opened the view entirely. The noticeable width of this walkway was necessary to accommodate the ladies in their voluminous crinoline dresses. There are 36 pots along the edge, paid for by the Gordons distillery company, following the discovery of juniper, an ingredient of gin, during restoration work here.

Walk to the right toward the centre of the terrace and down the steps to the beds at its foot. These have a mainly green colour scheme and an interesting plant texture – grape vines clothe the drop, with sage and rosemary bushes of the time, while other Mediterranean shrubs also flourish in the shelter of the borders: cistus with papery pink and white flowers, myrtle and scorpion senna, for example.

The terrace has an open view across a grid of eight turf 'plats' (plots) separated by wide gravel paths. The shape was revealed in aerial photographs taken by the Ministry of Defence during World War II. These eight plats were reshaped in 1976 out of what had become one

lawn. In the days of the Lauderdales these would have been full of statues and other ornaments, and there are plans to replace some of these.

Follow the path to the east of the plats, where it runs between an informal alley of oak,
sweet chestnut and other trees, while apple and pear trees hug the wall. There is also a fig
tree. Another handsome wrought-iron screen interrupts the wall at the end of the path, giving
outward views. From this spot, looking back toward the house, you can gauge the real scale
of the terrace and also notice that the two ends of the once H-shaped Jacobean house have
been enclosed at a later date to create more interior rooms. This infill contains early examples of sash windows.

The Wilderness

From the screen, follow the path diagonally into the Wilderness. This is a unique example of
a popular, 17th-century garden feature. It was not wild in the modern sense, but rather formal,
its hedges creating garden 'rooms' entered by 'doorways'. It was not a maze; the alleys are
quite wide. Writers of the day called the spaces 'cabinets', 'green arbours' and 'galleries'; they
were seen as being an out-of-doors version of the more private rooms of the house, suitable
for politics, chats and even flirtations.

Before the restorations started in the 1970s there was nothing to be seen of the Wilderness
but a thicket of trees and bushes. This was clear-felled and the original pattern of paths was
replanted with hornbeam hedges, set at intervals with taller field maples, a native tree. The
four round summerhouses, reproducing those seen in an early engraving, are white walled,
painted blue inside, and roofed by wooden tiling topped by a gilded ball. They have their
backs to the sun since, in the 17th century, a tan was a sign of belonging to the working class.
There are wild flowers here and the wild grasses are left uncut in summer, except along the
paths. As a result, you may see blue and brown grassland butterflies.

This Ham Wilderness was centrally aligned to the house and to the grass plots in front
of it. Walk along the path to its hub, an open space set round with a few white-painted
cockleshell-backed seats, copies of the originals. There were also statues and boxes of
flowering shrubs.

From this central arena you can see the fine south gateway to the left, its ironwork also
painted in a copy of the 17th-century 'smalt' blue. The elaborate coat of arms on the overthrow
to the gates is of the Tollemache family, the motto (translated as 'No man can harm me with
impunity') is of the Order of the Thistle. Beyond the gates, focused on the south front of the
house, is a great avenue of trees.

The Orangery Garden

Turn along the diagonal path to the right, leading westward through the Wilderness, which
ends at a fine gateway leading into the southern end of the Orangery Garden. The gateway, a
recent copy, is gilded in places; notice the gilt flowers on top of it. Proceed along the Ilex Walk,
which stretches ahead of you. Ilex trees, or Holm oaks (*Quercus ilex*), are evergreen oaks from
the Mediterranean; they keep their dense foliage in winter. These trees first became popular
in the 18th century.

Turn to admire the fine sweep of the Orangery Lawn, with a tall native oak at its centre. The lawn is edged with monochromatic rose beds – one yellow, one pink, one red, and so on. Old plans show that this garden was once wholly compartmented with plant beds and was probably a kitchen garden, and there are hopes that part of it might eventually be restored. Against the shelter of the east wall is a border with an interesting medley of herbaceous plants, including an almost black hollyhock, irises and sweet peas. These flowers are often cut for the house.

The Orangery

Turn to the right at the top of the Orangery Lawn and onto the Orangery Terrace, and walk along it. The Orangery is in rich, mellow red brick, clad in wisteria, and was probably built for the Lauderdale gardens in the 1670s. It is one of the oldest orangeries to be seen in Britain. Its west end has been converted into a café, The Garden Room. On the north side of the Orangery a door leads to a summer tea garden; and as you walk along the terrace you will see that its east part is a restaurant. Inside there are sets of sculptured busts, 19th-century copies of antique models. Orangeries such as this were originally heated by stoves and were used to protect delicate shrubs in winter, and to force flowers to early blooming. Today, in summer, the Orangery terrace is set with lemon or orange bushes in tubs.

The Ice House

Leave the Orangery Garden by the corner gateway. You have to your right the west courtyard to Ham House; there is a handsome lead water butt on the right. From the courtyard you can see the domed roof of the old ice house. It was built in brick, but coated in concrete during World War II, when it was used as an air raid shelter. Its entrance is alongside the gateway leading to the front of the house and the Main Gate, where the walk ends.

MARBLE HILL PARK

LOCATION About 8½ miles (13.7 kilometres) southwest of Charing Cross.

TRANSPORT St. Margaret's and Twickenham stations (overground trains from Waterloo and Clapham Junction) are ten minutes' and 20 minutes' walk away respectively. Buses 33, 490, H22, R68, R70. There is a ferry across the Thames from Ham House (*see* page 135). There is a car park off Beaufort Road on the east side of the park.

ADMISSION Open daily dawn–dusk. Admission is free.

SEASONAL FEATURES Horse chestnuts in flower in late spring; ancient black walnut and other fine trees in leaf in summer.

EVENTS Concerts on the south lawn in summer.

REFRESHMENTS Coach House Café open Apr–Oct daily 10:00–17:30 hours; weekends only Nov-Mar.

The surrounding park forms a marvellous setting for Marble Hill House, a perfect small Palladian villa which dominates its grounds. Its surroundings have changed from the original layout. The shrubberies which embrace it to each side have grown up where once its outbuildings stood, while the gently sloping lawns reveal only slight traces of the original terracing (despite its name, the house is not on a hill). Nevertheless, the park makes for a very satisfying visit, with some historic trees, an ice house and (especially) a grotto, a landscape conceit which was very popular when the house was built.

There could have been no better location for the house. Twickenham was then a riverside village in charming countryside, yet within easy enough reach of London to guarantee entertaining neighbours – the poet Alexander Pope (1688–1744) and the novelist and politician Horace Walpole (1717–97) among them – for the fashionable residents.

The house was built in 1724–9 for Henrietta Howard (*c.* 1698–1767), the mistress of George II, who paid for it with money from the king. She was also Mistress of Robes to Queen Caroline, and later became Countess of Suffolk. Colen Campbell was one of the architects, but Henry Herbert – later Lord Pembroke, and an amateur architect – was among the many friends who flocked to help with the work. The restrained façades were to be much copied. Jonathan Swift, author of *Gulliver's Travels*, advised Henrietta on her wine cellar; Alexander Pope helped with advice about the gardens and grounds, which were laid out by the queen's landscape designer Charles Bridgeman (*see* page 9). Lord Bathurst sent lime trees from Cirencester Park and Lord Islay (the future Duke of Argyll) planted a black walnut (*Juglans nigra*), which is now huge. 'Every thing as yet promises more happiness for the latter part of my life than I have yet had a prospect of,' wrote Henrietta Howard in 1731 to John Gay, the author of *The Beggars' Opera*, who lived in Richmond. 'I shall now often visit Marble Hill.' Having had a disastrous first marriage,

MARBLE HILL PARK

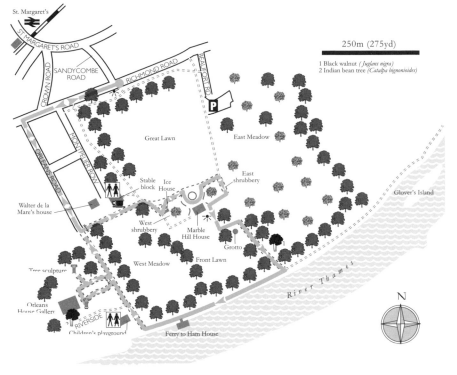

250m (275yd)

1 Black walnut (*Juglans nigra*)
2 Indian bean tree *(Catalpa bignonioides)*

she lived happily at Marble Hill for 36 years with her second husband, George Berkeley, until his death in 1753.

The house was later occupied by another royal mistress, Mrs. Fitzherbert (1756–1837), the secret wife of the then Prince of Wales, later George IV. It became empty for some years around the turn of the 20th century, until, in 1902, London County Council took it over for use as tea rooms. In 1966 the house was restored and opened as a museum of paintings and furniture, some of which had survived from its first years, and in 1986 English Heritage took charge of it.

THE MARBLE HILL PARK WALK

Start and finish The Orleans Road gate. **Time** Allow 45 minutes.

Enter the park via the gate in Orleans Road, and walk straight ahead until you come to converted stabling, now the Coach House Café, to the left. From about the 1720s, 'Gothick' architecture came into vogue, and among its adherents were some of Henrietta Howard's neighbours, including Horace Walpole, who had built Strawberry Hill House in that style. Under their influence Henrietta was persuaded to convert a barn into a

Gothick 'priory' somewhere in this area, but it had been pulled down by 1770. Horse chestnut trees were popular when the estate was planted, and some good specimens survive in this part of the park. There is also a magnificent plane tree.

Continue ahead, past the stabling and a fenced minipark for toddlers and parents, and you come to a corner of one of the densely tangled shrubberies which form natural wings to each side of the house. Turn right down the short path at the corner to see the 18th-century ice house, in which river or lake ice, packed tightly in straw, could last up to two years. It originally had a domed brick roof, but it is now capped with smooth mortar, obscured by a covering of ivy. All ice houses were domed, presumably because the dome shape was found most efficient in controlling the circulation of air; drainage considerations meant that they were always sited some distance from the main house. This ice house is kept locked, unfortunately, so visitors are unable to admire the skilled brickwork inside.

Ice was a summer luxury in the 18th century, its value shown by some lines of a friend of Henrietta Howard, Jonathan Swift: 'No more the Dean, that grave Divine,/Shall keep the Key of my No-wine;/My Ice-House rob, as heretofore,/And Steal my Artichokes no more...'.

The North Front

Continue along the main path to the north face of the house. The Great Lawn, to the left, is now often occupied by sports pitches. The house is elegantly winged by arcs of wall. In front of these walls are lollipop-trimmed bay shrubs in white-painted containers; ornaments such as these were popular in the 18th century. From the east shrubbery opposite, which hides the site of the service wing of the house, to Richmond Road stretches a superb double avenue of horse chestnut trees. This was the original main driveway to the house. The path skirting the eastern shrubbery has been planted with lime trees and two right turns along it bring you out in front of the elegant Palladian south face of the house.

The River Thames, to the south, is obscured by trees for most of the year, but in winter, when the trees are bare, you can see how well chosen was the situation, with the river providing a ready-made water feature and a misty distance beyond. The lawn bears traces of broad turf terraces, now framed by trees on each side; these terraces were possibly Bridgeman's contribution to the garden scheme. Eighteenth-century prints of the house from the river show what Pope called an impression of 'amiable simplicity' produced by the grass terraces and curved lines of trees. The atmosphere at that time may have been much the same as today, although some argue that the bankside trees should be cut down to leave the river view open, as it was originally.

Lady Suffolk's Grotto

Follow the edge of the east shrubbery round to the left, and you come to a grotto on the right, down in a small hollow hidden by dense shrubbery. Grottoes were a popular fad of the 18th century, a pleasing destination when promenading the grounds, or a place to sit while chatting with friends. The idea for such a feature came originally from Italy, and there was a well-known example in Alexander Pope's villa nearby. To the right of the path you see steps descending to the grotto. Go down them and look inside to see a puzzling, well-like pit and a round stone table. The walls would probably have been decorated with sea shells and perhaps pieces of coloured glass. From outside the grotto there is a view to Richmond Hill, but in summer it is obscured by foliage.

The Black Walnut

From the grotto, continue right along the path toward the river. To the left is a giant black walnut (*Juglans nigra*), one of the largest in the country, protected nowadays by a fence. Its girth at shoulder height is 17 feet 6 inches (over 5 metres), and its massive side boughs do not need support. It was planted for Henrietta Howard by Lord Islay (later Duke of Argyll). A native of North America, its leaves have more leaflets than Britain's native walnut, they are sharply toothed, and the ridged nut is very hard. This tree miraculously survived the great storm of 1987, which felled some tall Lombardy poplars nearby.

The River Walk and Tree Sculpture

Follow the path down to the river, go through the gate that leads to the river walk, and turn right (westward) along it. From this walk you catch glimpses through the trees of what is now a famous aspect of the house.

Follow the walk past Orleans Road and the children's playground to the left, to the sign-posted entrance to Orleans House Gallery. The name comes from a French connection: Louis Philippe, the Duc d'Orléans (who was later to become King of France), lived in Orleans House between 1793 and 1814. All that really remains of his house is the 1720 Octagon by James Gibbs, a handsome pavilion in ochre-coloured brick, with red-brick pilasters and dressings of Portland stone. There is an art gallery in the wing to one side.

In front of the gallery is a magnificent Indian bean tree (*Catalpa bignonioides*), with large, light green leaves, intricate white blossom in July, and hanging pods looking like beans in winter. To the far side is the unmistakable dark green mass of the Holm oak, and on the shade alongside the Octagon is a cast (slightly dented) of Diana the huntress in her short tunic; 1944 is the earliest record of this figure.

There is a more surprising work still to be seen. Walk back, as if to return to the river, and where the path curves to the right by a lamp post, a winding earth path branches off to the left, into the open woodland. It brings you to a recent tree sculpture, not all that large, on top of a post in a small clearing. It is the root end of a tree trunk, with eight root spokes radiating from a central face, each ending in a club of rootlets. It is partly gilded, with melted sheets of green glass attached to some roots.

Return to the main path and continue along it to the gate leading into Orleans Road, where the walk ends.

VICTORIA PARK

LOCATION	About 5½ miles (8.8 kilometres) northeast of Charing Cross.
TRANSPORT	Cambridge Heath Station (overground from Liverpool Street); Mile End, Bow Road and Bethnal Green Underground stations. Buses: D6, D7, 8, S2, 277, 333.
ADMISSION	Open daily, 08:00–dusk. Admission is free.
SEASONAL FEATURES	Spring bluebells; Flower Garden in spring and summer; autumn tree colour.
EVENTS	Occasional tea dances by the bandstand; pop concerts; model boat meetings; political gatherings.
REFRESHMENTS	Lakeside Pavilion Café open daily 09:00–18:00 hours.

Victoria Park is four times the size of Green Park, but remains relatively unknown to many Londoners, chiefly because it lies away from the West End and its tourist attractions and does not have its own Underground station. Yet this 'people's park' is easily accessible by train from Liverpool Street. Split into two – Victoria Park West and Victoria Park East – it has an atmosphere markedly different from its more famous neighbours, being used by people who live locally rather than visitors. It offers a variety of attractions, from glimpses of London's canal history and relics of old London Bridge, to strange sculptures and hidden flower gardens. It also affords some unusual views of the city's towers.

This park truly deserves the appellation 'the people's park' because that is precisely how it came into being. In 1839, a Registrar of Birth, Deaths and Marriages came to a grim conclusion: East London had the highest mortality rate in the capital. The rich lived in West London where the air was comparatively cleaner; the poor lived in the East End, where they were at the mercy of the prevailing westerly winds which blew the coal smoke and factory fumes from the city over their backyards. A report to Parliament suggested that a park would provide some much needed fresh air and open space for East Enders, although their concern may have been as much about preventing an epidemic spreading to the West End as about the well-being of their poor neighbours. In 1840 East Londoners took matters into their own hands. Some 30,000 of them signed a petition to persuade Queen Victoria that East Londoners needed a park for their health and recreation.

The Crown Estate purchased 218 acres (88.2 hectares) for £50,000 and the park was laid out between 1842 and 1847 by the architect Sir James Pennethorne, an assistant of John Nash, who worked on many projects in Victorian London, including Somerset House in the Strand. It wasn't all plain sailing, however. Despite the queen's blessing, officials were concerned about the amount of time and money being lavished on the project. Pennethorne ignored their concerns and by 1845 the park fences were in place and a superintendent's lodge had been built by Crown Gates, the park's main entrance.

Other lodges were planned for the north and east gates in order, so a periodical of the time put it, 'to safe-keep the regulations of the park, in so distant and lawless a neighbourhood as Hackney Wick'. Many of the park's original features still remain, including the handsome carriageway that encircles it, the ornamental entrance gates in Approach Road, the former bathing lakes and some lovely flower beds. The park is also bordered by the Regent's Canal to the west and the Hertford Union Canal to the east, which offer fascinating glimpses of 19th century history.

In 1848 the Chartists – the 19th-century movement that pressed for greater democracy and parliamentary reforms – held a huge rally in the park, a gathering that was to set the park's tone for years to come. Victoria Park has always been the dissenters' park, with a reputation for radicalism which continued late into the 20th century. George Bernard Shaw spoke here at one of its many impromptu speakers' corners, as did the Socialists William Morris and Annie Besant, who led the famous 'match girls' strike of 1888.

On 30 April 1978 the Anti-Nazi League and Rock Against Racism staged a landmark concert here, with The Clash and The Tom Robinson Band headlining. The park is still noted for its open-air music festivals, often ones linked with a political cause, and marches and demonstrations still often begin or end here. This Grade II listed park is also popular with artists and musicians who live locally and who maintain its reputation for questioning the status quo. In 2008, the London listings magazine *Time Out* voted 'Viccy Park', as it is known, London's Best Local Park. The Olympic Stadium is close by and, as this book went to press, plans to use the park during the 2012 Games were being discussed.

THE VICTORIA PARK WALK

Start and finish The Bonner Gates **Time**: Allow 1½ hours

The walk begins at the grand Bonner Gates, named after Bishop Edmund Bonner, a Tudor Lord fond of burning heretics at the stake. His ghost is said to haunt the park on moonlit nights. The gates are not the originals: they were dismantled, along with the park railings, during World War II to aid the war effort. Note the lovely views up and down the Regent's Canal from this point.

The Dogs of Alcibiades

Ahead is one of the park's most curious sights – the *Dogs of Alcibiades*, a sculpture of a pair of hunting dogs. Alcibiades was an Athenian politician and general, and he'd be sad to see the state of his faithful friends today. Based on the work of an ancient Greek sculptor, the figures were presented to the park in 1912 by Lady Regnart. The writer Iain Sinclair, who lives locally, describes them as 'frosty albinos [who] howl in perpetual torment'.

Turn left at the crossroads and join the path which runs beneath a lovely line of lime trees bordering the canal. Join the tarmac carriageway as it bends to the right and note the Indian bean trees (*Catalpa bignoniodides*), with their seed pods hanging like cigars

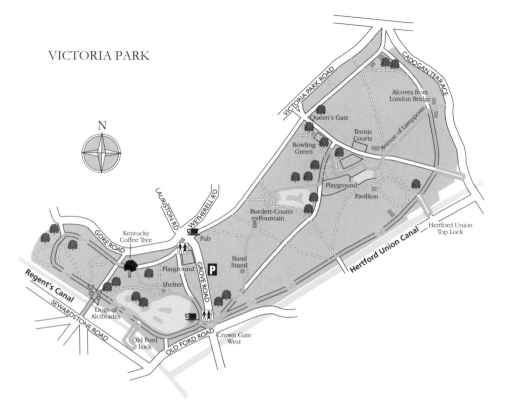

VICTORIA PARK

from the branches. Follow the road around and when it straightens out, notice on your left a tall, labelled turkey oak (*Quercus cerris*), so called, some say, because their leaves look like the bird's feet. Or is it that their acorns are often eaten by turkeys? Or, perhaps, it is simply because this species was found growing in the wild in Turkey. No one seems quite sure, although the latter is a safe bet. Much has been done to improve Victoria Park after it suffered badly from vandalism in the 1970s. Elegant benches line this carriageway and neat, engraved litter bins.

The Kentucky Coffee Tree

Pass through the gates and over the roadway to find an elegant, fan-tail flower garden sitting in a natural dip on your right. The beds change, but note the six small palms standing guard. Behind them, to the right, is a leaning cider gum tree (*Eucalpytus gunnii*), with its distinctive peeling trunk. Australian in origin, these trees take their name because the sap, when fermented and bottled, resembles apple cider. Behind the right-hand triplet of palms is a Kentucky coffee tree (*Gymnocladus dioicus*), a fairly rare tree introduced to England in the 18th century. The early settlers of Kentucky are said to have roasted the seeds to make a coffee-like drink.

147

A Natural Umbrella

Turn right and follow the secluded path to the little shelter. Just before the path turns to reach it, look across the open grass to your left to see a giant, magnificent narrowleaf ash (*Fraxinus angustifolia*), the largest ash tree in the park, with a pendulous crown that is a trademark of the species. To its left is the dark mass of a Turner's oak (*Quercus x turneri*), an oak hybrid that was first raised by a Mr. Turner in his Essex nursery in 1783.

The shelter has tree trunk supports for its roof. Turn sharp right and very quickly you come to a lovely weeping beech (*Fagus sylvatica* 'Pendula'), sheltering the path like a natural umbrella. It has an extraordinary top-heavy trunk. Walk onto the grass here and down to the leaning grey poplar (*Populus canescens*), whose roots bind the lakeside bank together. Now head up the grassy bank to the right-hand corner, where there is a sweet chestnut (*Castanea sativa*), noted for the edible nuts which are roasted and eaten in winter. From here, follow the edge of the lake on your right and head straight for the bulbous trunk you can see ahead of you; this belongs to an ash (*Fraxinus excelsior*), an important timber tree with light-coloured wood that is strong and hard-wearing, and commonly used to make furniture.

Keep to the lake edge until you rejoin the path beneath the unmistakeable dark mass of an Evergreen/Holm oak (*Quercus ilex*), common in parks, gardens and roadsides in Britain, where it has been cultivated since the 16th century. Continue around to the Lakeside Pavilion Café, its design based on an original Victorian building. Customers include old generation East Enders who claim to have known the Kray brothers and, increasingly, fashionable, artistic, middle-class newcomers: where once this café might have served egg and beans with two slices, now it is all organic carrot cake, lattes and celebrity sightings. In 2009 comedians Josie Lawrence, Lee Hurst and Sean Locke were regulars, while pop singers and musicians such as Ladyhawke and Bobby Gillespie from Primal Scream have also been seen here.

The Burdett-Coutts Fountain

Leave Victoria Park East through Crown Gates and pass the elegant Llanover Lodge, the former park superintendent's residence, now occupied by a park ranger. Cross at the zebra crossing to enter Victoria Park West and take the central road. The holly clump on your right was first planted in 1857 and later enlarged. A wide lawn opens to your left, at the edge of which is a mini forest of London planes (*Platanus x hispanica*), with their distinctive mottled bark, rather like camouflage. The ground beneath is kept wild, with glorious daffodils in February and lovely spring bluebells.

Cross to the bandstand and note the compass inlaid in its wooden ceiling. Walk across to a little common-like area, which has longer grass, to find a stone parish boundary marker from 1898; beyond it, beneath horse chestnuts, lies another.

Now make your way to the elaborate Burdett-Coutts Fountain, donated to the park by the wealthy Victorian philanthropist Angela Burdett-Coutts (1814–1906), granddaughter of the founder of Coutts bank. She provided the fountain after hearing that the park had no adequate drinking facilities, and it was a typically generous act by a woman who also founded the National Society for the Prevention of Cruelty to Children and to whom Charles Dickens dedicated his novel *Martin Chuzzlewit*. The 54-foot (16.5-metre) high, Grade II Star listed granite fountain is covered with decorative stonework which includes four winged cherubs – Iain Sinclair calls them *putti*, the early modern Italian word for child. They sit astride dolphins, each in slightly different postures. Sadly, the structure has suffered much from vandalism but a further restoration was planned as this book went to press.

A Giant Tree's Companion

Take the path opposite the statue of a boy with a flagon on his shoulder and pass football fields on your right. Victoria Park East tends to be quieter than its neighbour during the week, but at weekends it is busy with matches being played. A report in *Harper's Magazine* in 1888 describes the scene here: 'On the big central lawn are scattered numerous groups, some of which are very closely packed. Almost all the religious sects of England and all the political and social parties are preaching their ideas and disputing ...'.

At the end of the path, head straight across the grass, passing a large, rocket-shaped Wellingtonia (*Sequoiadendron giganteum*). This specimen looks modest enough, but in the Sequoia National Park in California a Wellingtonia – known as the 'General Sherman' tree, after the American Civil War general – is acknowledged to be the world's largest living thing, the girth of its trunk measuring 102.6 feet (31.3 metres). Visitors to the 'Viccy Park' Wellingtonia in centuries to come may well be amazed by its size.

Turn right and walk along the lake path with the water on your right. Park staff have built nesting stations for the white-beaked coots here. If you see one striding about on the grass, note its giant feet – they have distinctive lobed flaps of skin on the claws which act like webs when swimming. And how do you remember the difference between a coot and a moorhen? Easy – moorhens have red beaks and 'moorhen' has an 'r' in it.

The Flower Garden

As the lake path ends, there is a Caucasian elm (*Zelkova carpinifolia*) on your left, with its distinctive, and somewhat hypnotic, split trunk. Turn left, follow the road, and then turn sharp right, almost back on yourself, to enter the Flower Garden. This is a delightful, tucked-away gem, more formal in lay-out and atmosphere than the surrounding park. One could imagine frock-coated Victorians walking here. The beds are bordered by box privet, with bulbous ewe hedges on the corners. It ends in a circular flower bed, hidden behind ewe hedges reminiscent of the Hampton Court maze. Pass through and take the left-hand exit to emerge behind the children's playground, where you turn right.

Memories of London Bridge

Immediately on your left is the deer enclosure which has four resident deer, although the rangers say that they like to hide, so sightings can be a bit hit-and-miss.

Beyond this is the Boating Pond, home to the oldest model boat club in the world, the Victoria Model Steam Boat Club, founded in 1904. The club originally favoured a more traditional, purist approach to the hobby, eschewing radio-controlled boats and practising what is called 'straight running' – setting the boat down in the water and sending it toward a colleague at the other end of the pond. In recent years, however, radio-controlled boats have been allowed.

At the end of the pond take the left path, then the next left. Cross the main carriage-way, then turn right, following a slightly comical avenue of lampposts. In the distance you can see what look like two curved, free-standing shells. These are a real London discovery – two original stone alcoves from the old London Bridge which was demol-ished during the 18th century. They were presented to the park in 1860, having appar-ently been discovered by chance in a builder's yard. Look up inside the curve to see the insignia of the London Bridge Association. Legend has it that these alcoves have some-thing in common with the famous Whispering Gallery at St. Paul's Cathedral, in that such was the perfection of their proportions that if a person whispered in one of them, their voice could be heard in the opposing alcove, despite the noise of horse-drawn carriages on the street.

Classic Views

Facing the alcoves, turn right to walk along a splendid double avenue of plane trees, the tree that perhaps most symbolises London. As the carriageway curves, note two other symbols of London that appear on the horizon away to your right: Richard Rogers' rocket-shaped (and rather Wellingtonia-like) 30 St Mary Axe, nicknamed 'the gherkin', and the stepped silhouette of the International Finance Centre. At the pretty lodge by St. Mark's Gate, a short detour out of the park can be made to view the edge of the Olympic Stadium. It can be seen by turning right after the lodge and looking to the left at the bridge. Return to the park, rejoin the avenue and turn left. Another detour to the left is worthwhile, through Lockhouse Gate to Hertford Union Top Lock. It's also worth stepping onto the canal path here to see the pretty, listed canal cottages. The Hertford Union Canal opened in 1830 and links the Regent's Canal to the Lee Navigation.

Return to the park and turn left. Planted in 1919–20, this avenue is now a single line of planes, letting through more light. To your left, between the canal-side willows and flats, you may catch glimpses of Canary Wharf, with its summit pyramid. Frenchman Alain Robert, the self-styled 'spiderman', climbed the outside of this building in 1995.

Canalside Stables

Follow the majestic plane trees back to Crown Gate and retrace your steps back into Victoria Park West, taking the path to the left of the lake. Note the London plane on your left, near the café, which was planted by the Mayor of Tower Hamlets. It was a symbolic gesture, marking the Bow Parks Board's intention to regenerate the tree pop-ulation in the park after the destruction wrought by the great storm of 1987.

There is an avenue of relatively young limes (*Tilia x europaea/platyphyllos* 'Rubra') here, planted in 1991, with more mature specimens further on that were planted in 1985 by the former Greater London Council. Look out for motionless herons on the island, 'a bloom of cloud on a tilting stalk', as the poet Ted Hughes described these birds.

Where the avenue straightens out, walk up the slope to Arcade Gate and turn left to see Old Ford Lock and the brick stables once home to the horses that pulled the barges. At regular intervals along the canal are brick ramps which were used to help the horses climb out of the water after they had fallen in.

Return to the park and continue along the avenue of limes. The Glade is a tucked-away lawn on your right, edged with pretty blue lilac. Immediately afterwards you come to the *Dogs of Alcibiades* where you turn left for Bonner Bridge, where the walk ends.

MILE END PARK

LOCATION	About 5 miles (8 kilometres) east of Charing Cross.
TRANSPORT	Bethnal Green Underground Station (Central Line); Cambridge Heath Station (overground from Liverpool Street); buses 8, 25, 277, 323, 339, D6, 425.
ADMISSION	Open daily dawn–dusk. Admission is free.
SEASONAL FEATURES	Spring and summer displays in the Terrace Garden; autumn tree colour.
EVENTS	Occasional lectures in the Ecology Centre and exhibitions in the Arts Pavilion.
REFRESHMENTS	The Palm Tree Pub, in the middle of the park, is open 12:00–24:00 hours or later.

This area of London takes its name from a milestone that marked the point one mile east of the boundary of the City at Aldgate. Occupying a former residential area of Victorian terraces, this innovative park is one of the most unusual open spaces in the capital.

Following World War II bomb damage, the area was cleared by the Greater London Council as part of the Abercrombie Plan, the vision for London drawn up the town planner and architect Sir Patrick Abercrombie (1879–1957). At that time motor traffic wasn't yet the blight it has become today, and Abercrombie's plan was for strips of parkway to enhance the proposed new arterial roads. In east London, the notion was to create a long, narrow park running alongside the Grand Union Canal, but, unfortunately, the result was less than satisfactory. The park was dissected by railway viaducts and roads – notably the busy Mile End Road – and had a fragmented feel. It never had the chance to develop the character of a coherent park and fell into disuse, so much so that by 1990 it had become a semi-derelict jumble of underused land.

In 1995 the Mile End Park Partnership was formed and an outline plan for the park's improvement was produced. The following year the Millennium Commission awarded a grant of up to £12.3 million and town planners Tibbalds, whose varied projects have included Lords Cricket Ground and Weymouth Esplanade, drew up a masterplan. Their plan was to link the disparate areas of the park with a serpentine path and cycleway running from north to south, connecting several different themed 'parks within a park'.

It was a bold scheme involving one daring and extraordinary feature: the creation of a 'green bridge' over the Mile End Road, the experience of which alone makes a visit to the park worthwhile. A debate still rages over whether all of the park's artificially created features work, but the care that has been lavished on a neglected part of London is to be praised. Two routes can be taken through the park – an upper one, which crosses a number of green roofs on the park's modern buildings, or a lower one which stays closer to the canal. This walk enjoys a little of both.

THE MILE END PARK WALK

Start and finish Roman Road **Time** Allow 1 hour

Leave the busy Roman Road after you cross the Grand Union Canal and take the steps down into the greenery. The modern-style Mile End Park sign greets you, which sets the mood for much of what you will see on the walk. Follow the tree-lined path until you see the Ecology Centre on your left.

The Ecology Centre

This building has a green roof that carries a footpath and cycleway. It is the first publicly owned earth-covered building in the U.K., a feature which both reduces its visual impact and makes it extremely energy efficient. The sloping windows are gas-filled and triple-glazed, making the building one of the cheapest to heat. The centre hosts various activities, such as Creepy Crawly Weeks and Spider Safaris. It sits in a network of lakes enjoyed by coots, herons, mallards and moorhens. Some anglers have thrown carp into the lakes from the canal and this predator has reduced the lakes' fish population. However, according to staff, the herons enjoy frogs as much as fish. The coots are easy to spot, with their brilliant white beaks and their short, staccato, percussive cry, which sounds a little like a dripping tap. Moorhens are smaller and have red beaks. Yellow flag iris grows along the edges; it is also known as Jacob's sword because of the blade-like character of the leaves.

Unfortunately, there has been a slightly comical problem with the Ecology Centre. Buildings used for public speaking are meant to have an echo of around one second, but acoustic technicians have discovered that the Ecology Centre has an echo of just over seven seconds. Thus a conversation at one end of the long, curved room can be heard at the other end, making meetings difficult at times.

The Palm Tree Pub

Cross the wooden bridge, noticing the willows that line the lakeshore, and continue over the second bridge. The wind turbine that you pass on your left powers a pump which circulates the water between the lakes.

Standing isolated in front of you is a real East End gem – the Palm Tree Pub, which dates from 1666 and does indeed have a palm outside. It survived demolition and is a throwback to the East End of the Krays, with an original interior that makes it a favoured place for location filming by film and television companies. At the time of writing, it even retained its manual cash register.

Follow the path leftward past the gates and into the short Haverfield Road. The delight-ful row of listed cottages here miraculously survived the Blitz and is now a treasured reminder of how much of this area once looked. Note the curved first-floor windows, the raised stoops and the elegant lamps – and indeed, the equally elegant street lights.

Return through the gates and follow the road around to the Mile End Climbing Wall, housed in an old pipe engineering works on the edge of the canal. Here, urban mountaineers can rope up and try their chalked hands at different artificial slabs and

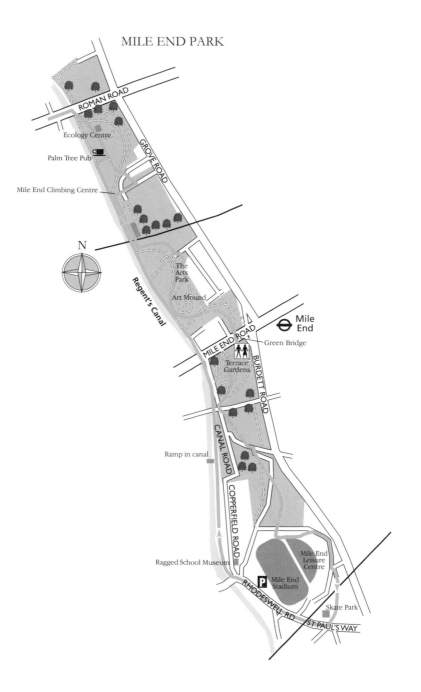

MILE END PARK

ROMAN ROAD

GROVE ROAD

Ecology Centre

Palm Tree Pub

Mile End Climbing Centre

N

Regent's Canal

The
Arts
Park

Art Mound

MILE END ROAD

Mile
End

Green Bridge

BURDETT ROAD

Terrace
Gardens

Ramp in canal

CANAL ROAD

COPPERFIELD ROAD

Ragged School Museum

Mile End
Leisure
Centre

Mile End
Stadium

RHODESWELL RD

Skate Park

ST PAUL'S WAY

overhangs, as well as indulging in 'bouldering' – short climbs without a rope, so called because it is often simply a large boulder that provides the challenge.

Skirt the edge of the climbing wall along the canal, pass under the railway bridge and then turn left to re-enter the park. Now climb up on to the grass area on your right.

The Arts Park

This is the ArtsPark, and, if you were in any doubt, two brightly coloured sculptures adorn the grass, looking like giant sweets. Like the Ecology Centre, the Arts Pavilion sits behind another artificial lake and is also an earth-covered building with rooftop pathways. During the summer and autumn various exhibitions are held here.

It is worth pausing on the grass to register the multiplicity of sights, the collision of old and new London. You are surrounded by change. To your right is the Grand Union Canal, its 19th-century warehouses long gone, now replaced by exclusive apartments. Formerly the Grand Junction Canal, it was laid out at the end of the 18th century and still links London to Birmingham. It became the Grand Union in 1929 after a merger between the Grand Junction, Regent and Warwick Canal companies. You may see a brightly painted barge, a reminder of when canals were of huge importance. The speed of a train behind you will demonstrate just why the canals' commercial importance faded. Above, planes begin their descent into London City Airport, while down on the canal path cyclists purr by. Ahead, the towers of Canary Wharf and the H.S.B.C. building show that it is not goods that are manufactured here anymore; it is the invisible world of commodities and shares – all too invisible during the banking crisis that began in 2009.

The Art Mound

Cross the gentle undulations of the lawn to the rise in the distance which has the silhou-ette of a church beyond. This is the Art Mound, described in the park's advertising as 'a dramatic topographical feature, the top of which can be accessed by means of a spiralling path or giant turf steps'. In reality, few use the giant turf steps which seem something of a gimmick, and, rather than showcasing art, the top is a rather forlorn affair, although it does give a good view, particularly of the 'green bridge'.

An information board here notes that this was the site of New Globe Tavern Gardens, 19th-century pleasure gardens from which ascents by hot-air balloonists would take place. On the canal, lovely willows frame Mile End Lock. The walk now drops down to reach the park's most innovative feature – the Green Bridge, also called 'the banana' because of its yellow underside.

The Green Bridge

Designed by Piers Gough, the modernist architect who described Prince Charles' opin-ions on architecture as 'baleful' in 2009, the Green Bridge is a bold, dramatic piece of work that creates an aerial park that sweeps over one of London's busiest roads. It has been described as 'growing' out of the landscape on one side and 'diving' into it on the other. Grass, shrubs and small trees cover the surface, alongside a footpath and cycleway.

The roots are contained within large fibreglass plant pots buried in the structure of the bridge, while rainwater runs off into tanks on either side from which it is pumped back on the bridge and recycled. This is necessary because the soil at the top of the bridge is slightly drier since it is at a higher level.

It opened in June 2000 with a performance of the 'Green Bridge Horn Concerto', an avant garde piece by contemporary composer Stephen Montague that involved 16 antique and modern cars, a bus, a dustcart, 15 cyclists and 15 pedestrians. Montague conducted them all from aboard a cherry picker which took him aloft so that everyone could see him. It was a suitably unconventional opening for an unconventional structure – one that went on to win the Institute of Civil Engineers Award of Merit as well as a commendation at the British Construction Industry Awards.

Yet the Green Bridge has its detractors who point out that its cycle lane is simply not used, most riders preferring to follow the canal path which passes under the Mile End Road. However, even they must admit that it is a brave solution to the problem of linking up the two halves of the park.

On your right is the Guardian Angels Roman Catholic Primary School where, in 1995, one of the first community planning weekend for the park took place. Piers Gough, then living locally, was at the meting, and it was here that he first heard the idea of a green bridge put forward by another resident. He could now argue, therefore, that if people don't like it, it is not entirely his fault.

From the crest of the span, to your right, you can see the rocket-shaped tower at 30 St Mary Axe, popularly called the 'gherkin', and the International Finance Centre. The contrast between the noise of the traffic below and the relative peace and quiet where you are standing is both surreal and pleasing. Beneath your feet are bars and restaurants, which help to finance the park, but you should focus on the lovely view ahead, which gives the impression that you are dropping down into a natural wood from which a forest of concrete, steel and glass emerges, the latter consisting of the towers of Canary Wharf.

The Terrace Garden

Follow the tree-lined slope and notice the terraced beds to your right, which are rich with shrubbery and drop down to a water feature. This Terrace Garden is well worth a little time for exploration, which you can do by turning right at the bottom of the slope. There are irises, heather and lavender, with rushes by the water, and the overall planting is designed to provide a range of colours, textural variety and scents which change and develop with the seasons.

Return to the main path and, opposite some horse chestnuts, turn left and walk diagonally across the open lawn to the far corner – easy to identify because Canary Wharf rises above it. Follow the path up the slope between an astro-turf pitch and an adventure playground. There is a London plane tree (*Platanus orientalis*) in a dip by the pitch. Note the old refurbished warehouse on the other side, with the name of the original company – Adam Ltd. Falcon Works – at the top. This is a typical scene in this part of London, as the grimy industrial past gives way to a 'latte and lifestyle' future.

Mile End Stadium

Turn left to skirt the famous Mile End Stadium, built in the 1950s on the site of the Edinburgh Castle, a music hall that was converted into a working men's club and people's mission hall. This was run by Dr. Barnado, the 19th-century philanthropist better known as the founder of homes for destitute children, and later for orphans. It was originally called the King George V Stadium, and took its current name after Sir Arthur Gold (1917–2002) officially opened its synthetic track on 9 September 1990. Gold was a leading figure in the administration of British athletics and a tireless campaigner against the use of drugs in sport. He was Chairman of the British Olympic Association from 1988 to 1992 and led British teams to the Mexico, Munich and Montreal games. It is an approved pre-Olympics training ground for athletes competing in the 2012 games close by, and it is home to the Victoria Harriers Athletics Club, the first club of triple jumper Phillips Idowu, who won a silver medal at the Beijing Olympics in 2008. There are fine views of Canary Wharf tower in the docklands.

Modern and Historic Graffiti

Follow the curve past Mile End Park Leisure Centre, which was refurbished in 2005–6 at a cost of £15 million, and exit in between mini-soccer pitches to pass under a railway arch which has a sanctioned graffiti wall for local street artists. Beyond the skate park, turn right along the road and notice the words 'George Davis is innocent' daubed in white at the top of the railway bridge. This refers to the man who was wrongly imprisoned in 1975 for an armed payroll robbery in Ilford, Essex, the previous year. After a high-profile campaign, supported by such celebrities as Roger Daltrey of The Who, he was released in 1976. In the 1980s he was tried and convicted of two further robberies. The words 'George Davis is innocent' are well known in London; they are seen on many road and railway bridges, but with the passage of the years more and more people have forgotten their origin.

The Ragged School Museum

Soon after the railway arch you come to the King George V gates on your right, which marks the entrance to what was once King George's Fields. His crest can be seen on the pillars. Across Copperfield Street is the Ragged School Museum, opened in 1990 in what was once the largest ragged school in London. These schools were so named because those who attended could not afford proper clothing. The museum gives a taste of what life was like for poor East End schoolchildren.

The Grand Union Canal

It is now possible to retrace your steps through the park, but it is more fun to walk alongside the canal which forms the park's western edge. Cross over the bridge and take the steps down to the towpath where you turn right. The park appears next to you, after the buildings, and as you walk along keep an eye on the water's edge. Before the Gunmakers Arms Bridge, you will see a stone ramp in the water, coming up to the towpath.

These ramps are a familiar site along the canal edges and were constructed to help the barge horses clamber out of the water if they fell in.

After the Gunmakers Bridge, you come to Mile End Bridge, and after that you will reach Mile End Lock. Note the listed lock-keeper's cottage and its extremely modern extension, and wonder, perhaps, as others have undoubtedly done before, how they ever got the necessary planning permission. People fish along the canal, catching carp, tench, roach and bream, the latter breeding in the deep water of Limehouse Basin.

There are clusters of rushes after the railway bridge where you may see the odd motionless heron, or the white question mark of a swan. Pass the back of the Palm Tree Pub and walk up on to the bridge over the Roman Road, where the walk ends.

DULWICH PARK

LOCATION	About 6¾ miles (11 kilometres) south of Charing Cross.
TRANSPORT	West Dulwich Station (overground from Victoria); North Dulwich Station (overground from London Bridge). Buses P4 (College Road) and P13 (Dulwich Common).
ADMISSION	Open daily, 08:00–dusk. Admission is free.
SEASONAL FEATURES	Rhododendrons in early summer; autumn tree colour.
EVENTS	Films in the park during the summer; Dig the Park on the first Saturday of the month; occasional open air Shakespeare; Dulwich Festival every summer.
REFRESHMENTS	Pavilion Café open Mon–Fri 08:30–17:30 hours, Sat and Sun 09:00–17:30 hours.

Nestling at the foot of the slopes of Crystal Palace in south London, beneath the Eiffel-like B.B.C. television tower, Dulwich Park is an elegant late-Victorian park that does much to make this exclusive London village one of the most desirable in the capital.

The land – originally farmland and a group of meadows known as Five Fields – was given to the Metropolitan Board of Works in 1883 by the Governors of Dulwich College school on condition that it was made a public park. The original design was the work of Charles Barry, Junior (1823–1900), whose father, Sir Charles Barry, was Architect and Surveyor to Dulwich College.

His design was amended and improved by Thomas Blashill, who was at that time the President of the Architectural Association, and went on to become Architect to London County Council. He gave the park a design that related more closely to nature, a scheme that favoured curves rather than straight lines. The horticulture was the responsibility of Lt.-Col. J. J. Sexby, Surveyor to the Metropolitan Board of Works, who was later to become London County Council's first Superintendent of Parks. Work began in January 1887, with the oak trees that lined the fields remaining in place, some of which can still be seen today. By October 1888, the artificial lake was ready, filled at a cost of £85, and the following month plans were drawn up for the park's two lodges.

The park was opened on 26 June 1890 by Lord Rosebery (1847–1929), the Chairman of London County Council, who served under Gladstone as Foreign Secretary and who became Prime Minister in 1894. Despite the dampening effect of the steady drizzle which continued until the afternoon, it was a grand occasion, with the park *en fête*. The South London Press described the scene thus: 'There was music, and a big crowd of well-dressed ladies and gentlemen, and guardians and vestrymen and policemen; indeed a right down genteel, aristocratic affair.' Standing on a 'cane-bottomed chair' inside the College Road entrance, Lord Rosebery declared 'In the name and by the authority of the London County Council, I have the great honour and satisfaction of declaring this park open, and dedicated to the service of the public for ever.' Although one of the chair legs was sinking into the rain-softened ground as he spoke, his lordship didn't falter; there were cheers and applause and the public flocked into the park. Lord Rosebery then addressed the schoolboys at Dulwich College, whose pupils would later include the writers P. G. Wodehouse and Raymond Chandler.

Today, the 72-acre (29-hectare) park is managed by Southwark Council, and run by a head gardener and apprentice, with four maintenance staff. It benefits from an extremely effective Friends group that organises voluntary work at the weekends and has successfully lobbied various bodies for grants. They have added a number of features to the park which are on the route of this walk, and their work shows just how much can be achieved if the grass-roots' (forgive the pun) will and support are there.

Dulwich Park received one of the Mayor's Green Flag awards for 2008–9, providing money for further improvements. Although aircraft beginning their descent into London City Airport are a regular reminder that central London is only a few miles away, this park actually gives the impression of being far from the city – and offers welcome relief from the urban mass of southeast London.

The proximity to the city makes this park popular for photo-shoots and filming. The commercial for a recent Julio Iglesias album was made here – which may, or may not, be an encouragement to visit the park, although no such added enticements are necessary.

THE DULWICH PARK WALK

Start and finish Old College Gate **Time** Allow 2 hours

Enter the park at Old College Gate, with its six grand pillars, redolent of the days of empire. The white building opposite is Old Dulwich College, completed in 1618. It bears the name Edward Alleyn House, after the Elizabethan actor manager who founded the charity Alleyn's College of God's Gift to provide education and accommodation for the poor of Dulwich Village. It became the original home of Dulwich College until the New College was opened in 1870, and is now an almshouse, as per Alleyn's original wish.

A 'Living Fossil'

The building on the left is College Lodge, the former home of the park's superintendent but sadly empty and boarded up at the time of writing. At the corner of the garden is a Tree of Heaven (*Ailanthus altissima*), with a dry, cracked trunk, like parched earth. This tree takes its name because, although not especially tall, *ailanto* comes from the Indonesian meaning 'reaching for the sky', while *altissima* is a Latin superlative meaning very high or tallest, from *alta*, meaning high.

At the end of the lawned area on the left is a dawn redwood (*Metasequoia*), easily recognised by its very straight trunk and delicate needles. These trees are known as 'living fossils' since the species dates back to prehistoric times. Continue up the grand Carriage Drive, crossing to the right to see a magnificent common oak (*Quercus robur*), one of the original oaks around which the park was laid out.

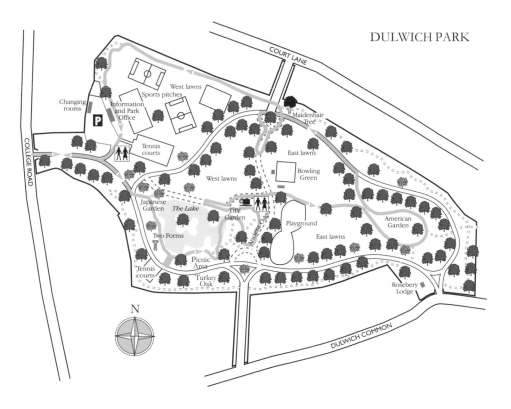

DULWICH PARK

Bear right at the gate and, just past the tree-covered traffic island, take the path on the left which brings you to the lakeside path. Busy beds include yellow iris (*Acorus*) and purple and white foxgloves.

The Barbara Hepworth Sculpture

Turn right and walk up to the bridge. On your right is the Japanese Garden, or, more accurately, the Victorian notion of a Japanese garden. The eye is drawn down beyond the water to the brilliant Japanese acer (*Acer palmatum*) by the other bridge. There are irises bordering the edge of the stream, while the view on the other side is across the lake and the West Lawns. On the left, at the lakeshore, is a weeping elm (*Ulmus glabra*), and, to the right, another of the park's ancient oaks.

Continue along the lake path. Opposite a splendid willow is Barbara Hepworth's *Two Forms (Divided Circle)*. This is a cast of the 1969 original, owned by the Tate Gallery, and was bought by the Greater London Council in 1970 for £15,000. The gallery explains that the sculpture's 'bifurcated form seems to draw the viewer in while the narrow spacing between the two halves denies a passage through'.

161

The Turkey Oak

Next to the willow is a tall, sweet gum (*Liquidambar styraciflua*), from the Latin *liquidas*, liquid, and *ambar*, amber, alluding to the fragrant resin obtained from the bark. Take the path to the right shortly after the sweet gum to see one of the park's most splendid trees – the enormous turkey oak (*Quercus cerris*), which is one of the Great Trees of London, as a plaque notes. The species was introduced to this country in 1735 and this example must have been planted soon after. It takes its name, so one theory has it, because its leaves resemble a turkey's foot. Gazing up into the branches of this fine specimen is dizzying.

Retrace your steps to the lake, noticing the '1500m' painted on the driveway for the benefit of runners. Continue to the right at the lake and, immediately on your right, in a small glade, is a pair of Caucasian wingnut trees (*Pterocarya fraxinifolia*), with their telltale hanging catkins and rather drooping, oblong leaves. This tree originates from the Caucasus Mountains and was introduced to the U.K. early in the 19th century. The female catkins are long and thread-like and strung with small seeds, each surrounded by a whitish-green papery wing, hence its name.

Opposite the wingnuts is the small Japanese Peace Garden, its pillar inscribed with the words 'May Peace Prevail on Earth'. This is one of a number of such gardens in the capital, provided by Japanese religious bodies. There are yuccas here, and beyond these the dense shrubbery has been cut back to reveal the oak by the water's edge. The paler yellow irises you may see are *Pseudo-acorus*. Note also the goose-proof fencing!

A little further along, take a short detour to the picnic area on your right. Beyond the tables and leaning over Carriage Drive is a golden catalpa (*Catalpa bignonioides* 'Aurea'), the glowing variation of the common Indian bean tree, sometimes called the cigar tree because of the shape of its long, hanging seed pods.

Now retrace your steps to cross the boardwalk, one of the park's best features.

The Boardwalk and Lake

Built in 2006, the Boardwalk snakes across the water and affords good views of the lake's wildlife and ecology. In the same year, thanks to a lottery grant, the lake was cleared and destocked, and a pump put in to circulate the water (this pump was still being fine-tuned in 2009). Careful planting was introduced to control the algae. The reeds, which include *Typha minor* and *Typha major*, suck out the nutrients in the water on which the algae feeds, and also provide habitat for wildlife.

Stop in the centre, by the decking platform. If you look across the water to the far island you can see an artificial sandy cliff with concealed holes to encourage kingfishers. Little grebes also breed on the lake, as well as the familiar emerald-necked mallards, who often sit on the wide banister. Other birds seen in the park include nuthatch, black caps, chiffchaff, willow warbler, whitethroat and both the green and the greater spotted woodpecker.

Looking the other way, across the decking, you can see purple loosestrife (*Lythrum salicaria*), an ordinary enough plant with a long and fascinating history. *Lythrum* is from the Greek *lythron*, meaning gore, from the purple colour of the flowers, and *salicaria* is from *salix*, meaning willow, from the shape of the leaves.

Purple loosestrife has many names – purple grass, herb willow, long purples, purple loose-strife, red Sally, soldiers and spiked willow herb. In John Clare's poem 'Village Minstrel', it is called long purples: 'Gay long-purples with its tufty spike She'd wade o'er shoes to reach it in the dyke'.

Toward the end of the boardwalk, you can see water forget-me-not, water veronica and watercress. As you leave it, take the path opposite, which runs straight ahead and then curves to the right.

A Quirky Quercus

Pass through the gate into the Nature Conservation Area where the grass has been left wild. Follow the cinder path, passing a copper beech (*Fagus sylvatica purpurea*) on the right. On your left you come to one of the park's most unusual trees – an oak – which is a favourite of head gardener, Ric Glenn. One branch has fallen away, taking a third of the trunk with it as it fell. In the cavity that remains you can see an aerial root that looks like a giant parsnip, or a cream-coloured stalactite. The tree has put down a root into itself, believing its own base to be the earth.

The line of gnarled oaks to your right probably marks one of the original boundaries of the Five Fields. Follow this line to what you could call the 'toilet oak'. This last tree is probably the most splendid of them all, despite its location next to the public conveniences. Opposite is a collapsed Indian bean tree (*Catalpa bignoniodes*), which makes a perfect low-level climbing frame for children while their parents are in the café.

The Dry Garden

Now pass to the left, around the back of the café, and take the little gap in the border just before the pale-barked cider gum (*Eucalyptus gunni*), a native of Tasmania and a tree that provided the only alcohol enjoyed by Aborigines before the arrival of the Europeans.

Turn immediately right and right again to find the Dry Garden with its lizard sculpture in the floor, laid out by children at the Dulwich Festival in 2008. The planting here includes lamb's ear (*Stachys Byzantium*), hardy geraniums (*Pratense* and *Endressii*), raised beds of *Euphorbia Wulfenii*, the pale grass *Miscanthus sinensis*, cat mint ('cat nip', from Nepeta) and the yellow flowering *Phlomus russeliana* by the palm.

After exploring the garden, walk a short way down past the first shelter for another view of the lake. Boats may be hired in the summer although, as this book went to press, tenders from new operators were being considered.

The American Garden

Retrace your steps and pass the front of the café. Cross the lane and follow the signs for the American Garden. There is a view across the playground and the East Lawns to your right, up to the Norwood hills and the B.B.C. television tower at Crystal Palace, built in 1956 and some 719 feet (219 metres) high.

At the next junction take the right-hand path. Planted in 1890–91, the American Garden – actually a rhododrendron garden – is less formal than many Victorian gardens.

The emphasis is on curves, on reflecting nature itself which, as the saying goes, abhors right angles. Sexby (*see* page 159) was influenced by the work of garden designers Gertrude Jekyll and William Robinson, and included many species from the U.S.A. Follow the path straight ahead, ignoring the path by the large oak to the right. This takes you deep into the rhododendron garden, one that rivals the Isabella Plantation in Richmond Park (*see* page 123).

Follow the path that forms an oval, passing the wooden shelter which replaced the thatched original from the 1930s. There is a hidden glade in a slight dip to your left. There are silver birch here, older ones on the edge and younger ones within. It is a delicate tree, rather brittle – which is why you see so many broken ones.

When you return to the entrance to the American Garden, turn right. Just before you meet Carriage Drive, there is a lovely acacia on the left, with glorious white flowers in May and June. This one has a deeply crevassed, twisting trunk.

Turn left on Carriage Drive which has more ancient oaks. Unusually, this park does not have many London planes – contrast this Drive with Victoria Park – although you soon meet one on the right with its familiar camouflage-like bark.

The Maidenhair Tree

Continue along Carriage Drive until you see a large horse chestnut on your right, almost at the crossroads where turning right takes you to Court Lane Gate, and left takes you down Snakes Lane towards the café. There is an innocuous-looking tree here that it is worth taking the time to find. The maidenhair tree (*Gingko biloba*) is one of nature's most unusual species. It is the first tree on the right, after the horse chestnut, just before the left turn and just past the '900m' marker on the road. It lies at the edge of the longer grass, approximately 20 feet (6 metres) from the road.

Maidenhair trees are among the oldest trees on the planet. They may be relatively common on our streets, but they should not be taken for granted. This Asiatic species is known as a 'living fossil' because 65 million-year-old gingko fossils have been found in the U.S.A. and Canada. Gingko is from the Chinese *yin-kuo*, meaning 'silver apricot' and refers to the edible inner kernel of the seeds. *Biloba* is from the Latin *bilobus*, meaning two-lobed, a reference to its leaves.

It takes its common name from the fact that its fan-shaped leaves resemble the maidenhair fern, but that only begs the question, why is the maidenhair fern so called? There is nothing more fascinating than how trees and plants get their common names. The Latin name for the maidenhair fern is *Adiantum capillus-veneris*. *Adiantum* is from the Greek *adiantos*, meaning 'not wetting' and refers to the fern's ability to shed water without getting wet. *Capillus* is Latin for hair and *veneris* means the goddess Venus. The roots of the fern have fine and delicate hairs, like the hair of Venus. So, the literal meaning is 'Venus's hair' which, over time, became 'maiden's hair'.

These trees are tough maidens indeed. They have developed a resistance to most pests and diseases, allowing them a very long lifespan – one tree in China is thought to be around 3,000 years old. Several are also know to have survived the atomic bomb that devastated Hiroshima, Japan, in 1945.

Gingko leaf extract is believed to have medicinal properties, with traditional Chinese medicine using it to improve health, circulation, memory and attentiveness. According to Kew Gardens, clinical trials have yet to prove conclusive, but the value of worldwide sales of Gingko biloba is estimated at a staggering half a billion U.S. dollars a year.

The Winter Garden

Turn left after the green traffic island, and then immediately right on the sandstone paving slabs. This brings you into the Winter Garden, a gift of the Dulwich Park Friends in 2002. The aim was to provide winter colour. The plants here include Winter Beauty (*Cornus alba sanguinea*), pampas grass (*Cortaderia selloana*) and the scented *Daphne bholua*. Explore at your leisure and then return to Carriage Drive, cross straight over and head across the grass to the park edge where you turn left.

Now follow this grassy, tree-lined avenue, with the park fence on your right. Trees here include lime, copper beech, ash, young oak and sycamore. There are sports fields on your left and views down to the Francis Peek Information Centre, named after the Victorian tea merchant who lived close by and who gave his support (and money) when the park was being planned.

The Village Copse

Just before the end of the main path, take the smaller path on the left, between fairly young poplar trees. You are now in the Village Copse, established in 2007 by the Dulwich Village Preservation Society. The path snakes along to reach a miniature meadow with seats. The grass has been kept deliberately long, to encourage wild flowers and insects, and a view has been created across the lawns.

Keep to the path and at the end you may see on the right, amid the long grass, the delicate nodding heads of snake's head fritillary (*Fritillaria meleagris*), one of the U.K.'s relatively rare wild flowers. The head gardener planted 10,000 in the park during 2008.

Walk to the left of the Information Centre and pass the offices of Recumbent Bikes, with all manner of unusual bicycles for hire, including the yellow 'banana bikes', which look rather like go-karts. On the subject of unusual vehicles, if you see a red truck trundling across the lawns with 'FIDO' written on it, you may wonder what it is. F.I.D.O. stands for Faeces Intake Disposal Operative. So now you know.

This path rejoins Carriage Drive where you turn right and return to Old College Gate where the walk ends.

CANNIZARO PARK

LOCATION	About 9½ miles (15.2 kilometres) southwest of Charing Cross.
TRANSPORT	Wimbledon Station (overground from Waterloo, and District Line Underground) is a 20-minute walk; bus 93.
ADMISSION	Mon–Fri 08:00–dusk; Sat, Sun, Bank holidays 09:00–dusk.
SEASONAL FEATURES	Spring crocuses and bluebells; summer rhododendrons and azaleas; autumn tree colour.
EVENTS	Occasional open-air theatre; Cannizaro Festival (depending on sponsorship).
REFRESHMENTS	Café open Sun 14:00–18:00 hours.

Lying like a giant green necklace on the edge of Wimbledon Common, the beautiful, slightly mysterious Cannizaro Park is probably the least-known park in this book. In fact, it is so tucked away, and its entrance so nondescript, that many pass it by, understandably lured by the delights of Wimbledon Village. They are missing the opportunity to experience one of the capital's finest collections of trees and to discover secret garden upon secret garden, curious follies, surprising sculptures and hidden walkways. This is a park that taps you on shoulder and whispers, 'Let's see what's around *this* corner'.

It all begins with a spelling mistake. The park takes its name from the Duke and Duchess of Cannizzaro who lived in Cannizaro House (now the Cannizaro House Hotel) between 1817 and 1841. After the couple died, local officials referred to the house by their name, but could never get the spelling correct, and 'Cannizaro' finally became the accepted version in 1874.

The house itself dates from the early 18th century, when it was known as Warren House. It was built by William Browne, a wealthy London merchant, who lived in a large mansion house close by and leased Warren House to affluent friends – an early example of the buy-to-let phenomenon so common today.

This pattern continued for many years with the occupants of Cannizaro House invariably being wealthy or distinguished, or both. They included M.P.s and future Prime Ministers. The Scottish M.P. and socialite Henry Dundas, Viscount Melville, who was a close associate of Prime Minister William Pitt, lived there from 1785 to 1806. He liked to entertain, and Pitt was a frequent visitor. During walks in the grounds they thrashed out the problems of the day, including the war with France. He married Lady Jane Hope and celebrated the wedding by planting Lady Jane Wood which still exists today.

George III visited the house when reviewing the troops on the Common and, in 1801, enjoyed 'a glass of Mr. Dundas's excellent Madeira to the health, the happiness and the prosperity of the inhabitants of this house'.

In 1801 the new Prime Minister, Henry Addington, took up residence at Cannizaro House and in 1806 it became the home of the future Prime Minister, George Gordon, Earl of Aberdeen. Then, in 1817 the Duke and Duchess of Cannizzaro arrived. Born in Sicily as Francis Platamone, Count Saint Antonio, the Duke is believed to have taken his title from the little village of Cannizzaro, which lies on Sicily's eastern coast. The Duke's wife, Sophia, was, by all accounts, not very bright, but vivacious and good-humoured, and had a passionate interest in music.

As in Melville's time, the house once again became well known for its parties. The Duchess hosted frequent concerts at the house, occasionally hiring operatic stars of the day to perform works by Rossini. Guests at one concert included the Duke of Wellington and Napoloeon's brother, Lucien. An echo of these concerts has been enjoyed at the annual Cannizaro Festival, at which singers such as Elkie Brooks and Katriona Taylor have performed, as well as comedians Bill Bailey and Jimmy Carr.

From 1879 to 1896 the widow of Leo Schuster, a director of the Union Bank of London and Chairman of the London and Brighton Railway, lived at the house. She hosted garden parties at which guests included the Prince and Princess of Wales and the writers Henry James and Oscar Wilde.

During World War I the house was used as a convalescent home for wounded soldiers. In 1920, the most important chapter in the long history of Cannizaro began when the house and park were bought by Kenneth Wilson, a wealthy businessman from Hull, whose family were ship-owners. Wilson and his wife, Adela, moved from Yorkshire to Cannizaro, bringing with them the wrought-iron gates that bear the family monogram. They were both keen gardeners and members of the Royal Horticultural Society and the Rhododendron Association. They employed a landscape architect and a head gardener and created rhododendron, camellia and magnolia walks, and they funded plant-hunting expeditions to the Far East that brought back rare trees.

The park was used by the Home Guard during World War II and became neglected. The Wilsons died just after the war and their daughter Hilary sold the house and 34 acres (13.7 hectares) to the Corporation of Wimbledon for £40,000 in 1948. The park was opened to the public later that year, while the house was used as an old people's home from 1950 to 1977. It then fell empty until, in 1985, after much debate over its future, it was sold to Thistle Hotels, who opened it as 'London's first country house hotel'.

Today, its terrace remains one of the loveliest places to take (expensive) afternoon tea – and during that particular fortnight at the end of June you may find yourself sharing it with a famous tennis player or two.

THE CANNIZARO PARK WALK

Start and finish Park Gates **Time:** Allow 2 hours

The walk begins at the park gates that bear the monogram of the Wilson family. Almost immediately you come to a delightful fountain that could be straight out of *Alice in Wonderland*. It takes the form of a multi-spouted tea pot, which fascinates children, and was installed here to celebrate the new millennium. It is the work of Richard Rome, who used to teach sculpture at Wimbledon School of Art.

Follow the path until you reach the 'Gothick' aviary, built in the 1970s by park staff and apparently modelled on an Italian cathedral, although no one is sure whether it is Pisa or Turin. Turn left, passing a splendid oriental plane tree (*Platanus orientalis*) on your right, and note the enormous magnolia tree (*Magnolia delavayi*) at the corner of the house.

An Arboreal Theatre

Make your way to the central path which bisects the lawns. The view here is superb. It is like standing in a grand arboreal theatre and it is hard to believe that central London is only 8 miles (12.8 kilometres) away. Follow the path down. The two fir-like trees ahead of you are both Brewer's weeping spruce (*Pica breweriana*), from the Siskiyou Mountains in California, and named after the American plant explorer, William Henry Brewer. The much larger tree to the right, with star-like triplets of leaves at the ends of its branches, is a shagbark hickory (*Carya ovata*) from the eastern U.S.A. Mature specimens have loose, shaggy bark, hence the name. Its nuts are edible and the word 'hickory' is derived from *pawcohiccora*, the Algonquin Indian word for the tree's oily nutmeat.

Continue down the steps to the pond, passing an ivy-covered swamp cypress (*Taxodium distichum*). Look for one of its knobbly roots, rising like a knee near the water's edge. Roots like these are called pneumatophores, and rise above the water level in order to reach the air. The pond is sheltered by oaks which reflect in the water.

The Kitchen Garden

Pass through the gates into a walled garden, formerly the Kitchen Garden, where produce was grown for residents of the house in its heyday. In the 1950s glasshouses stood here, growing flowers for municipal displays in the borough of Wimbledon. Today, this is a picnic area, although a hint of the lower Italian Garden has been created in the top right-hand corner with a cluster of olive trees. Also, the warm colour of the wall here – the original Kitchen Garden wall – gives it a slightly Tuscan feel.

In the far left corner is a glory tree (*Clerodendrum trichotomum*), a native of China and Japan, and believed to have medicinal properties. Some say its flowers smell like lemon-scented towels, while its name may refer to the sepals that surround its turquoise berries like a four-pointed star.

The Italian Garden

Pass through the hedge to find the Italian Garden, where there this park's magical atmosphere begins to take hold. Note the gate in the wall, through which it is very easy to imagine an Edwardian gardener appearing. Blue-berried mahonia grows in the bed to the left. Drop down into the garden proper, with its wood and brick arbor covered with climbing roses and wisteria.

Take the central path between a pair of swamp cypresses from the southeastern U.S.A. Opposite these, on the right-hand border, is a sweet buckeye (*Aesculus flava*), with

Marble Hill Park: *Designed as an Arcadian retreat from the noise of 18th-century London, Marble Hill House still retains a sense of peace and grandeur*

Victoria Park: *Tranquil reflections in Regent's Canal*

Dulwich Park: *Japanese gardens were popular with Victorians and this one forms a green corridor along a little stream*

Mile End Park: *The Ecology Centre's wind turbine which powers a water pump to circulate the lake water*

Dulwich Park: *This cast of Barbara Hepworth's 1969* Two Forms (Divided Circle)
creates new perspectives as you pass

Cannizaro Park: *The formal beauty of the Sunken Garden by Cannizaro House Hotel*

Lincoln's Inn: *Lavender beds help keep London's traffic fumes at bay and provide a pleasing sheen of colour*

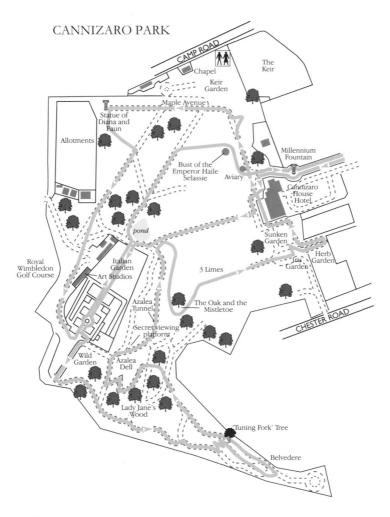

CANNIZARO PARK

chestnut-like leaves. Also from the southeastern U.S.A., it takes its name from the resemblance of the seeds to the brown eye of a buck (male deer).

Drop down again on to the lower terrace, which has a faded grandeur. It is all silent balconies, cracked stone balustrades, missing pillars, empty beds, lonely urns and a circular stone base, its statue long gone. It is as if everybody has just upped and left, as in the famous Lost Gardens of Heligan in Cornwall. On weekdays during term time this garden can be very quiet – what visitors there are in the park tend to stay up near the hotel – and it is possible to be alone in these lower sections; just you and those watching trees.

It is almost disappointing to discover that this Italian Garden is entirely fake, created by the council in the 1970s using young, would-be bricklayers working on a Youth Training Scheme. There are certainly those who feel that the house's original Kitchen

Garden should have been recreated and its derelict greenhouses rebuilt – but, as ever, it is all a question of funding. Yet there is still an appealing, slightly melancholy atmosphere in what has been created, which feeds the imagination.

The Wild Garden

Pass through the final gate to find yourself in another area with an atmosphere all of its own. On the left is the Wild Garden, a kind of green dell behind an old metal fence with woodland rising majestically behind. It has a lush display of plants – acers, primroses, rhododendrons, azaleas, magnolias and, in front of the third of a line of oak trees, a snow-drop tree (*Halesia carolina*), famous for its pendulous white flowers.

On the right is a Wet Garden, along the banks of a little, hidden stream. There are two young swamp cypresses here amid some astounding gunnera whose enormous leaves look like giant, upturned umbrellas.

Cross the little stone bridge, which marks the deepest point of the park, and take the right-hand path past the Berlin poplar (*Populus berolinensis*). Close to the bridge, there are a pair of firs with red trunks: you should pass the one with the single trunk and the nesting box. Follow this shady path with rhododendrons to your left, among them some young Perfect Lady and Silver Skies. Keep to the right, passing two pale-barked black pines (*Pinus nigra*) beyond which you soon reach one of the park's oldest trees, an enormous common oak (*Quercus robur*), with its deeply crevassed trunk.

The Mediterranean Garden and Belvedere

After the oak, take the log-lined, zigzag path on the left which brings you up into the light and into the Mediterranean Garden. Note the comical black pine at the top of the path, which looks like a giant tuning fork. Black pines are resistant to salt water and are often found by the coast in southern Europe. They like full sun and you can almost feel them reaching up to the light on this slope of the park. Gaze up into their crown against a blue sky and, just for a second, you might feel as if you are at the coast.

Turn right at the top and, just beyond another black pine, you will pass beneath the branches of a pagoda tree (*Sophora japonica*), so called because they are often found outside Buddhist temples in Japan.

A curious monument, like a small, abandoned Greek temple, now appears through the trees. This is the Belvedere, 'a raised structure with a fine scenic view', built as a folly in the 1980s with pillars that were brought from another park. Even though this is fake, a mysterious mood has been achieved in this tucked-away corner of the park that is redolent of the Greek island described by John Fowles in *The Magus*. Nothing is happening, and yet it can seem as if something is about to happen.

Lady Jane's Wood

Retrace your steps along the path and beyond the 'tuning fork' pine you walk through ferns, rhododendrons and oak to enter Lady Jane's Wood. At the first junction, marked by two oaks, turn left and drop down a dark path beneath holly, laurel and rhododendrons.

There are badgers on these slopes and in 1999 the size of the main sett was estimated to extend underground for more than 1,600 feet (500 metres).

Turn right at the bottom and then take the first right, on a path that has a triplet of oaks stretching away from you. At the second oak, take the stone steps to the right which lead to a secret viewing platform with two sculpted 'stacks' marking its entrance. Continue up the steps and pass through an azalea tunnel. The path snakes up until you turn left at the top. Carry straight on at the junction beneath giant laurel and go into a rhododendron tunnel which brings you out close to the pond.

The South Lawn and Iris Garden

Turn right passing an Indian horsechestnut (*Aesculus indica*) from the Himalayas, with its pinkish candles rising high in June. Keeping the trees to your right, walk along the lawn until you come to a wild meadow area, where you will find in the grass a sculpture from 1993 called *The Oak and the Mistletoe*. Cannizaro Park has a tradition of showing works of art, especially pieces by students at Wimbledon College of Art.

Walk across the lawn to the three limes in the middle of the grass. Here, turn right and head for the path at the edge of the longer grass, peeling off to the right as you reach it to make for the clearing.

Make your way between hollies into the Iris Garden, another one of Cannizaro's tucked-away little treasures. There is a classical urn in the centre, and on the far side is a magnificent cork oak (*Quercus suber*), with its unmistakable gnarled trunk. The thick bark can be harvested every nine to 12 years without harm to the tree since it grows back. It was once believed that cork could prevent cramp, and sufferers would sleep with cork beneath their pillows.

The Sunken Garden and Herb Garden

Retrace your steps, turn right by the leaning Holm oak and make your way to the pretty sunken garden by the side of the hotel. Planting in the beds here includes petunias, patience, marigolds, asters, lavender and English roses. There are benches with interesting and touching dedications and, on the left, the Mayor's Tree – a *Magnolia acuinata*, sometimes called a cucumber tree because of the shape of its seed pods. It was planted on 2 April 1949 by the Mayor of Wimbledon to mark Cannizaro's opening as a 'public pleasure ground'.

The row of narrow cottages that can be seen behind the high wall were built in 1770 and are among the oldest in Wimbledon. A triplet of gnarled acacias leads into the Herb Garden whose gates have twin dogs, possibly put there by the Wilsons who had a number of dogs. This is a lovely secret, walled garden that you can often enjoy in solitude. Herbs here include varieties of thyme, feverfew, St. John's wort, evening primrose and Roman chamomile. There is an elegant brick and slab path, and an ancient gate and seating area.

After exploring the herb garden, make your way across the front of the hotel and past the aviary which has a huge Atlantic cedar (*Cedrus atlantica*) on the far side.

The Pet Cemetery

Follow the path through rhododendrons (yet more!) until you come to a fallen tree trunk on your right with a small meadow behind. At the time of writing, it was possible – but not easy – to scramble in and see the remains of the Wilsons' pet cemetery. If you want to take a look, enter the shrubbery behind the tree marked 'Forty', follow the path to the left and turn left at the park wall. There is a leaning tree here, so you may have to come back a few feet to scramble through. The dogs' headstones lie in a sad jumble. Two read: 'Vic My Friend, Aged 12 Years'; 'My Susie, June 1936, Aged 10 and a half years'. It is easy to imagine them gambolling in what must surely have been the ultimate garden for dogs.

Statues and Cottages

Return to the path by the tree trunk and at the junction turn left and head for the white statue in the distance. Note the Australian *Eucalyptus dalrympleana* to your right, with its gleaming, bleached bark. It was planted in 1990 and is estimated to grow approximately 40 inches (1 metre) every year. The house glimpsed through the trees was built around 1838 for a Catholic priest who used to conduct services in a neighbouring chapel. The Wilsons were great supporters of the Scouts and Guides movements and allowed them to use their land. This continues to this day, with a local Brownies pack running a tea garden here during summer weekends.

Follow the avenue of maples, planted in the 1920s and 1930s by Wilson, which perfectly frames the statue of Diana. On your right you pass a walled rose garden, once part of the adjoining house called The Keir. A Golden-rain tree (*Koelreuteria paniculata*) spreads over the beds, and another 19th-century cottage seems to grow out of the park wall. This one was built for The Keir's gardener and is now privately owned.

The statue of Diana and the faun dates from 1841 and originally stood at the back of the house. Turn left here and notice a fabulous oak with a hollow trunk on your left; where branches have fallen away there are holes, and children love to play here. Return to the path where there is a ghostly cedar (*Cedrus Atlantica*), which seems to glow at twilight. Turn right and, after more cedars, notice on your left, at the edge of the lawn, a Roble beech (*Northofagus obliqua*), very tall and straight, with drooping branches touching the lawn. This is the fastest-growing hardwood in the U.K.

Artistic Peace

Continue your descent until a long single-storey building appears on your left, marked by an ancient oak. This used to house the garden nursery and is now home to Cannizaro Studios, whose occupants usually include woodworkers, sculptors, potters and painters. Looking up from the studios, back up the path down which you have just walked, you can see what must be one of Wimbledon's most delightful houses – a pretty cottage, tucked away by itself. No one is certain, but there is some evidence that one of Cannizaro's butlers lived here. There used to be a dairy at the back, and some of the original tiling and slate benches for cooling and separating the milk still remain. The house has the same postal address as the hotel and occasionally each receives the other's mail.

Head down across the lawn, with Royal Wimbledon Golf Course away to your right, and follow the lawn around to the left to re-enter the Italian Gardens. Enjoy the curious lost atmosphere of this garden again and make your way up to the pond, where you should turn left, then right, behind the bamboo that skirts the pond.

An Unexpected Visitor

Walk up the slope through the trees and as you near the top, take a rough path to your right which heads into bamboo. On your left is a Caucasian wingnut (*Pterocarya fraxinfolia*), which gets its common name from the fact that on its hanging catkins each seed has its own whitish-green wing.

In a clearing to your right, where a tennis court once stood, is something rather unexpected: a bust of the Emperor Haile Selassie of Ethiopia (1930–75). This secret corner of Wimbledon has become a Rastafarian pilgrimage point, particularly on 23 July, the emperor's birth date. Haile Selassie took refuge in London in 1936 when the Italians invaded his country. He stayed near to Cannizaro at the Wimbledon home of Sir Richard Seligman, a leading metallurgist and entrepreneur. Seligman's wife, Hilda, was a sculptor and active campaigner against the British appeasement of the Italian invasion. During his stay, the Emperor sat for Hilda, and the result was the bust that now adorns this quiet glade. It was restored in 2005 and was unveiled at a ceremony attended by descendants of both the Emperor and the sculptor.

Retrace your steps, keeping the shrubs and beds to your right, pass a collapsed tree trunk and join the path where you turn right. This leads back up to the aviary where you turn left for the park gates where the walk ends.

LINCOLN'S INN FIELDS, LINCOLN'S INN AND INNER TEMPLE GARDENS

LOCATION	About 1 mile (1.6 kilometres) northeast of Charing Cross.
TRANSPORT	Holborn Underground Station (Central Line and Piccadilly Line); buses: 19, 59, 68, 91, 168, 171, 243.
ADMISSION	Lincoln's Inn Fields: open 08:00–dusk; Lincoln's Inn Gate and Wildy & Sons Archway: open Mon–Fri 07:00–19:00 hours; Inner Temple Gardens: open Mon-Fri 12.30–15:00 hours.
SEASONAL FEATURES	Spring colour on Foxglove Trees in Lincoln's Inn Fields; year-round colour in Lincoln's Inn and Inner Temple Gardens.
EVENTS	Regular guided tours of Lincoln's Inn; occasional concerts in Inner Temple Gardens.
REFRESHMENTS	Many cafés close to Lincoln's Inn Fields; Terrace in the Fields restaurant (booking required, tel: 020 7430 1234)

This walk begins in the rough-edged democratic scruffiness of Lincoln's Inn Fields, one of London's most pummelled squares, and ends in the tidy formality of the Inner Temple. On the way it passes through one of the capital's best preserved 17th-century squares.

Lincoln's Inn Fields is one of the oldest open spaces in London, and was reputedly one of the inspirations for New York's Central Park, whose co-designer, Calvert Vaux, was born in England and studied in London. It dates back to the 14th century when two 'waste common fields' were used for recreation by students from the neighbouring Lincoln's Inn, one of the Inns of Court. Lincoln's Inn itself is believed to have been named either after Thomas de Lyncoln, the King's Serjeant of Holborn, or from Henry de Lacy, 3rd Earl of Lincoln, whose family acquired land nearby.

During the 16th century, the Fields were used for executions, among them those of the Roman Catholic martyrs, Robert Morton and Hugh More, in 1588. Although fashionable housing began to be built around its edges, the square itself remained a place of danger. In his *Trivia*, published in 1716, the poet and dramatist John Gay wrote: 'Where Lincoln's Inn, wide space, is rail'd around/ Cross not with venturous step; there oft is found/The lurking thief ...'.

There were proposals to build on the land over the years, but the Society of Lincoln's Inn and the adjoining parishes always objected, believing that 'for their general Commoditie and health [the fields should be] converted into walkes' – an idea which was supported by Charles I. However, in the 1630s one William Newton of Befordshire persuaded the king to allow 32 houses to be built, but with the proviso that most of the fields should 'for ever and hereafter remain open and unbuilt'. It was that agreement which gave the Fields the shape they have today.

The Fields are managed by the London Borough of Camden. During the 1980s the square acquired a dubious fame because of the number of homeless sleeping there. It resembled a shanty town. In 1992 the square was cleared and new railings erected. In marked contrast, Lincoln's Inn and the Inner Temple are tidier and more formal. They each have their own management and to walk through these Inns of Court is to enter a strange, enclosed world; one steeped in tradition and encrusted with history. They are described thus: 'The Inns of Court are ancient unincorporated bodies of lawyers which for five centuries and more have had the power to call to the Bar those of their members who have duly qualified for the rank or degree of Barrister-at-Law.' They are called Inns because they offered hospitality to their members.

An extraordinary atmosphere pervades these Inns of Court – part Oxbridge, part freemasonry, and all with a dollop of Harry Potter.

THE LINCOLN'S INN FIELDS, LINCOLN'S INN AND INNER TEMPLE GARDENS WALK

Start Remnant Street **Finish** Temple Underground Station **Time** Allow 1½ hours

The walk begins at the northwest corner of Lincoln's Inn Fields, opposite Remnant Street. As you face the square, look down its right-hand side. You can see Nos. 57 and 58, with a curved balcony. Charles Dickens' friend and eventual biographer, John Forster lived at No. 58, and it was here, in December 1844, that Dickens read his Christmas story, *The Chimes*, to a group of friends.

The dilapidated water fountain was here in Dickens' day. It dates from 1861 and bears the inscription: 'The fear of the Lord is a fountain of hope'. Enter the square and turn left. You soon come to a lovely statue and seat commemorating Margaret MacDonald, the feminist and social reformer, who was wife of the first Labour Prime Minister, Ramsay MacDonald. It shows her with nine children, her arms outstretched protecting them. Margaret and Ramsay lived at No. 3 Lincoln's Inn Fields, which is where she died in 1911. Behind the statue is Sir John Soane's Museum, which boasts an unusual and eclectic collection of antiquities and works of art, housed in the architect's home. He bequeathed his collection to the nation in 1833 and died in 1837.

The B.B.C.'s *Time Team* excavated in the Fields in 2009 and found evidence that refugees came here during the Great Fire of London. Charred timber posts were found deep in the ground.

On the corner of the first right-hand path there is a *Paulownia tomentosa*, more commonly known as a Foxglove Tree because of the similarity of its large, bell-like flowers to those of foxgloves. It has huge leaves like green handkerchiefs. This species is named for Anna Paulowna (1795–1865), daughter of Tsar Paul I of Russia.

Symbols of London

Turn right here and head down to the bandstand, noticing the tall, thin, maidenhair tree (*Gingko biloba*) on your right, just before the rose beds. This spacious central area may be slightly scruffy, but it does boast some of the finest, and oldest, plane trees (*Platanus acerifolia*) in the capital. The nine trees here were planted early in the 19th century and their enormous, spreading branches turn this piazza into an arboreal cathedral. The tree on your right as you enter is particularly impressive, since pollarding has spread its branches out very wide.

The plane tree is arguably a symbol of London and it is famous for its ability to cope with pollution which it absorbs and then passes out through its bark which it sheds, as if it was a large, vertical, moulting snake.

Take the exit on the left, passing beneath what is possibly the square's oldest plane tree – its trunk has the most enormous girth – and stop to wonder what it might have witnessed during its lifetime.

The Bamboo Garden

Turn right into a delightful, but somewhat under-appreciated eastern-style bamboo garden. On your left is a *Fatsia japonica*, also known as the glossy-leaved paper plant. This is an evergreen shrub that grows well in shade. Follow the little winding path through a veritable mini-Kew, passing the tree fern *Dicksonia antarctica*, named after the British botanist James Dickson (1738–1822). Little gardens-within-a-garden such as this are a great credit to the gardeners of London's parks.

On emerging, turn immediately left and walk across the grass to the path where, opposite, is the Coronation Magnolia, planted in 1953 to celebrate the coronation of Queen Elizabeth II. Facing the tree, turn right and walk down to the gates where, on the right, is a Dry Garden which includes *Ophiopogon planiscarpus nigescens*, the Latin mouthful more commonly known as black grass.

Exit through the gates, passing another drinking fountain (this one from 1880) and cross to the main gate of Lincoln's Inn opposite. Note the lion and shield above the doorway, the symbol of Lincoln's Inn. Each Inn of Court has its own symbol: the lamb and flag for the Middle Temple and the Pegasus for the Inner Temple.

The Best Lawns

Keep to the left-hand pavement until you reach the grass, where you should take the left-hand path beneath an avenue of planes, believed to be at least 150 years old. These trees are undoubtedly magnificent, but they pose a problem in May, when their bauble-like seed pods burst and the air becomes full of fine seeds. During this time the gardeners wear masks when working here.

The Great Hall is now on your left. The barristers are allowed to dine here, while the Inn's three gardeners and other staff eat down in the basement. The gardeners refer to the lawns in this area as the Best Lawns or the Bencher's Lawns (after the barristers' original seat in court). The Benchers' Border includes two *Magnolia grandiflorias*, various

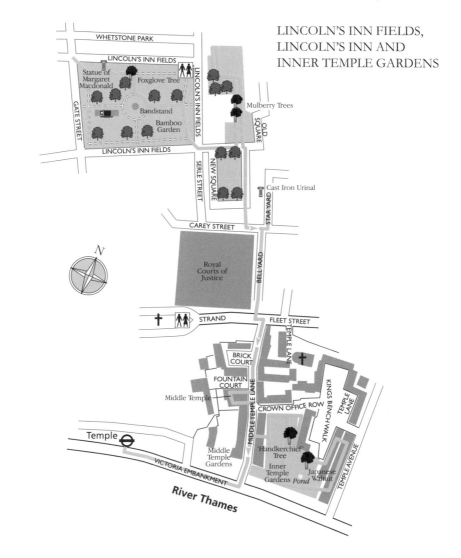

LINCOLN'S INN FIELDS,
LINCOLN'S INN AND
INNER TEMPLE GARDENS

climbers – including star jasmine (*Trachelospermum jasminoides*) – tree peonies, day lilies, delphiniums, aliums and hostas.

The West Border

Note the little Grade I listed Gardener's Cottage on the right, which was formerly a gatehouse. There are three mulberry trees on the lawn opposite the cottage, which produce much fruit each summer. Turn left, to walk past the library and then follow the gravel path up on to the raised West Border. The cottage you will see on your left is known as the Colonel's House and is the residence of the Inn's Under-Treasurer, who is head of the Inn. Planting along this raised walk includes *Cercis canadensis*, whose flowers can be used in salads, *Napeta* (better known as catnip), *Phlomis*, orange day lilies, white *Pittosporum*, *Euphorbia*, irises and *Thalictrum*. Unfortunately, the odd syringe has also been found in these borders, tossed over the wall by some of the homeless who gather for the nightly soup kitchen on the other side. You will see a number of chairs along this walk, marked for 'Benchers Only'.

Turn right at the end where the border includes hellebores, pink valerian, *Salvia* and the *Campanula*, with its purple bell-shaped flowers. The long white building opposite is called Stone Buildings and has been used by film-makers to double as Buckingham Palace. The sun dial dates from the late 18th century.

A Perfect Georgian Square

Now follow the lower path back past the Gardener's Cottage, along the avenue of planes and into New Square, perhaps the finest and most complete 17th-century square in London. It was built between 1682 and 1693, with the central lawn dating from 1843.

On your left, note the red-brick Old Hall which dates from 1490. In its long history, the hall has been used not only as a court of justice, but also by barristers for 'eating, drinking and debating'. Yet its immortality lies not in history books, but in a novel. This was the setting for the famous opening scene of Charles Dickens' *Bleak House*, with its memorable description of London fog: 'London. Michelmas Term lately over, and the Lord Chancellor sitting in Lincoln's Inn Hall. Implacable November weather ... Fog everywhere. Fog up the river, where it flows among green aits and meadows; fog down the river, where it rolls defiled among the tiers of shipping, and the waterside pollutions of a great (and dirty) city ... And hard by Temple Bar, in Lincoln's Inn Hall, at the very heart of the fog, sits the Lord High Chancellor in his High Court of Chancery'. Today, when it is not required by the Inn, it is a sought-after venue for dinners, receptions, meetings and other functions.

Continue along the left-hand side, where a fig tree grows up the front of New Square Chambers at No. 12 and there is a magnificent wisteria next door. The little garden on your left is the former kitchen garden. In amid the prettiness there is a *Dracunculus vulgaris* by the railings, otherwise known as a stink lily because of its foul smell. Its pollinators are flies, which it traps for one night and then releases – hence the smell.

As you pass the doorways of the chambers, you can see the names of the barristers on elegant wooden panels. The Inn's barristers include Fiona Shackleton, who represented Paul McCartney and the model Jordan (Katie Price) in their respective divorces.

At the far left-hand corner of the lawn are three robinia trees, which almost seem to glow in the summer. In the semicircular rose bed next to them is a walnut tree planted by Princess Margaret.

The Pissoir Detour

Leave the square through the archway by Wildy & Sons, legal booksellers, who have occupied this site since 1830. Turn left on exiting and notice the line of four dawn redwoods (*Metasequoia glyptostroboides*) at the rear of the Royal Courts of Justice.

Before turning right into Bell Yard, take a short detour up Star Yard to see one of London's most curious sights. Attached to the wall is a listed, cast-iron urinal, looking for all the world like a Parisian-style *pissoir*. This is a splendid relic of a London that has long gone. In his classic The London Nobody Knows by the writer and artist Geoffrey Fletcher, he observes: 'There are several of these lavatories remaining in London, most frequently down dark alleys, lit by the zinc yellow light of a gas lamp, the whole scene being unchanged from the time of Jack the Ripper...'. That was in 1962. These cast-iron gems are now extremely rare, and the one in Star Yard is the only one remaining in Central London.

The Middle Temple

Retrace your steps and follow the quiet, narrow street down to the noise of the Strand. Opposite is Middle Temple Gate, with its lamb-and-flag emblem. Enter through the doorway and notice how the bustle of the Strand immediately drops away. It is as if you have stepped through a time portal and gone back 200 years to the cobbled streets of horse-drawn London, an impression that is hardly diminished even if the first person you might see is an American tourist talking on their mobile phone. Pass Brick Court to reach the second courtyard, where you turn right to find Middle Temple Hall. Dating back to 1562, this is acknowledged as the finest Elizabethan building in the country.

It was here, in 1602, that Shakespeare's *Twelfth Night* was first performed, while 400 years later, the after-show party for the premiere of *Harry Potter and the Half-Blood Prince*, attended by the film's stars and author J. K. Rowling, was held here.

Walk into the courtyard and along to the fountain, with its two leaning mulberry trees. A plaque notes that this fountain is featured in Dickens' *Martin Chuzzlewit*, in which its 'liquid music' is described. Middle Temple Gardens lie just to the other side, and parts can be viewed from the outside, or from the raised terrace found by walking down the steps. Like much of the Inner Gardens, its opening hours are somewhat arcane and our walk now goes instead to its larger neighbour in the Inner Temple.

The Inner Temple Gardens

Return to Middle Temple Lane, turn right and soon turn left through the archway to find Inner Temple Gardens on your right. Medieval records talk about an orchard here, while in the 14th century its roses were being described. Shakespeare used it as the setting for the meeting between Richard Plantagenet and John Beaufort which led to the Wars of the Roses. The garden's shape changed when Joseph Bazelgette laid out the Embankment in the 19th century, but it remains green and tranquil, and unknown to many Londoners.

Pass through the decorated iron gates, which date from around 1730, and turn left to walk along the top terrace of 1591. Here are magnificently tall echiums, thistle-like cardoons, asters, heleniums, perennial sunflowers, tulips, geraniums, aliums and clematis.

Turn right and walk down the Long Border which is usually planted with alternately coloured roses to represent the Wars of the Roses – white for York and pink/red for Lancaster. The chambers on your left are curiously called Paper Buildings, after the timber and plaster 'paperwork' of the original building that stood on this site, which was destroyed by fire in 1838. The chambers opposite suffered extensive bomb damage during World War II and were rebuilt in the 1950s.

The Dove Tree

After the Atlantic cedar (*Cedrus atlantica*), there is a weeping pear (*Pyrus salicifolia Pendula*), behind which is a handkerchief tree (*Davidia involucrata*), which takes it common name from its hanging white flowers. It is also known as the dove tree for the same reason. Beyond it, almost opposite the corner, lies a large black Japanese walnut (*Juglans ailantifolia*), planted in the 1960s.

As you turn left, there is characteristically spindly maidenhair tree (*Ginko biloba*) on the grass and a foxglove tree (*Paulownia tormentosa*) just beyond. Growing up the wall of the chambers opposite is a *Magnolia grandiflora*. However, you will find your eye drawn immediately to the splendid, pre-war Indian bean tree (*Catalpa bignonioides*), with its famously large leaves and hanging, bean-like seed pods. Like many catalpas, this one needs cables to support its branches – such is the weight of all those leaves that the branches can often break.

The Blackamoor Garden

Follow the path around to the left into the Blackamoor Garden, a reference to the statue of a black boy bearing aloft a sundial at its centre. The barristers sometimes refer to this as the 'black boy garden'. Blackamoor is a dated term referring to the stylistic representation of black people in sculpture, jewellery and other artistic forms.

A large black mulberry (*Morus nigra*) shelters the statue, and varieties of peonies grow in the borders. The land behind the mulberry was originally an orchard because the alluvial soil was good for the fruit trees.

As you leave the Blackamoor Garden there is a large cherry tree on the right, with its tell-tale striations on the trunk. Around its base is a woodland border, with hostas, foxgloves, heart's tongue fern and hellebores.

The 'Wrong' Mulberry

Just beyond the cherry is a handsome dawn redwood (*Metasequoia glyptostroboides*), but arguably the most interesting tree in the gardens lies just behind it. It is the very small mulberry, still a relatively new planting, which sits more toward the middle of the lawn. It may look inconspicuous, but this tree is grown from a cutting taken from the black mulberry planted at Charlton House in Greenwich in 1608. Charlton House was home to Sir Adam Newton, tutor to Henry, Prince of Wales, the eldest son of James I. When the impoverished king realised that large fortunes could be made within the silk industry he imported a number of trees from the Low Countries, believing them to be the white mulberry (*Morus alba*), the host plant of the silkworm. However, it is said that the Dutch deliberately supplied black mulberry because they wanted to prevent competition to their own thriving silk trade.

Giant Survivors

Follow the path past a mature *Paulowia tormentosa* which has a Judas tree (*Cercis siliquastrum*) standing opposite, named because it is believed to be the tree from which the biblical Judas hanged himself. There is a woodland spring border on the left. Now follow the path up to the top terrace, passing a natural hedge of hawthorns, blackthorn, dogwood, spindle and hollyhocks beside the gardeners' yard.

Turn right at the top, passing a statue called *The Wrestlers* (nicknamed 'foreplay' by the barristers), into an avenue of plane trees. Miraculously, this avenue survived the Blitz. The three plane trees in the middle of the lawn show the original width of the river before the Embankment was created. There used to be a line of five trees here, but two fell during World War II.

The Queen's Visit

Drop down to the pond on the lawn with its Peter Pan-like statue and displays of gunnera, irises and arum lilies. On this lawn in 2008, the Queen joined celebrations marking the 400th anniversary of the Inn. Now head for the 'Mediterranean' steps that lead back to the main gate. Tender species are grown here: salvias; cistus; the yellow, foxglove-like verbascum; and the red Maltese Cross (*Lychnis chalcedonica*). There is also purple and bronze fennel, *Buddleia asiatica* and lion's paw (*Leonotis*), a native of south Africa. The rose beds on either side of the steps include the wonderfully named 'kiss-me-over-the-garden-gate' (*Persicaria orientalis*), which does indeed lean over as if its pink flowers are waiting to be kissed.

Exit through the gates, turn left and pass back through the archway to Middle Temple Lane where you turn left. Follow the cobbled lane down to the river, where you turn right to find Temple Underground Station, approximately 250 yards (230 metres) on your right, where the walk ends.

FURTHER INFORMATION

OPENING TIMES

LONDON HISTORIC PARKS AND GARDENS TRUST

Duck Island Cottage, St. James's Park, London SW1A 2BJ. Tel: 020 7839 3969; www.londongardenstrust.org
Membership: Standard £21, concessionary £15.
An independent charity concerned with conserving and restoring London's historic parks and gardens, and providing education about them. The Trust organizes guided walks and visits, exhibitions, study days and seminars.

OSTERLEY PARK

Jersey Road, Isleworth TW7 4RB. Tel: 01494 755 566; www.osterleypark.org.uk.
Osterley Park House open 4 Mar–1 Nov: Wed–Sun 13:00–16:30 hours; 5–20 Dec, Sat–Sun 12:30–15:30. Admission £7.60 adult, £3.80 child, parking £3.50 (National Trust members free). Facilities for the disabled.
The house and park are in the care of the National Trust.

SYON PARK

Park Road, Brentford, Middlesex TW8 8JF.
Tel: 020 8560 0881; www.syonpark.co.uk.
Syon House open 18 Mar–31 Oct: Wed, Thu, Sun and Bank Holiday Mon 11:00–17:00 hours (last admission 16:00 hours). Admission £9 adult, £8 concession, £4 child.
Syon Park is the London home of the Duke and Duchess of Northumberland, and has been in their family for around 400 years.

FULHAM PALACE GARDENS

Bishop's Avenue, London SW6 6EA. Tel: 020 7736 8140 or 3233; www.fulhampalace.org.
Fulham Palace Museum and Gallery open Mon–Tue 12:00–16:00 hours, Sat 11:00–14:00 hours, Sun 11:30–15:30 hours.
Admission free.
The palace is operated jointly by Hammersmith and Fulham Council and the Fulham Palace Trust.
Bishop's Park is managed by the London Borough of Hammersmith and Fulham. For information tel: 020 8748 3020.

HOLLAND PARK

The Stable Yark, Ilchester Place, W8 6LU.
Tel: 020 7361 3003; www.rbkc.gov.uk.
Ecology Centre Tel: 020 7471 9809.
Theatre box office Tel: 020 7602 7856.
Holland Park is managed by the London Borough of Kensington and Chelsea.

KENSINGTON ROOF GARDENS

99 Kensington High Street, London W8 5SA.
Tel: 020 7937 7994;
www.roofgardens.virgin.com
The Roof Gardens are owned and managed by the Virgin Group.

KENSINGTON GARDENS

The Magazine Storeyard, Magazine Gate, Kensington Gardens, London W2 2UH.
Tel: 020 7298 2000; www.royalparks.org.uk.
Kensington Gardens are managed by the Royal Parks Agency.
For events information, tel: 020 7298 2066 or consult website.

Kensington Palace, the State Apartments and Royal Ceremonial Dress Collection open Mar–Oct daily 10:00–18:00 hours (last admission 17:00 hours); Nov–Feb daily 10:00–17:00 hours (last admission 16:00 hours). Admission £12.50 adult, £6.25 child. Tel: 0844 482 7777; www.hrp.org.uk
The Serpentine Gallery tel: 020 7402 6075 for details of shows.

HYDE PARK

The Ranger's Lodge, Hyde Park, London W2 2UH. Tel: 020 7298 2100; www.royalparks.org.uk
Hyde Park is managed by the Royal Parks Agency.
For events information, tel: 020 7298 2066 or consult website.
The Serpentine Lido and Paddling Pool is open Jun–mid-Sep daily; weekends in May. Tel: 020 7706 3422; www.serpentinelido.com

THE REGENT'S PARK

The Store Yard, Inner Circle, The Regent's Park, London NW1 4NR. Tel: 020 7486 7905; www.royalparks.org.uk.
The Regent's Park is managed by the Royal Parks Agency.
For events information, tel: 020 7298 2066 or consult website.
London Zoo open daily from 10:00 hours (closing time varies seasonally). Admission £16.80 adult, £15.30 concession, £13.30 child, under 3s free. Tel: 020 7722 3333; www.zsl.org.

KENWOOD ESTATE

Hampstead Lane, London NW3 7JR. Tel: Estate office: 020 7973 3893.
The Kenwood Estate is managed by English Heritage. The Estate Office Manager and Rangers, based at the Estate Office, Mansion Cottage, near the Brew House Restaurant,

provide information about planting and new developments on the estate and answer visitors' queries.
Open-Air Concerts: book through Ticketmaster, tel: 0870 4000 700 or 0161 385 1138; www.ticketmaster.co.uk
Kenwood House open daily 11:30–16:00 hours. Tel: 020 8348 1286.

GREENWICH PARK

Park Office, Blackheath Gate, Charlton Way, London SE10 8QY. Tel: 020 8858 2608; www.royalparks.org.uk
The park is managed by the Royal Parks Agency.
The Old Royal Observatory open daily 10:00–17:00 hours (last admission 16:30 hours). For planetarium ticket information, tel: 020 8312 6608; www.nmm.ac.uk
The Ranger's House open early Apr–30 Sep: Mon, Tue and Wed, by guided tour only, at 11:30 and 14:30 hours; Sun 11:00–17:00. Admission £5.70 adult, £4.80 concession, £2.90 child (English Heritage members free). Tel: 020 8853 0035; www.english-heritage.org.uk

VICTORIA EMBANKMENT GARDENS

The gardens are managed by Westminster City Council. For information contact the Parks and Open Spaces Department: tel: 020 7641 2696; www.westminster.gov.uk

VICTORIA TOWER GARDENS

The Gardens are managed by the Royal Parks Agency. The Park Manager is based in St. James's Park. Tel: 020 7930 1793; www.royalparks.org.uk
The Museum of Garden History 5 Lambeth Palace Road, London SE1 7LB. Tel: 020 7401 8865; www.museumgardenhistory.org.
The museum is run by the Tradescant Trust.

Open daily 10:30–17:00 hours (closed 1st Mon of month).
Admission £6 adult, £5 senior citizen; child under 16 free.
Lambeth Palace Garden is open to the public three times a year: in April (the date is published in the National Gardens Scheme diary); and in June and September. For information tel: 020 7898 1200.

GREEN PARK

The St. James's Park Office, The Storeyard, Horse Guards Road, St. James's Park, London SW1A 2BJ. Tel: 020 7930 1793; www.royalparks.org.uk
For events information, tel: 020 7298 2066 or consult website.
The park is managed by the Royal Parks Agency.
Spencer House, entrance: 27 St. James's Place, London SW1A 1NR. Tel: 020 7499 8620 (information line).
Public tours 1 Feb–31 Jul, and 1 Sep–31 Dec: Sun 10:30–17:45 hours (last admission 16:45 hours). Admission £9 adult, £7 concession; no children under 10.

ST. JAMES'S PARK

The Park Office, The Storeyard, Horse Guards Road, St. James's Park,, London SW1A 2BJ. Tel: 020 7930 1793; www.royalparks.org.uk
For events information, tel: 020 7298 2066 or consult website.
The park is managed by the Royal Parks Agency.

BATTERSEA PARK

Wandsworth, SW11 4NJ. Tel: 020 8871 7530; www.wandsworth.gov.uk.
The park is managed by the London Borough of Wandsworth. For information about events in the park, tel 020 8871 7534.

Children's Zoo open daily from 10:00 hours, last admission 16:30 in summer, 16:00 in winter. Admission £6.50 adult, £4.95 child.
Tel: 020 7924 5826;
www.batterseaparkzoo.co.uk

CHELSEA PHYSIC GARDEN

66 Royal Hospital Road, Chelsea, London SW3 4HS. Tel: 020 7352 5646, ext 228; www.chelseaphysicgarden.co.uk
The garden is run by an independent charity.

RICHMOND PARK

Superintendent's Office, Holly Lodge, Richmond Park, Surrey TW10 5HS.
Tel: 020 8948 3209; www.royalparks.org.uk
The park is managed by the Royal Parks Agency.

THE ROYAL BOTANIC GARDENS, KEW

Richmond, Surrey TW9 3AB. Tel: 020 8332 5000 (switchboard) or 020 8332 5655 (24-hour visitor information); www.kew.org
The Royal Botanic Gardens are run by an independent charity.
Kew Palace Open mid-Apr–late Sep only. Admission (in addition to Kew Gardens ticket price) £5 adult, £4.50 concessions, children under 17 free.

HAM HOUSE GARDENS

Ham Street, Ham, Richmond-upon-Thames, Surrey TW10 7RS. Tel: 020 8940 1950; www.nationaltrust.org.uk
Ham House open mid-Mar–end Oct: Mon–Wed, and Sat, Sun 12:00–16:00 hours (last admission 15:30 hours). Admission (house and gardens) £9 adult, £5 child.
The house and gardens are in the care of the National Trust.

MARBLE HILL PARK
Richmond Road, Twickenham, TW1 2NL.
Tel: 020 8892 5115;
www.english-heritage.org.uk
Marble Hill House and gardens are managed
by English Heritage.
Marble Hill House open 1 Apr–1 Nov: Sat
10:00–14;00 hours, Sun and Bank Holidays
10:00–17:00 hours. Admission £4.40 adult,
£3.70 concession, £2.20 child.

VICTORIA PARK
Grove Road, Bow, E3. Tel: 020 7364 2494;
www.towerhamlets.gov.uk
The park is managed by Tower Hamlets
Council.

MILE END PARK
Tel: 020 7364 2494; www.towerhamlets.gov.uk
The park is managed by Tower Hamlets
Council.
Ragged School Museum 46–50 Copperfield
Road, E3 4RR. Tel: 020 8980 6405;
www.raggedschoolmuseum.org.uk
Open Wed and Thu 10:00–17:00 hours, first Sun
in month 14:00–17:00 hours. Admission free.
The museum is run by an independent charity.

DULWICH PARK
College Road, Dulwich Common, Court Lane,
Dulwich Village SE21. Tel: 020 7525 2000;
www.southwark.gov.uk
The park is managed by Southwark Council.

CANNIZARO PARK
Dunstall Road, Wimbledon. Tel: 020 8545 3678
or 020 8545 3930; www.merton.gov.uk or
www.cannizaropark.org.uk (Friends of
Cannizaro Park).
The park is managed by Merton Council.

**LINCOLN'S INN FIELDS/LINCOLN'S
INN/INNER TEMPLE GARDENS**
Lincoln's Inn The Honourable Society of
Lincoln's Inn, Lincoln's Inn, WC2A 3TL. Tel: 020
7405 1393; www.lincolnsinn.org.uk
Inner Temple Gardens The Honourable
Society of the Inner Temple, Inner Temple,
EC4Y 7HL. Tel: 020 7797 8243;
www.innertemple.org.uk

IDENTIFICATION GUIDES

*Photographic Field Guide to the Trees of Britain
and Europe* (New Holland Publishers 1993) by
Bob Press.
Field Guide to the Trees of Britain & Europe
(Kingfisher, 1990) by David Sutton.

INDEX

Adam, Robert 16, 18, 24, 67, 68, 71, 98, 121
Aiton, William 125
Albert, Prince Consort 9, 48, 50
Albert Bridge 106
Albert Memorial 50
alleys 9
allotments 31
America, plants from 11, 29–30
American ambassador's residence 63
American Garden, Dulwich Park 163–4
Anne, Queen 9, 45, 47, 49, 100
Anne of Denmark 73
Apsley Gate 56
arboretums
  Holland Park 37
  Kew Gardens 126
archaeological finds 29, 79, 89
Archbishop's Park 88, 92
aromatic plants 114
Art Mound, Mile End Park 155
Arts Park, Mile End Park 155
ash, narrowleaf 148
Augusta, Princess of Wales 125, 126, 127, 130, 133
avenues 9
  Ham House Gardens 136
  Inner Temple Gardens 181
  Kensington Gardens 46
  Kenwood 69
  Lincoln's Inn Fields 176
  Osterley Park 17, 21
  Regent's Park 62
  Victoria Park 150, 151
azaleas 37, 51, 83, 123–4, 167

ballooning 94, 155
bamboo 117, 129, 176
bandstands 78, 96
Banister, Rev. John 11, 29–30
Banks, Sir Joseph 11, 117, 125–6, 129
banqueting houses 8, 138
Barry, Charles junior 159
Barrie, J. M. 49, 51, 84

Bath House, Kenwood 71
Battersea Park 7, 105–11
bead tree 78
Beales, Edmund 54
bedding plants 10, 11, 51, 56, 59, 62, 111
bee boles 33–4
beech, weeping 57, 148
Belvedere, Cannizaro Park 170
birds
  Battersea Park 110
  Dulwich Park 162
  Greenwich Park 78
  Kenwood 72
  Kew Gardens 130
  Mile End Park 153
  Regent's Park 65
  Richmond Park 122, 123
  St. James's Park 100–1, 102–3
Birdcage Walk 104
Bishop's Park 34
Blackamoor Garden, Inner Temple 180
Blackheath Gate, Greenwich 78–9
Blashill, Thomas 159
Bligh, Captain William 92
Boardwalk, Dulwich Park 162
Bonner, Bishop Edmund 146
botanic gardens 8, 22
box hedges 8, 32, 91
Bridgeman, Charles 9, 45, 46, 48, 96, 141, 143
Brompton Nurseries 30
Brown, Lancelot 'Capability' 10, 24–5, 26, 27, 125, 129, 130, 131
Buckingham Palace 53, 97, 98, 100, 103–4
Burdett-Coutts Fountain, Victoria Park 148–9
Burton, Decimus 56, 61, 63, 65, 126, 131, 132
Butterfield, William 30, 34
Buxton Memorial, Victoria Tower Gardens 88–9
Byron, Lord 56

cable frieze beds, Regent's Park 62
camellias 11, 51, 124, 167
camera obscura, Greenwich 76

canals 9

Cannizaro Park 166–73

Caroline, Queen (wife of George II) 9, 45, 48, 52, 58, 96, 100, 125, 127, 141

Caroline, Queen (wife of George IV) 79

carpet bedding 56, 111

cascades 41, 66, 106, 109

cattle 20

Cavell, Edith 129

cedars 17–18, 31, 34, 37, 171, 172

Central London Mosque 63

Chambers, Sir William 9, 16–20, 50, 125, 127, 130–1, 132, 133

'champion trees' 107, 110

Charles I, King 24, 52, 119, 175

Charles II, King 7, 9, 74, 75, 93, 97, 99, 100, 104, 137

Chartists 146

Chelsea Physic Garden 8, 11, 112–18

cherries, flowering 132, 138

chestnuts
    horse 37, 62, 79, 143
    sweet 31, 48, 50, 74, 76, 78, 96, 148

Children's Zoo, Battersea Park 108–9

Chilean wine palm 131

Chinese influences 17, 38

Chiswick Park 9

cider gum trees 147, 163

cistus 114

clairvoyee 138

Classical style 26

Cleopatra's Needle 81

Coade stone 136

Coalbrookdale Gates, Kensington Gardens 50

College Gardens 88

Compton, Henry, Bishop of London 29, 30, 31

concerts 71, 101

conservatories 11, 24, 27–8

Constance Fund Fountain, Green Park 97, 98

Constitution Arch 98

Constitution Hill 97–8

Cope, Sir Walter 35

cottage gardens 10–11

Cromwell, Oliver 60, 74

Crystal Palace Park 58

Cubitt, Thomas 105

Cumberland Terrace 62–3

deer 7, 78, 109, 120, 149

The Dell, Greenwich 79

The Dell, Hyde Park 57

Devonshire Gate, Green Park 95–6

Diana, Princess of Wales Memorial Fountain, Hyde Park 58

Dogs of Alcibiades, Victoria Park 146

Dry Garden, Dulwich Park 163

Duck Island, Regent's Park 63

Duck Island, St. James's Park 101, 102–3

Dulwich Park 159–65

Dutch gardens 36, 46, 135

dye plants 113

Dysart family 135

Ecology Centre, Mile End Park 153

Elizabeth, the Queen Mother 56, 103

Elizabeth I, Queen 8, 16, 31, 60, 73, 76

Elizabeth II, Queen 84, 133, 176, 181

enclosures 38, 119–20

English Heritage 68, 142

Epstein, Jacob 59

Evelyn, John 17, 45, 52, 89, 100, 104, 135

exotic plants 11, 116

Festival of Britain (1951) 82, 106, 108

fireworks 93–4

Fitzherbert, Mrs 142

flamingos 42

Flamsteed, John 75

Flamsteed House, Greenwich 75–6

Flaxman, John 53

flower gardens
    Greenwich Park 78
    Hyde Park 56
    Kensington Gardens 50–1
    Kenwood 69
    Regent's Park 62
    Victoria Park 149

flower shows 11, 81

formal gardens 10, 28, 62

fountains

Battersea Park 107

Cannizaro Park 167–8

Children's Fountain, Hyde Park 59

drinking fountains 10, 57, 63, 98, 148–9, 175, 176

Hyde Park 56

Kensington Gardens 49

Kensington Roof Gardens 41, 43

Regent's Park 62

Fowler, Charles 27

Fox, Henry 35, 38

foxglove trees 175, 180

fruit trees 32, 113

Fulham Palace Gardens 8, 11, 29–34

Garden Museum 11, 87, 89–91

gardens 7

gazebo, Kew Gardens 127

George II, King 9, 45, 58, 93–4, 141

George III, King 125, 166

George IV, King 53, 61–2, 97, 103, 142

geraniums (pelargoniums) 36, 125

Gibbons, Grinling 47, 48

Gibson, John 107, 111

gillyflowers 8

glory trees 168

golden rain trees 24, 57, 172

good King Henry 113

goosefoot (*patte d'oie*) 9

Gothick style 142–3

Gough, Piers 155–6

graffiti 157

Grand Union Canal 155, 157–8

grasses, Chelsea Physic Garden 117

Great Exhibition (1851) 50, 52, 58, 105–6

Green Bridge, Mile End Park 155–6

Green Park 93–8

greenhouses 11, 27

Chelsea Physic Garden 114

Kew Gardens 126, 131–3, 134

Greenwich Meridian 75

Greenwich Park 9, 73–9

Gresham, Sir Thomas 16, 20

grottoes, Marble Hill Park 141, 143–4

Guards Memorial, St. James's Park 101

gunnera 25

ha-has 10, 130, 136, 138

Haile Selassie, Emperor of Ethiopia 173

Ham House Gardens 8, 10, 135–40

Hampstead Heath 67–70

Hancock, Ralph 40, 43

Hanover Terrace 64

Hawksmoor, Nicholas 47

Heather Garden, Richmond Park 123

Henry VIII, King 7, 52, 73, 75, 76, 85, 93, 99

Hepworth, Barbara 69, 110, 161

herb gardens 7

Battersea Park 107

Cannizaro Park 171

Chelsea Physic Garden 114

Fulham Palace Gardens 32

Greenwich 74

Kew Gardens 127

herbaceous borders 10, 66

hickory, shagbark 168

Highgate Ponds 68

Historic Tree Clumps 20

Holland, Lady 35

Holland Park 11, 35–9

The Holme, Regent's Park 65

Holocaust memorial, Hyde Park 57

Hooker, Sir Joseph 11, 126, 129

Hooker, William 11, 126

hornbeam 138

Horse Guards Parade 101

Horseshoe Fountain, St. James's Park 103

Horticultural Therapy Garden, Battersea Park 109

Howard, Henrietta 141–4

Hudson, W. H. 59

Hutton, Barbara 63

Hyde Park 9, 11, 46, 52–60

Hyde Park Corner 56, 98

ice houses

Ham House 140

Holland Park 36

Marble Hill Park 143

Osterley Park 20

ilex trees 139, 148

Indian bean trees 25, 27, 85, 92, 117, 144, 146–7,

162, 163, 180
irises 39, 123
Isabella Plantation, Richmond Park 119, 120, 123–4
Italian gardens 10, 133
   Cannizaro Park 168–70, 173
   Kensington Gardens 48–9
Ivy Tunnel, Kenwood 69

Jacobean houses 9, 35, 135
James I, King 7, 52, 73, 100, 104
Japanese gardens 11
   Dulwich Park 161, 162
   Kew Gardens 129, 130
   Kyoto Garden, Holland Park 11, 38
Jesuits' Bark 126
Jones, Inigo 22, 36, 73–4, 84
Judas trees 82, 115, 181

Kensington Gardens 9, 45–51
Kensington Palace 52
Kensington Roof Gardens 11, 40–4
Kensington Square 40
Kent, William 9, 48, 50, 58
Kentucky coffee tree 147
Kenwood 10, 67–72
Kenwood House 67, 68, 69–71
Kew Gardens 7, 8, 9, 10, 11, 125–34
Kew Palace 127
King Henry VIII Mound, Richmond Park 121
kitchen gardens 31–2, 168
knot gardens 7–8
   Fulham Palace Gardens 32
   Ham House Gardens 138
   Tradescant Garden 91
Kylins 133
Kyoto Gardens, Holland Park 11, 38–9

laburnum walk, Kew Gardens 127
Lady Jane's Wood, Cannizaro Park 170–1
lakes 9, 10, 17
Lambeth Bridge 89
Lambeth Palace 87–8, 89, 92
Lancaster, Osbert 107
landscape gardens 9–10

Lansbury Lido, Hyde Park 58
larch, European 89
Lauderdale, 1st Duke of 135
Le Nôtre, André 74, 76, 99
leaf-shredding 50
lilac 129
lime trees 43, 46, 62, 69, 94, 136, 151
Lincoln's Inn 174–81
Lincoln's Inn Fields 174–81
liquidambar 11, 17, 27, 30
Lodge Garden, Regent's Park 65
London, George 48
London Bridge 150
London Zoo 63
Long Water, Kensington Gardens 49, 57
loosestrife, purple 162–3

Macartney House, Greenwich 79
magnolia 11, 30, 34, 51, 168, 171
maidenhair trees 33, 51, 101, 118, 164–5, 176, 180
The Mall 101–2
Marble Arch 53
Marble Hill Park 9, 141–4
Mary II, Queen 9, 29, 40, 47, 74, 85
The Meadow, Hyde Park 59
medicinal plants 8, 112, 116, 127
Mediterranean Garden, Cannizaro Park 170
medlars 25, 32
Melancholy Walk, Ham House Gardens 137–8
Meridian Line, Greenwich 75
Middle Temple 179
Middlesex Forest 61
Mile End Park 152–8
Mile End Stadium 157
Miller, Philip 112, 117
Mitchell, Alan 107, 110
monkey puzzle trees 130
Moore, Henry 72, 110
Moorhouse, Peter 31
mounts and mounds 121, 127, 138, 155
mulberry trees 115, 177, 179, 180
Murray, William 67, 68, 71
Museum of Economic Botany, Kew Gardens 133

Nash, John 10, 53, 61–6, 97, 100, 103, 126
Nash beds, St. James's Park 103
National Trust 16, 135, 137
'natural' look 9–10, 16, 17
Nesfield, William 10, 62, 132
North, Marianne 131
nurseries, Hyde Park 59

oak trees 20, 27, 34, 37, 119, 121–2, 160, 163
    cork 18, 114, 132, 171
    holm 139, 148
    Queen's Oak, Greenwich 76
    stag-headed 20, 120–1
    turkey 147, 162
    Turner's 148
Old English Garden, Battersea Park 107
Old Royal Observatory, Greenwich 74, 75–6
olive tree 113
orangeries 8, 27
    Ham House 140
    Holland Park 35, 39
    Kensington Gardens 47
    Kenwood House 71
    Kew Gardens 127
Order Beds
    Chelsea Physic Garden 118
    Kew Gardens 134
Orleans House Gallery, Marble Hill Park 144
Osterley Park 16–21

pagoda tree 25, 170
pagodas
    Kew Gardens 9, 125, 130–1, 132
    Peace Pagoda, Battersea Park 107, 108
Palm House, Kew Gardens 132–3
Palm Tree Pub, Mile End Park 153
Pankhurst, Emmeline 88
Park Lane 56
parks 7
Parliament Hill 68
parterres 8, 127
patte d'oie (goosefoot) 9
pavilions 17
Peace Pagoda, Battersea Park 107, 108
pelargoniums (geraniums) 36, 125

pelicans 100–1
Pembroke Lodge, Richmond Park 121
Pen Ponds, Richmond Park 122–3
Pennethorne, Sir James 48, 105, 145
Pepys, Samuel 52, 100
pergolas 32, 56
pet cemetery, Cannizaro Park 172
Peter Pan 49, 51
physic gardens 8, 112–18, 134
pine, Corsican 127
pine pits 31
Piper, John 107
plane trees 18, 26, 31, 40, 80–1, 85, 92, 94, 100,
    127, 148, 150, 176, 181
Planetarium, Greenwich 76
plant introductions 11, 12
plats 138–9
pleached trees 138
pleasure grounds 31, 107, 155
poisonous plants 116
pollarding 120
pollution 113
pomegranate trees 113
Pope, Alexander 141, 143
poplars 94, 148
Primrose Hill 62
Princess of Wales Conservatory, Kew Gardens 134
Pump House, Battersea Park 109

Queen Anne's Gate 104
Queen Charlotte's Cottage, Kew Gardens 130
Queen Elizabeth Gates, Hyde Park 55
Queen Mary's Gardens, Regent's Park 66
Queen Mary's Steps, Victoria Embankment
    Gardens 85
Queen Victoria Memorial 96, 97, 102, 103
Queen's Garden, Kew Gardens 127
Queen's House, Greenwich 73–4, 76
Queen's Oak, Greenwich 76
Queen's Walk, Green Park 95, 96–7

Ragged School Museum 157
rainforest plants, Chelsea Physic Garden 114
Ranger's House, Greenwich Park 79
Ranger's Lodge, Hyde Park 59

redwoods 84, 130, 160, 178, 180
Reform League 54, 60
Reformer's Tree, Hyde Park 60
Regent's Canal 63
The Regent's Park 10, 61–6
Rennie, George 58
Rennie, Sir John 58
Repton, Humphry 10, 67, 68, 69, 71
rhododendrons 122, 123–4, 129, 163–4, 167
Richmond Park 119–24
Rima Monument, Hyde Park 59
The Ring, Hyde Park 52
rockeries
  Chelsea Physic Garden 117
  Kew Gardens 134
  St. James's Park 101
Romans 7, 120
Roof Gardens, Kensington 40–4
rose gardens
  Chelsea Physic Garden 114
  Greenwich Park 79
  Holland Park 39
  Hyde Park 56
  Kew Gardens 132
  Queen Mary's Rose Garden, Regent's Park 66
  St. James's Park 103
rose hips 134
Rotten Row 52, 56
Round Pond, Kensington Gardens 46, 48, 49
Royal Botanic Gardens, Kew 7, 8, 9, 10, 11, 125–34
Royal Naval College, Greenwich 74
royal parks 7
rubber trees 126
rushes 118

St. James's Park 9, 10, 99–104
St. John's Lodge, Regent's Park 65
St. Mary-at-Lambeth 11, 87, 89, 91
Secluded Garden, Kew Gardens 134
The Serpentine, Hyde Park 57
Serpentine Bridge, Hyde Park 58–9
Serpentine Gallery 50
7 July, 2005 Memorial, Hyde Park 55
Sites of Special Scientific Interest (S.S.S.I.s) 26, 68
Slezer, John 135

Sloane, Sir Hans 112, 117
Society of Apothecaries 112
Spanish Garden, Kensington Roof Gardens 43–4
Speakers' Corner 53–4
Spencer House 96–7
spruce, Brewer's weeping 168
stove houses 11, 27, 29, 140
strawberry trees 91, 110
strewing plants 127
Sub-Tropical Gardens, Battersea Park 110–11
sumach 26
summerhouses 139
sundials 34, 36, 82, 91, 127, 129, 138, 178
sunken gardens
  Cannizaro Park 171
  Kensington Gardens 46
  Kew Gardens 127
  Regent's Park 69
Sussex Place 64
swamp cypresses 25, 57, 66, 72, 91, 103, 133, 168
sweet gum (liquidambar) 11, 17, 27, 30
Syon House 132
Syon Park 9, 10, 11, 22–8
Systematic Order Beds, Chelsea Physic Garden
  118

tazzas 62
Temperate House, Kew 131–2
Temple Gardens 11, 174–81
Temple Place Gardens 81
temples
  Kew Gardens 132, 133
  Queen's Temple, Kensington Gardens 50
  Temple of Pan, Osterley Park 18
Terrace Garden, Mile End Park 156
theatres, open-air 36, 66
Thomson, James 10, 121
topiary 47, 85, 137
Tradescant, John 11, 87, 89–92
Tradescant, John junior 11, 25, 87, 89–92
Tradescant Garden 11, 91–3
Tree of Heaven 160
tree sculpture 144
trespass, legal 96
Tudor Garden, Kensington Roof Gardens 43

Tudors
  deer parks 7
  gardens 8, 22
  houses 29, 31
tulip trees 27, 46, 62, 78, 91, 123
Turner, Dr. William 22
Tyburn stream 93
Tyburn Tree 53

urinal, Star Yard 179

Vanbrugh, Sir John 47, 74, 76–8
Vanbrugh Castle, Greenwich 76–8
vegetables 113–14
Victoria, Queen 9, 21, 34, 45, 46, 48, 50, 53, 58,
   94, 97, 103, 121, 126
Victoria Embankment Gardens 10, 80–6, 87
Victoria Park, Hackney 9, 145–51
Victoria Tower Gardens 87–92
Village Copse, Dulwich Park 165
Villiers, George 84–5
vines 28, 32
virginia creeper 11, 91
Virginia Trading Company 89
vistas 48, 59, 62, 68, 71, 98, 121, 132, 138, 156

walnut, black 31, 91, 107, 141, 144, 180
wardian cases 116
water gardens 26
water gates 84–5
waterlilies 17, 72, 84, 132–3
Waterloo Bridge 82
Watts, G. F. 37, 48
Wellington, Duke of 55, 58, 98, 105, 167
Wellingtonia 149
Westmacott, Sir Richard 55
Westminster Bridge 86
Wet Garden, Cannizaro Park 170
White Lodge, Richmond Park 123
Whitehall 61
Wild Flower Meadow, Hampstead Heath 68
Wild Garden, Cannizaro Park 170
wilderness gardens 8
  Battersea Park 109

Ham House Gardens 139
Holland Park 37
Kenwood 72
William III, King 9, 29, 40, 45, 46, 47, 52, 74
William IV, King 74
Wilson, E. H. 123–4
Winfield House 63
wingnut trees 25, 114, 162, 173
Winter Garden, Dulwich Park 165
Wise, Henry 48
wisteria 32, 43
Wolfe, General James 75, 79
woodland gardens 42, 118, 133
Wren, Christopher 47, 48, 49, 73, 74, 75, 80, 85
Wyck, Jan 135

York Gate, Regent's Park 66
York Terrace 66

zoos
  Children's Zoo, Battersea Park 108–9
  London Zoo 63